Since the last edition of *Endnotes* in 2013, the global economic train-wreck has juddered forward. No real recovery has taken place, but neither has there been a return to depression-like conditions. It is unclear how much longer this interim period will last. The wrapping-up of extraordinary measures has been declared many times, most recently in September 2015, when the US Federal Reserve was expected to raise its prime rate (this move would have ended a six-year stretch in which the fed funds rate was at zero). But this, too, was cancelled at the last minute. In a by-now familiar scene, technocrats shuffled onto the stage, shuffled some papers, and then shuffled off again. Another round of quantitative easing is anticipated. With little changing, the high-income countries' economies continue to tick over.

Meanwhile, uncertainty and economic turbulence are extending themselves from the high-income countries to the low-income ones, which not so long ago were thought to be the scene of a possible economic "delinking". Today, the news from Brazil looks grim, and the news from China is getting grimmer by the month. This is already impacting economies across the low-income world, so much of which depends on China's demand for commodities. Are we about to see another "Third World Debt Crisis" unfold, as we did in 1982?

Even more so than when we published *Endnotes 3*, it is hard to say what is likely to happen next. Complex developments are taking place, which look quite different when viewed from Ferguson, Missouri, or Athens, Greece — or along the route of refugees fleeing Syria on their way to Germany. In some places, new social struggles are taking place; in others, there has been a return to calm; in still others, there is unending civil war. Some countries have seen the resurgence of a milquetoast parliamentary left, yet the prevailing order remains decidedly unshaken.

THE IN-FLIGHT TEAM WILL BE COMING AROUND IN A MOMENT WITH ANOTHER ROUND OF DRINKS...

The world is apparently still trapped within the terms of the holding pattern that we described in *Endnotes 3*.[1] This pattern is defined by a partial petrification of class struggle, attendant on a similar petrification of the economic crisis. This social stasis has been maintained only by means of massive ongoing state interventions, which have ensured that the crisis remains that of some people, in some countries, instead of becoming generalised across the world. How long can this holding pattern be maintained?

1 See 'The Holding Pattern', *Endnotes 3*, September 2013.

As they did in the earlier years of the decade, states continue to spend vast quantities of money in order to stave off catastrophe. At the end of 2014, debt levels as a percentage of GDP were still rising across the high-income countries, reaching 90 percent in the UK, 95 percent in France, 105 percent in the US, and 132 percent in Italy (the exception was Germany, where debt levels fell from 80 percent in 2010 to a still-high 73 percent in 2014). Yet all this state spending has not led to economic recovery. Following an initial period of growth in 2010–11, high-income countries' economies have once again returned to a state of relative stagnation. The main exceptions are the US and UK, where a small measure of recovery has taken place. By contrast, across continental Europe and in Japan — ECB manoeuvres and "Abeconomics" notwithstanding — growth rates have remained low or negative. Greece's GDP has, of course, shrunk significantly.

Such lackluster developments continue a trend that has been in place for decades: in the high-income countries GDP-per-capita growth rates have been ever slower on a decade by decade basis, falling from 4.3 percent in the 1960s, to 2.9 percent in the 1970s, to 2.2 percent in the 1980s, to 1.8 percent in the 1990s, to 1.1 percent in the 2000s. The 2010s seem set to continue this quantitative trend, with a growth rate of around 1.0 percent between 2011 and 2014. However, there are signs at present that we are at a qualitative turning point; the world economy is threatening to go down, in a Titanic fashion. Politicians can be seen, everywhere, trying to bail the inflowing water out of the sinking ship. But they are doing so with a set of hand pails which are themselves leaking. As we argued in 2013, these politicians are locked into a dance of the dead, for the following reasons.

States are taking out debt to prevent the onset of a debt-deflation spiral; however, their capacity to take out this debt is based on the promise of future economic growth. A combination of slow growth and already high debt levels has meant that government officials have found themselves trapped between two opposed pressures. On the one hand, they have needed to spend huge quantities of money to prevent recession from becoming depression. On the other, they have already spent so much over the past few decades that they have little left to give.

Thus, instead of spending even more, governments in the richer countries engaged in campaigns of austerity: to show their creditors that they remained in control of their finances, they cut social services at the same time as they handed out money to bankers. Austerity has had devastating consequences for workers. Public employees found themselves without jobs. The costs of education and healthcare rose just as households' incomes were pinched. Meanwhile, without a boost to demand for goods and services, private economies stagnated. Creditor nations have been remarkably successful in preventing any departure from this line among debtors.

A PROBLEM OF COMPOSITION

This contradictory logic, we argued, shaped the unfolding crisis and so also the struggles that erupted in response to it. Many people claimed that government officials were acting stupidly or even crazily: shouldn't they have been making the banks pay in order to bail out the people, rather than the other way around? The main explanation offered for this irrationality was that governments had been captured by moneyed interests; democracy had given way to oligarchy. It was in this way that the form of the crisis determined the form of class struggle in this period: it became a contest of real democracy against austerity. Real democracy could, according to the logic of the protests, force the state to intervene in the interest of the nation, rather than that of crony capitalists.

In reality, governments have few options available to them, regardless of who is at the helm, for this crisis is one not of "crony" or "neoliberal" capitalism but rather of capitalism itself. The latter is beset by ever slower rates of economic growth. As productivity levels continue to rise in this context, the result has been an ongoing production of surplus populations alongside surplus capital, excesses which the economy has trouble absorbing. The social order persists, but it is slowly unraveling. The categories of our world are increasingly indistinct. When protesters have come together in this context, they have typically found it difficult to locate a common ground on which to build their struggle, since they experience the crisis in such diverse ways — some worse than others. The perspectives of the old workers' movement are dead and gone, and thus unavailable as a substantial basis for common action. How are we to account for the failure of that movement to revive itself when workers everywhere are getting screwed?

In this edition, we reconsider in depth the long emergence and dissolution of an affirmable worker's identity (and, with it, the crisis of "the Left") in "A History of Separation". European socialists and communists had expected the accumulation of capital both to expand the size of the industrial workforce and, at the same time, to unify the workers as a social subject: the collective worker, the class in-and-for itself. However, instead of incubating the collective worker, capitalist accumulation gave birth to the separated society. The forces of atomisation overpowered those of collectivisation. Late capitalist civilisation is now destabilising, but without, as yet, calling forth the new social forces that might be able, finally, to dissolve it.

An intake from Chris Wright, "Its Own Peculiar Decor", looks at the same story through the optic of suburbanisation in the United States. Initial waves of proletarianisation that gathered people in factories and cities, constructing the collective worker, gave way to never-ending suburbanism, where the absence of any link to the countryside was combined with a near full-achievement of atomisation. This was a suburbanisation constructed on a rejection of the unruly poor, the non-homeowner, and through the inevitable racialisation of these categories.

In *Endnotes 3* we described this structure of rejection and racialisation in the context of the English riots of 2011 as a process of abjection.[2] Both the 2011

2 See 'A rising tide lifts all boats', *Endnotes* 3, September 2013.

British student movement and the US Occupy movement — which were initially struggles of a white middle class fighting against an ongoing impoverishment — were followed by struggles on the part of racialised populations whose impoverishment and exclusion had long been an everyday reality. In "Brown v. Ferguson", we trace the unfolding of Black Lives Matter, situating this movement in the history of race politics and struggles in the US. We look at the shifting meaning of black identity in a context of growing surplus populations managed by incarceration and police violence.

But it would be too hasty to deduce from such struggles the emergence of some new, potentially hegemonic figure of the "surplus proletarian", or "the abjected", to which we might hitch our revolutionary aspirations. Rather than unifying all workers behind a specific subject, growing superfluity has meant a decomposition of the class into so many particular situations — fragments among fragments — pitting the interests of those with stable jobs against precarious workers, citizens against undocumented migrants, and so on. Proletarians thus increasingly face a "composition problem", lacking any firm basis for unity in action. In "An Identical Abject-Subject?" we consider the political meaning of surplus populations.[3]

3 This text updates our account of surplus populations in 'Misery and debt', in *Endnotes* 2, April 2010.

Struggles do not all try to solve this problem in the same way. In "Gather Us From Among the Nations", we look at a movement that received little international coverage: the February 2014 protests in Bosnia-Herzegovina. When workers from privatised factories — whose demands had been ignored by authorities for years — were attacked by police in Tuzla, thousands took to the streets, storming the Canton government buildings. During the following months, citizens held large assemblies, where they rejected the ethnic divisions that had plagued the country for more than two decades. Participants in these assemblies tried to solve the composition problem in an unusual way, by marshalling an ever-proliferating multiplicity of demands, so that nobody's plight would be forgotten. But it remained unclear to whom these demands could be addressed and, above all, who might be able to fulfill them. That raised key questions about the protesters' relation to the state.

ΣΥΡΙΖΑ IS GREEK FOR DESPAIR

If, in retrospect, 2012–13 was the end of a high point in the movement of squares, these movements did not exactly disappear in the following years. Still, their development gave us no reason to be particularly optimistic. Sisi's coup in Egypt—shrouded in the mantle of Tahrir—introduced mass-shootings to the movements' repertoire. The following year saw another bloodied square in the Maidan, this time defended by fascist groups. Shortly thereafter Occupy Bangkok, organised by royalist yellow shirts, succeeded in bringing about a military coup in Thailand.

The conclusions of many social struggles were given by geopolitical manoeuvring. Various powers succeeded in taking the gains of destabilised situations. In the Maidan, tensions between nationalists and pro-EU liberals had been brewing for months, but they did not get much of a chance to play themselves out, for as soon as Yanukovych resigned, Russia—faced with the prospect of EU and NATO extension to another country in its "near abroad"—invaded the Crimea and began a proxy war in Eastern Ukraine. At that point, the rebellion became a civil war. In Egypt the conflicts between radicals and the Brotherhood, or Muslims and Copts, which had developed in the aftermath of Mubarak's fall, were ultimately submerged in a larger regional power game, as Saudi financial support helped Egypt's deep state to reestablish itself. Elsewhere, from Syria to Bahrain, Yemen and Libya, the hopes of the Spring were snuffed out in civil war, military intervention or both.

Similar limits were encountered by left-wing parliamentarians in Europe. There too it was ultimately the regional hegemon that would decide the fate of social movements, whatever came of their assemblies and government referendums. To understand the tepid nature of Syriza's proposals — calling for a primary surplus of 3 rather than 3.5 percent — it is necessary to recognise that Greece cannot feed itself without foreign exchange. Moreover, any sign of unilateral default would deplete the country of taxable revenue. This left Syriza few options, such that their "modest proposals" could easily be ignored by the troika of creditors.

As we prepared this issue for publication, an analogue of the Syriza developments seemed to be in preparation in the UK with the shock rise of a member of the Labour Party's long marginalised left-wing to its leadership. The political discourses greeting these developments have busied themselves with empty rhetorical distributions of the old and the new, but what is certain is that the social forces and situation that propelled Jeremy Corbyn to victory are different to those that caused the rise and fall of Tony Benn in the early eighties. The institutional brakers have of course stepped in to halt this upsurge, and are likely to be successful in the short term. But can a party that has already been looking cadaverous for years avoid sustaining an even greater loss of legitimacy in the process? The key question for the current strain of political anti-politics remains: how many instances of these vessels crashing on the rocks will it take to produce something qualitatively different, and what will that be?

In reality, despite the offers of Marxist economists "to save European capitalism from itself",[4] states will continue to find that they have very little room for manoeuvre, since they are beset by high debt levels and slow growth. It will therefore be difficult for governments to deal with the catastrophic events to come, whether

4 Yanis Varoufakis, 'How I Became an Erratic Marxist', *The Guardian,* 18 February 2015.

these are further economic crises, or the already emerging consequences of global climate change, regardless of who is in charge. These pessimistic conclusions are now becoming common, in a way that was not true in 2011–12, marking an important transition in public discourse. A growing, although still small portion of the population now understands that the state — even a real democratic state — will not be able to revive capitalist economies. To bring this onwards-grinding wreck to a halt, the passengers can only count on themselves.

BROWN V. FERGUSON

On 21 March 2012 a crowd assembled in New York's Union Square to hear two bereaved parents speak: "My son did not deserve to die"; "Trayvon Martin was you; Trayvon Martin *did* matter".[1] Summoning heavenly powers to their aid, a preacher led the crowd in prayer: "Hallelujah we are Trayvon Martin tonight...". The Million Hoodie March — a reference to the Million Man March called by Nation Of Islam leader Louis Farrakhan in 1995 — had been publicised on social media with the #MillionHoodies hashtag by a New York activist and ad agency worker alongside a change.org petition. Trayvon Martin's parents had themselves only found out about it last minute during a chance visit to New York. But it had gone sufficiently viral to bring out 5,000 to Union Square, and 50,000 across the country, at short notice. Within days the meme would make it into the House of Representatives. Bobby Rush, of Chicago's South Side, donned a hoodie for an address on racial profiling. He was escorted from the chamber by security while the chair droned over him: "the member is no longer recognised".

1 Thanks to Chino, Chris, Danielle, Idris, Jason, Mike and Shemon.

The Million Hoodie March took place while Occupy's flame was guttering, and a residual Occupy presence had been cleared from Union Square only the day before. There was an overlap of personnel, resulting in some off-message chants — "we are the 99%" — and the use of the people's mic. Along with the black nationalists and community organisers who commonly turned out for such events were members of a younger crowd: Zuccotti freaks, anarchists from Brooklyn, members of Occupy the Bronx — many of whom would go on to form the Trayvon Martin Organizing Committee. After the speeches, the rally fragmented, with some heading up to Times Square, and another crowd heading in the opposite direction, for downtown Manhattan, where one rode Wall Street's bronze bull, shouting "I am Trayvon Martin". The accidental symbolic dissonance of that gesture may be taken as marking a junction-point in the recent history of American struggles. Five days before, Occupy protesters had been rebuffed in an attempt to retake Zuccotti Park, and three days later they would march from there to Union Square, demonstrating against police brutality, but this was the waning phase of that movement. Another was waxing.

DESCENDING MODULATIONS

While political composition had tended to present itself as a fundamental, unsolvable riddle for the movements of the global 2011–12 wave, they were not compositionally static. There had been a tendency to produce descending modulations, with the worse-off entering and transforming protests initiated by the better-off: occupations initiated by students or educated professionals over time attracted growing numbers of the homeless and destitute; university demonstrations over fee hikes gradually brought out kids who would never have gone to university in the first place. Later, the Ukraine's Maidan protests, kicked off by pro-European liberals and nationalists, mutated into encampments of dispossessed workers. In England, such modulations had terminated with the crescendo of the 2011 riots, as the racialised poor brought their anti-police fury to the streets.[2]

2 See 'A Rising Tide Lifts All Boats' and 'The Holding Pattern' in *Endnotes* 3, September 2013.

If such compositional descent could bring questions of race into play in the struggles of a country where they are a largely post-colonial development, where less than 4% of the population identify as black, it was unsurprising that such questions would soon press to the fore in the movements of a nation founded substantially on the plantation, where the percentage is three times higher and the urban ghetto a reality. And if the riddle of composition, for movements like Occupy, had stemmed from the lack of any already-existing common identity, "black"—in this country more than any other—seemed perhaps to offer one. Though it was an identity which many of the Occupiers of course could not share, it might at least offer a pole of attraction, a leading edge for mobilisations. Early activists within this wave would thus consciously seek to solve Occupy's "whiteness" problem, which many imagined would facilitate the development of either a broad alliance of workers and the poor, or—for some—a new civil rights movement.

17-year-old Trayvon Martin had been shot and killed on 26 February 2012 during a visit to the suburban gated community where his father's fiancée lived. The homeowners of The Retreat at Twin Lakes in Sanford, Florida had suffered massive losses of equity in the years immediately following the crisis, the value of their homes collapsing, and a couple of recent break-ins had heightened the anxiety. Neighbourhood watch volunteer George Zimmerman was armed and patrolling the area, anticipating a return of the culprits. The appearance of an unrecognised individual, apparently fitting their racialised profile in Zimmerman's mind, prompted him to call the police, before getting involved in some confrontation. That Trayvon had been armed with only a packet of Skittles and an Arizona Ice Tea when shot, but had been clothed in a standard racial signifier—the hoodie—would establish the symbolic coordinates of the case.[3]

But old and new media were silent at first; then on 8 March the story broke in the national press. A social media trickle now began, which would quickly become a torrent as outrage spread at racial profiling and the killing of a teenager. Soon, local actions were being organised: a rally at a church in Sanford; another outside the Seminole County courthouse. But these were not reducible to the spontaneous response of a local community: the first was led by an evangelical preacher from Baltimore; the second was organised by student activists from a newly forming leftist grouping, "Dream Defenders", at the historically black Florida Agricultural

3 Why Trayvon's death in particular triggered such a reaction, in a country where a black man is killed almost every hour, is difficult to understand. Part of the reason may be Trayvon's background, his undoubted 'innocence', making him a safe object of middle class identification. But it is surely also the exaggerated symbolism of the scene: the 'white ethnic' coveting the value of his home, the mirage of a black intruder whose very presence seems to jeopardise it. Such suburban fears have long been entwined with dynamics of racialisation in the us. See Chris Wright, 'Its Own Peculiar Decor' in this issue.

and Mechanical University 300 miles away in Tallahassee, the state capital. By 17 March, the family's calls for Department of Justice intervention were making the *New York Times* — calls swiftly answered, with Emanuel Cleaver of the Congressional Black Caucus announcing an investigation into the case as a possible "hate crime". Four days later, with the Million Hoodie March, the demonstrations too went national.

VERTICAL MEDIATIONS

The next day, Al Sharpton was on the ground in Sanford, leading a demonstration. A TV host, ex-James Brown manager, founder and president of the civil rights organisation National Action Network (NAN), Sharpton is one half of America's celebrity black activist duopoly. The other — who was soon to follow, along with NAACP[4] president Ben Jealous — is Jesse Jackson: twice Democratic presidential candidate, colleague of Martin Luther King Jr., founder of the National Rainbow Coalition and Operation PUSH, as well as their current amalgamation. Sharpton and Jackson are both ordained Baptist ministers, following a standard pattern that entwines civil rights and organised religion; King too was a Baptist minister. With the arrival of such figures and their associated institutions, the nascent movement gained the imprimatur of long-standing civil rights figures and present-day "race leaders".[5]

That most of its leaders were, in living memory, subjected to violent state repression has not prevented the Civil Rights Movement from taking a special, sacrosanct place in national myth.[6] Here, the nation's foundation in the original sin of black chattel slavery is ritually sublimated in the Christ-like figure of King — in whose blood Jackson literally anointed himself. For his speeches, King now sits in the American pantheon alongside Lincoln and Jefferson, and like George Washington he has a national holiday in his honour. For American

4 NAACP (National Association for the Advancement of Colored People): a key African-American civil rights organisation formed in 1909 by a group including WEB Du Bois, initially focused on overcoming Jim Crow laws.

5 Cedric Johnson, *Revolutionaries to Race Leaders: Black Power and the Making of African American Politics* (University of Minnesota 2007).

6 With the knowledge of presidents Kennedy and Johnson, the FBI under J. Edgar Hoover – and its murky COINTELPRO programme – persecuted the movement

schoolchildren, MLK day signals the approach of Black History Month, during which they are told of proud Rosa Parks on the bus and subjected to newsreel footage of Southern cops attacking peaceful protesters. Together these furnish an airbrushed image of a social movement which, fleetingly emergent from the mire of American history, all can safely applaud. In this firmament, Civil Rights appears as the *ur*-model for political action per se, its constellations of historic leaders and events the major points for orientation and aspiration. It was through that movement that part of the black population managed to extricate itself from the descending fate of those who remained in the ghetto. The movement also left behind a significant institutional infrastructure.

and its leaders, including the now-venerated King. During Nixon's presidency it organised the assassination of Fred Hampton and other members of the Black Panther Party.

"Civil rights leaders" such as Sharpton and Jackson, often placed at the front of demonstrations, even have sufficient political heft to regularly get the ear of the President: at the time of writing, Sharpton had clocked up more than 60 invitations to the White House since 2009. If the wave of struggles that would later become known as #BlackLivesMatter has often seemed an exemplar of youthful hashtag activism, and if social media—as lawyers on both sides of George Zimmerman's murder trial would later agree—would be the making of the Trayvon case, it would thus be a mistake to emphasise some putative horizontality at the expense of these more vertical mediations, which were already in gear within a month of Trayvon's death. Such vertically integrated coordination is of course a commonplace of American history, in which the racial bonds among whites have always been stretched over a greater span. Slave owner and yeoman farmer, postbellum landlord and poor white sharecropper, WASP industrialist and Irish immigrant had even less in common than black political elites have today with the predominantly poor victims of racial violence. Yet the yeoman joined slave patrols and fought to defend slavery in the Civil War; the white sharecropper (after the brief interracial alliance of populism) would help to maintain Jim Crow segregation through lynch terror; and the Irish immigrant, though initially racialised himself, would brutally police black neighbourhoods on behalf of his protestant betters. Historically, the vertical mediations of whiteness were able to span these great distances not because of the affinity of culture or kin, but because they were embodied in the American state itself.

Now however, that state was topped by someone ostensibly outside this construct. However tenuously, blackness too now seemed capable — at least in principle — of spanning comparable social distances. Before a month was up, the reticent Obama had conceded to media pressure for a statement, with a lukewarm Rose Garden pronouncement that managed to quietly affirm a personal racial identification with Martin — "if I had a son, he would look like Trayvon" — while simultaneously brushing this under the rug of a common American identity: "all of us as Americans are going to take this with the seriousness it deserves". The rhetorical tension here — racial particularity vs. the universality of national citizenship — registered the constitutive contradiction of American society. This tension had beset Obama's campaign and presidency alike, with race both an asset and a liability.[7] Rhetorical oscillations between these poles would thus consistently structure his reactions to the coming wave of struggles.

MEDIATION AND CAUSATION

But the Al Sharpton or Jesse Jackson-led demonstration after the killing of another black person, typically at police hands, had been a familiar fixture of the American political landscape for decades; the rate of such deaths had been high for years — and may have been even higher in the past.[8] The capacity for a single fatality to set in motion what would — once it had met with some powerful cross-currents — become

7 Its function as an asset here was, of course, rather more novel, surely in some part a measure of the gradual filtering-through of Civil Rights gains. But such things appear distinctly ambivalent in the context of the rotting edifice on which they are perched. There was something disarmingly redemptive about an extremely unequal and grotesquely violent society selecting a black man to be President.

8 Data on police shootings are notoriously incomplete. The best evidence on trends over time is the FBI's charmingly titled 'justifiable homicides by law enforcement'. This series shows peaks in 1980 and 1994. Alexia Cooper and Erica Smith, 'Homicide Trends in the United States, 1980–2008', Bureau of Justice Statistics, 2010, p. 32.

the most significant wave of US struggles in decades thus demands some explanation, and it is here that the particularities of hashtag activism become more important, alongside other key factors. The recent mass uptake of easy-to-use digital tools had lowered the bar for political mobilisation, generalising capacities for active production and dissemination of information. This brought possibilities for countering or bypassing mainstream news agendas, and facilitating processes of questioning the standard practice of simply reiterating police reports within popular media. Other narratives could now be collectively constructed on the basis of relatively little effort on the part of individuals, pulling together particular instances that in previous times would not have been linked. It was through such mediations that a unified cause was to be constructed from a list of geographically and temporally scattered killings, and it is thus in part to these mediations that we must look if we are to grasp the articulation of this movement.

Also, having been more or less made taboo in the long push-back that had started under Nixon, with the wave of crisis-era struggles — and Occupy in particular — open protest had again become both visibly possible and increasingly legitimate. Lastly, the past few years were ones of political-economic and social crisis, with a dwindling of prospects worse in black communities than elsewhere: race is a marker for the most insecure fractions of the US labour force, who are inevitably hit disproportionately by generally declining conditions. It would be the combination of these conjunctural factors with the peculiar social and institutional structures of racial representation in the US that would enable the burgeoning of a singular mass movement. The death of Trayvon Martin was a signal flare illuminating a tortured landscape. There was thus nothing idle about the comparisons that would become commonplace between him and Emmett Till, the murdered 14-year-old whose mutilated features helped spur the civil rights movement.

Martin's parents soon started to undertake their own campaigns over the Trayvon case and related issues, while the demonstrations proliferated nationally and the social media chatter continued to grow. A 24 March 2012 Trayvon demonstration in Hollywood seems to have been the occasion for the first deployment of "Black Life Matters" as a slogan and hashtag, perhaps responding to Trayvon's father, Tracy Martin's assertion just a few days before at the Million Hoodie March, that Trayvon *did* matter. In Martin's case it seems to have been meant programmatically: that Trayvon would be *made* to matter through a campaign, in his name, for justice. Similar performative intent may be perceived in the slogans that emerged at this time. #BlackLivesMatter appeared — perhaps as a corruption of the existing slogan — in the response of @NeenoBrowne to the 12 April announcement that Zimmerman would be charged with murder; the meme may well have an older provenance than that.[9] Whether black people's lives "matter" is a question posed objectively in a country where they are so perfunctorily expended: 6,454 killings in 2012, a figure out of all proportion to the size of the black population.[10] Such memes surely catch on for a reason: they are thoughts already in everyone's heads.

9 blacklifematters.org was registered on 18 March 2012, in the run up to the Million Hoodie March, and appeared on placards at the Hollywood demo. This site links Trayvon actions to charter schools and church-based activism. #BlackLifeMatters remained more common than #BlackLivesMatter through 2012. The activists who would become known as the originators of the latter trace their own story back to the struggles of summer 2013, after Zimmerman was acquitted of all charges.

10 Source: FBI. Crime in the United States, 2012.

HITTING PLASTER

On 6 April Dream Defenders set out on a Civil Rights-model 40-mile march from Daytona Beach, Florida to Sanford. Then from late April another case entwined itself with Trayvon's, adding complexity and further outrage. In Jacksonville, Florida, Marissa Alexander was being prosecuted for aggravated assault after having fired a warning shot at her abusive husband — a shot that, unlike Zimmerman's, had only hit plaster. Florida's version of the "Stand Your Ground" law — which authorises those who are under threat to defend themselves — seemed to be at play in both cases, with distinctly different prospective outcomes.[11] On the one

11 According to the prosecutor, Angela Corey, who also tried the Zimmerman case, Alexander's Stand Your Ground defence failed because she had left the house to retrieve

hand, a man who had killed an unarmed black teenager, invoking the right of self-defence. On the other, a black woman who had harmed no one while defending herself against the threat of violence, and who stood to spend a long time in prison. The bleak combination of these two cases seemed demonstration enough — even before the results of the trials were in — of the racial (and gendered) character of the legal system. The 20 May sentencing of Alexander — given a mandatory minimum of 20 years in prison — only confirmed expectations.[12]

a gun from her car. Although the Twin Lakes police chief had initially cited Stand Your Ground as a justification for releasing Zimmerman without charge, his lawyers did not actually appeal to Stand Your Ground, opting for a standard self-defense plea.

12 Alexander was released on appeal in January 2015, having done three years, with two more to serve under house arrest, wearing an ankle monitor.

The Trayvon case in particular had by now become a national media spectacle and, since Obama's statement, had summoned familiar reactions. From a straightforward national villain, Zimmerman was increasingly celebrated as a folk hero by conservatives. A mediatised battle over representation ensued, with Zimmerman claiming he was being victimised, while Trayvon was given the usual treatment meted out to that elite class of the racialised deceased whose deaths ignite significant protest: his digital presence muckraked by media for any indications he might have been anything less than an "angel". That he was a middle-class kid from a Florida suburb did not prevent such attempts — but it limited their plausibility, and thus probably their efficacy. The outcome would almost certainly have differed had Trayvon actually been a child of the ghetto — as would Obama's capacity to conjure up a parental identification. But still, while the case waited, and Trayvon's family kept plugging away at small-scale activism, the media coverage gradually dropped off, and the social media torrents reduced to a plaintive trickle.

Then on 23 November another name was added to the list: Jordan Davis, 17, shot and killed, also in Jacksonville, Florida, by Michael Dunn. Davis's offense was that he played loud hip-hop in his car, for which he earned ten shots from a 9mm handgun, three of which hit and killed him. This was a random act of rage from someone with an antipathy to what he saw as "thug" culture, though Dunn too would claim self-defence, having felt threatened by a mysterious shotgun that was never to be found.[13] With another, similar Floridian case in so many months it was probably inevitable that #RIPJordanDavis would join #RIPTrayvonMartin. On 1 December, Dream Defenders staged a vigil for Davis a couple of hours away in Tallahassee. And the Davis family soon joined the sad daisy chain of the campaigning bereaved, linking up with Trayvon's family for anti-gun-violence events in the aftermath of the Sandy Hook school shooting. They drew on family history associating them with civil rights struggle, while Davis's mother would later tell a melancholy story linking the two fates:

> Jordan kept saying [of Trayvon Martin], "Mom, that could have been me. Mom, that could have been me." We talked at length. He said, "He didn't even do anything wrong." And I told him, "Jordan, you don't have to be doing anything wrong. You are a young black male and there are certain people who will never give you respect."[14]

Gun control and Stand Your Ground: these were the tangible and immediately prospectless campaigning issues at play at this time, in the long months while people waited for the Zimmerman trial to begin. But, of course, a generalised sense that there was something specifically *racial* at work in such things had never gone away. A late December demonstration in Oakland, California, drew links between Trayvon and a local black man, Alan Blueford, who had died at the hands of the cops, while in January 2013, *JET Magazine* — which had published the original photos of Emmett Till — placed Davis's portrait on its cover with the headline: Is your child next?

On 9 March 2013, 16-year-old Kimani Grey was shot and killed by plainclothes police in East

13 In autumn 2014, when America was boiling in the aftermath of Michael Brown's shooting, Dunn would be found guilty of three counts of attempted murder and sentenced to life in prison without parole.

14 Ta-Nehisi Coates, 'To Raise, Love, and Lose a Black Child', *The Atlantic*, 8 October 2014.

Flatbush, Brooklyn in an event whose contradictory accounts — gun-brandishing gang member or unarmed innocent executed in cold blood while fleeing for his life — would never be reconciled. This brought New York City the closest thing to an anti-police riot since the 1980s — a smashed pharmacy and cars in flames a few blocks from the site of the shooting, after teenagers broke away from a vigil — with further gatherings on subsequent nights as #BrooklynRiot spread on Twitter. Local council member Jumaane Williams showed up with heavies to shut things down in the name of the community, accusing Occupy of sending outside agitators. This was an early instance in a pattern that would become general, of existing black organisations claiming to represent the movement, their legitimacy in this respect a function of their ability to rein in the violence. But what distinguished protest for Grey from that for Trayvon and Davis was the confinement to a locality and relative lack of mediation: though it was soon added to the hashtag memorials, actions in Grey's name differed. In lieu of the solidarity protests of far-flung activists accompanied by waves of social media chatter in the weeks and months after an incident, the reaction to Grey's death was near in both time and space.[15] Such formal differences may be read as indexes of distinct compositions.

15 Flatbush may be seen as an instance of an older tradition of community riots in response to police shootings – one also evidenced in the 2009 Oscar Grant riots in Oakland. There local 'community leaders' found themselves largely outflanked due to their longstanding alliances with mayor Jean Quan. On Flatbush see Fire Next Time, 'The Rebellion Contained: The Empire Strikes Back', 15 March 2013; Nick Pinto, 'Everybody Wants a Piece of Kimani Gray', *Village Voice*, 20 March 2013.

THE PRESIDENT IS TRAYVON MARTIN

In June 2013 — in the summer that marked the fiftieth anniversary of the March on Washington — Black Life Matters activists were in Chicago's South Side responding to gun violence by "collecting dreams". Then came Zimmerman's 14 July acquittal on all charges. This brought the bellows to bear again on 2012's embers. On 16 July Dream Defenders started a several-week sit-in at Florida's Capitol building, demanding a Trayvon Martin Act to repeal Stand Your Ground and outlaw racial profiling, and with Twitter and Tumblr posts on the Zimmerman trial, the #BlackLivesMatter variant now reared its head again, this time under the stewardship of activists — Alicia Garza, Patrisse Cullors and Opal Tometti — who would later become leading figures in the movement and assert ownership of this slogan.[16] Meanwhile the state proffered carrot and half-concealed stick: under Democratic pressure, US Senate hearings on Stand Your Ground (at which Trayvon Martin's and Jordan Davis's families would testify) were announced on 19 July, while Obama now identified *himself* with Trayvon — and as a victim of racial prejudice — speaking at significant length on issues of race, suggesting that there may be some legislative reforms ahead, while simultaneously upholding the neutrality of the existing law, and warning against violent protest. Here was that tension again: "black" and "president" in some ways at odds; now, perhaps more than ever, the former rhetorically encroaching on the latter, probably in reasoned anticipation that the Trayvon Martin case would not quietly die.

16 Alicia Garza, 'A Herstory of the #BlackLivesMatter Movement', *The Feminist Wire*, 7 October 2014.

The next day, in customary fashion, Al Sharpton and the National Action Network announced demonstrations in "100 cities". The Martin, Alexander and Davis protests had so far been centred on their home state of Florida — with solidarity actions coming from America's two activist metropoles, New York City and the Bay Area. Demonstrations now spread to DC, Atlanta, Dallas, Cincinnati, New Orleans, Minneapolis, and on, though Florida remained a base, with protests in Jacksonville and Miami. The Alexander case was still on the agenda, with a Jacksonville rally called by Jesse Jackson. The latter — who lent his physical support to the Tallahassee sit-in — was also offering to mobilise institutional force in aid of the younger demonstrators. Florida was, said Jackson, an "apartheid state", and — singing from the standard Civil Rights hymnbook — "the Selma of our time". Though the standard power brokers of black politics could obviously not fill demonstrations and occupations all by themselves, now, as in spring 2012, this was evidently more than a spontaneous upsurge.

Indeed, the concerted push from student-led demonstrations and occupations — and, later, riots — as well as the institutional and personnel holdovers of Civil Rights activism, all the way up to the legislative organs of the American state, with diplomatic mediation and concessions announced by the President, is one of the most remarkable aspects of this wave of struggles. Set against Occupy or the anti-globalisation movement, it has had a peculiar social and institutional "depth" — one only possible, perhaps, in a country beset by race's constitutive contradiction, where Civil Rights legacies perform important social and ideological functions. With a now-sizeable black middle class still prone to identify along racial lines before any other, and with an active black presence in higher state institutions, there is a social basis, it would seem, for substantially vertical modes of movement composition which defy traditional storytelling about radical upsurges and their inevitable cooptation. This was the composition that "black" brought.

Before long even Oprah Winfrey — a *Forbes* rich list member worth $3 billion — was wading in, drawing parallels between Trayvon Martin and Emmett Till. And within a month came the mediatic spectacle of the March on Washington anniversary and the "National Action to Realize the Dream March", bringing out the Obamas, Bill Clinton and Jimmy Carter (but notably no Bushes; Carter pointedly identified Democratic fortunes with Civil Rights gains) to glory in Civil Rights as national myth. Sharpton took a historic opportunity to criticise black youth culture and its "sagging pants", to much applause. But attendance estimates were much lower than anticipated — probably somewhere in the 10,000s. While the symbology of Civil Rights is never far away in this wave of struggles, this was evidence, perhaps, that the sentiments exposed by the Trayvon case were looking for something other than monuments to a previous generation's heroism; Luther dons the mask of the Apostle Paul.

FUCK THE FEDS

At this stage activist strategy remained largely confined to a Civil Rights playbook. First highlight local instances of racist violence or institutional discrimination in order to draw in the federal government. Then use Department of Justice or FBI investigations into "civil rights violations" to extract concessions from state and local officials.[17] This orientation to the federal government might seem surprising — especially given its role in crafting policies that have adversely affected African Americans. But race and the US state have had a long and intimate relationship in which the latter's role cannot simply be reduced to either abuse or accommodation, and it would be a mistake to read the function of the state here as a matter of the simple incorporation of a previous generation's insurgent black politics. Black people in America have been continually exposed to high levels of arbitrary violence. This violence has often been inflicted directly by agents of federal, state and municipal governments; at other times by private actors with the tacit or explicit approval of the state. But jurisdictional conflicts between different levels of government have also allowed black movements, in certain periods, to play one off the other. Indeed their attempts to do so have shaped the existing division of powers in the United States.

17 This game plan has been tacitly assumed by most actors in the current wave, from Dream Defenders and Organization for Black Struggle at the local level, up to NAN and the NAACP at the national level, whether the immediate demand was repeal of Stand Your Ground or police reform. As a strategy it was more visible in the early days, but it would return to prominence in summer 2015, with the approach of the Democratic primaries.

18 Lisa Miller, *Perils of Federalism* (Oxford 2008).

Prior to the Civil War, tight restrictions on federal power had been introduced into the Constitution explicitly to forestall any potential for Congress to undermine or outlaw slavery in the Southern states, and federal legal protection had been largely limited to slaveowners — the Constitution's Commerce and Fugitive Slave Clauses confined the federal enforcement of property rights

19 Federal support for Civil Rights was partly explained by the incompatibility between Jim Crow and the role of the US as 'leader of the

to the kind of property that had a tendency to flee across state lines. But after the war the 14th and 15th amendments, together with the Enforcement Acts, gave Congress unprecedented powers to overrule state law in order to protect the former slaves from their former masters. These amendments, along with a beefed-up interpretation of the Commerce Clause, still underlie federal power over state judiciaries today. The question of race is thus bound intimately to the very structure of political power in America.

But the intended beneficiaries of these developments were abandoned almost immediately by the newly empowered federal government amid a backlash against Reconstruction, led by a revanchist Southern elite. A series of Supreme Court decisions culminating in Plessy v. Ferguson (1896) succeeded in depriving Southern blacks of their newfound constitutional protections. And even as federal judicial oversight and intervention expanded in the early twentieth century to cover organised crime, auto theft, drug and prostitution rackets — billed as "white slavery" — the federal government consistently ignored the appeals of anti-lynching campaigners.[18] It was only after Brown v. Board of Education (1954), when Jim Crow had become both unprofitable and a national embarrassment,[19] that Southern blacks were finally able to discount these constitutional promissory notes.[20] In a sense, black people were both the first and last to enjoy access to federal protection.

Of course today, as in the past, those protections remain very limited. The Department of Justice has been inconsistent in enforcing its civil rights mandate, and no-one imagines the feds are committed to racial equality. There is perhaps an analogy here with the role of the Chinese Communist Party in making an example of corrupt local officials in order to quell protest and preserve the wider system of corruption. The role of Congress in establishing the basis of mass

free world'. The key pre-condition for the movement's success in the South was that sharecroppers had been replaced by the mechanical cotton harvester, and the rigidly divided Jim Crow labour market proved a drawback to employers in burgeoning Southern cities. The principal beneficiaries of the Civil Rights Movement may have been the Southern white elite, who experienced an influx of regional investment in its wake. See Gavin Wright, *Sharing the Prize: The Economics of the Civil Rights Revolution* (Harvard 2013).

20 There was an ironic inversion here: the 14th amendment, originally addressed to the rights of former slaves, had been reinterpreted as protecting corporations from state regulation and was thus largely overlooked in the Civil

incarceration (see addendum, below) and the recent gutting of the Voting Rights Act by the Supreme Court leave no illusions about the trustworthiness of the federal government in this respect. But the history of Reconstruction shows that there is nothing new in the fact that the supposed saviours of black people can often be their worst enemies.

Rights Act, which instead relied on the Commerce Clause to make private race-based discrimination a federal offence.

BEING BLACK WHILE SEEKING HELP

On 14 September 2013 Jonathan Ferrell, 24, crashed his car in Charlotte, North Carolina and went to a nearby house in search of help. The homeowner called 911 and police officers soon arrived on the scene. Rather than helping Ferrell, police officer Randall Kerrick shot him 10 times.[21] On 2 November Renisha McBride, 19, crashed her car in Dearborn Heights, Michigan, in the Detroit metropolitan area, and went in search of help. Apparently intoxicated and confused, she knocked on Theodore P. Wafer's front door in the early hours of the morning. He responded with a shotgun blast to her face. The appearance of such strikingly repetitive patterns in this story is probably in part a product of the mediation of specific incidents: two cases that separately and with different timing might have drawn little attention in themselves coming to resonate together, the latter case amplifying the former, and both sounding out louder together. But it is surely also in part an artefact of generic structures of American society: the black person deposited in an unfamiliar neighbourhood by a car accident, rousing fears on the part of the resident to whom they attempt to appeal for help, ultimately leading to their death — the whole standard apparatus of suburban anxiety, racialisation and arbitrary violence towards black people shows itself.

21 In this case the NAACP actually *praised* police for promptly bringing charges against Kerrick, though the initial indictment failed. A second Grand Jury indicted him for voluntary manslaughter on 28 January 2014 – a fairly rare occurrence in this chain of events. However, a mistrial was declared in August 2015, with a hung jury reflecting a broader national polarisation over the issue of police killings.

Spokespeople for the McBride family seem to have resisted her insertion into the ongoing macabre narrative of Trayvon et al., but with Michigan's Stand Your Ground law potentially at stake, and Wafer's defence involving the claim that he thought his home was being broken into, the association was probably inevitable — as was Al Sharpton's prompt appearance on the scene, making the case. On the day of McBride's funeral, however, an attempt by Democrats to repeal Florida's Stand Your Ground law was defeated by overwhelming Republican opposition. In the weeks following McBride's death, demonstrations grew in Detroit, with vigils and rallies outside a police station using the Black Lives Matter slogan, while #JusticeForRenisha entered the national chatter. But the lack of Trayvon-esque levels of mobilisation was noted: did black women's lives matter even less?

In February 2014, though Jordan Davis's killer was convicted of 2nd degree murder, a hung jury meant that a full-scale murder charge was left pending further trial. This led to national outrage and Florida demonstrations for Davis. These were followed in major cities across the country by a new round of Trayvon Martin actions. A 10 March demonstration at Florida's State Capitol in Tallahassee, led by Martin's and Davis's parents, as well as the omnipresent Sharpton, demanded repeal of Stand Your Ground. Yet at this point Florida's Republican-dominated legislature actually appeared ready to *extend* this legislation — albeit with a view to cases like Marissa Alexander's where a warning shot is fired. While the country's pulse seemed to be palpably quickening over issues related to these killings, and the "New Civil Rights Movement" idea remained much in the air, it seems conceivable that things might have fizzled at this point into minor Stand Your Ground and gun control campaigns, had further events not intervened.

I CAN'T BREATHE

But at mid-summer, while Dream Defenders were organising "Freedom Schools" across Florida — modelled on the obligatory Civil Rights precedent — New

York cops added another name to the list, while managing to bring police brutality to the fore in the mix of live issues: Eric Garner, 43, killed in a chokehold on 17 July 2014 on Staten Island, New York City, by police officer Daniel Pantaleo. Garner apparently sold "loosies"—individual cigarettes purchased in neighbouring states like Pennsylvania or Delaware where taxes were lower—and had already been arrested multiple times in 2014 for this minor misdemeanor. For the cops this was a matter of clamping down not on crime but "disorder", part of the "broken windows" policing strategy made famous by the NYPD.[22] Garner's last arrest was captured in a video which was released 6 hours later to immediately go viral: Garner remonstrating with the police officers, referring to the arrests as a pattern of harassment, announcing that "it stops today"; Pantaleo throwing his arm around Garner's neck, while five other cops dragged him to the ground, piling on top of him. In another video we see a crowd gathering while cops insist "he's still breathing"; ambulance workers arriving on the scene fail to notice that he isn't. Garner died on the sidewalk surrounded by his killers, his dying words caught on camera: "I can't breathe. I can't breathe".

Perhaps because the ground had already been prepared by preceding events; perhaps because this event was captured so viscerally; perhaps because it took place in New York City rather than Florida or Michigan, it became clear around this time that a momentum was building. On 19 July demonstrations for Garner took place on Staten Island and in Harlem, with Al Sharpton and NAN involvement. In a speech criticising the police, Sharpton quickly announced a civil rights lawsuit against the NYPD. On 29 July Broadway stars staged a flashmob demonstration for Garner in Times Square. Then a further name: John Crawford, 22, shot and killed by police in Beavercreek, Ohio on 5 August 2014 after picking up a toy gun in a shop. Video of aggressive

22 It seems that the trigger for the clampdown on Garner's spot in the Tompkinsville Park area of Staten Island was the complaints of local shopkeepers and landlords, concerned about customers and property values. 'Beyond the Chokehold: The Path to Eric Garner's Death', *New York Times*, 13 June 2015.

police questioning of Crawford's girlfriend after the killing would further stoke controversy.

And another: on 9 August, 18-year-old Michael Brown Jr. was shot and killed by police officer Darren Wilson in Ferguson, Missouri, a suburb of St. Louis, unarmed, and — witnesses claimed — with his hands up in surrender. If events in this wave of struggles had hitherto largely followed the sanctioned Civil Rights standard of non-violent direct action, now came a shift of key: this was the Watts moment. And if actions had so far been mostly convened and driven by university students and professional activists, those descending modulations now kicked in again, bringing out a substantial cut of Ferguson's poor.

ADDENDUM: ON MASS INCARCERATION

With Ferguson approaching the brink, it probably made little difference to the overall pattern of events that on 7 August Theodore P. Wafer, Renisha McBride's killer, was found guilty of all charges and sentenced to 17–32 years. Indeed, even some activists were doubting whether they could honestly chalk this up as a victory. Patrisse Cullors, an anti-incarceration activist who had set up the Black Lives Matter Network along with Alicia Garza and Opal Tometi, began to worry that the movement was celebrating the very thing she had been campaigning against; she and Garza were actually debating this when Michael Brown's shooting rolled across the television news.[23] Ferguson would put this question on hold, but the fact that the first mass movement against mass incarceration would have, as one of its central demands, *more* incarceration (albeit only for cops and racists) would remain a point of contention.

In 1970 an obscure sociologist from Galveston, Texas, Sidney M. Willhelm, published a book with the incendiary title *Who Needs the Negro?*.[24] In it he argued that

23 Jamilah King, 'How three friends turned a spontaneous Facebook post into a global phenomenon', *The California Sunday Magazine*, 1 March 2015.

24 Sidney M. Willhelm, *Who Needs the Negro?* (Shenkman 1970).

a bitter irony was facing black America: just when the Civil Rights Movement was promising to liberate black people from discrimination in the workplace, automation was killing the very jobs from which they had previously been excluded. Willhelm painted a dystopian future that has proved eerily prophetic. He warned that African Americans were in danger of sharing the fate of American Indians: heavily segregated, condemned to perpetually high levels of poverty and dwindling birth rates — an "obsolescent" population doomed to demographic decline. At the time, in the heady days of Civil Rights success, Willhelm was dismissed as a kook. Today his book is remembered only within some small black nationalist circles.[25]

In retrospect many of Willhelm's predictions bore out, but even his bleak vision failed to anticipate the true scale of the catastrophe in store for black America. He wrote that "the real frustration of the 'total society' comes from the difficulty of discarding 20,000,000 people made superfluous through automation", for "there is no possibility of resubjugating the Negro or of jailing 20,000,000 Americans of varying shades of 'black'." Nowhere in his dystopian imagination could Willhelm envisage an increase in the prison population of the scale that actually occurred in the two decades after his book was published. Yet this was the eventual solution to the problem that Willhelm perceived: the correlation between the loss of manufacturing jobs for African American men and the rise in their incarceration is unmistakable.

Today in the US one in ten black men between the ages of 18 and 35 are behind bars, far more than anything witnessed in any other time or place. The absolute number has fallen in recent years, but the cumulative impact is terrifying. Amongst all black men born since the late 1970s, *one in four* have spent time in prison by their mid-30s. For those who didn't complete high school,

25 Automation has long been a central topic among black revolutionaries and nationalists in the US. C.f. James Boggs, *The American Revolution: Pages from a Negro Worker's Notebook* (Monthly Review Press 1963)

26 Bruce Western, *Punishment and Inequality in America* (Russell Sage Foundation 2006).

27 These reforms, along with new conspiracy charges that could be used to turn any associate into a state's witness, effectively gave sentencing power to prosecutors. Michelle Alexander, *The New Jim Crow: Mass Incarceration in the Age of Colorblindness* (New Press 2010). However, as James Forman Jr. points out, Alexander's backlash thesis overlooks the support of black politicians for this same legislation. James Forman Jr.,

'Racial Critiques of Mass Incarceration: Beyond the New Jim Crow' *NYU Law Review*, vol. 87, 2012.

28 For most of the 20th century, the black incarceration rate was much lower in the South, for Jim Crow lynch terror didn't require jails. With Southern urbanisation and the advent of civil rights this rate began to rise (strikingly it first reached Northern levels in 1965, the year of the Civil Rights Act). But although today the black incarceration rate is higher in the South, racial disparity is lower, for the white incarceration rate has grown even faster (Data: BJS Historical Statistics on Prisoners in State and Federal Institutions).

incarceration has become the norm: 70% have passed through the system.[26] They are typically caged in rural prisons far from friends and family, many are exploited by both the prison and its gangs, and tens of thousands are currently rotting in solitary confinement.

How to explain this modern hellscape? Wilhelm gives us an economic story: capitalists no longer have the capacity or motive to exploit the labour of these men; unnecessary for capital, they are made wards of the state. Michelle Alexander, in *The New Jim Crow*, gives us a political one: fear of black insurgency (a backlash against the successes of the Civil Rights Movement) led white voters to support "law and order" policies, like increased mandatory minimum sentences and reduced opportunity for parole.[27] Alexander underplays the impact of a very real crime wave beginning in the late 1960s, but it is true that these policies were first championed by a Republican "Southern strategy" that did little to conceal a core racial animus, and they began to receive bipartisan support in the 80s, when the crack epidemic united the country in fear of black criminality.

However, if white politicians had hoped to specifically target blacks with these punitive policies then they failed. From 1970 to 2000, the incarceration rate for whites increased just as fast, and it continued to increase even as the black incarceration rate began to decline after 2000. Blacks are still incarcerated at much higher rates, but the black–white disparity actually *fell* over the era of mass incarceration. This is partly a matter of wider demographic trends, such as urbanisation and inter-regional migration, but it means that black people are far from being the only victims of the prison boom.[28] Even if every black man currently in jail were miraculously set free, in a sort of anti-racist rapture, the US would still have the highest incarceration rate in the world.

> Ferguson is a picture of pleasant suburbia, a town of tree-lined streets and well-kept homes, many of them built for the middle class at mid-century. But Ferguson is in north St. Louis County, and the area is suffering from one of the region's weakest real estate markets.
>
> — *St. Louis Post Dispatch*, 18 August 2013

St. Louis has a long history of state mandated racial segregation in the form of redlining, segregated public housing, restrictive covenants and so on.[29] Out of urban engineering and "slum surgery" there came the 1956 Pruitt-Igoe project, which housed 15,000 people in North St. Louis. Modelled partly on Le Corbusier's principles by Minoru Yamasaki, the architect who would go on to design the World Trade Centre, this project became notorious almost immediately for its crime and poverty.[30] Local authorities solved the problem — and that of Pruitt-Igoe's large-scale rent strike — by simply demolishing it in the early 1970s in an event that Charles Jencks famously identified as "the day modern architecture died".[31] North St. Louis has remained heavily impoverished and racialised to the present, with 95 percent of the population identifying as black, and unemployment among men in their twenties approaching 50 percent in many neighbourhoods.

An incorporated city close to the northern edge of St. Louis, Ferguson had been an early destination for white flight, as both workers and jobs moved out of the city in the 1950s and 60s, to escape the desegregated school system and benefit from the lower taxes of suburban St. Louis County. But many of the refugees of the Pruitt-Igoe disaster too fled north to places like Ferguson when other white suburbs blocked the construction of multi-family housing, enforced restrictive covenants, or simply proved too expensive.[32] This was the beginning

29 In 1974 a panel of federal judges concluded that 'segregated housing in the St. Louis metropolitan area was … in large measure the result of deliberate racial discrimination in the housing market by the real estate industry and by agencies of the federal, state, and local governments.' Richard Rothstein, 'The Making of Ferguson: Public Policies at the Root of its Troubles', *Economic Policy Institute*, 15 October 2014.

30 See the 2011 documentary film directed by Chad Freidrichs, 'The Pruitt-Igoe Myth', for an exploration of the social history of this project.

31 With a certain historical irony, some would later view the other famous demolition of Minoru Yamasaki buildings as the day postmodernity died.

of another wave of out-migration — this time black — as crime and poverty swept the deindustrialised city through the 1980s and 90s. Whites now began to leave Ferguson, taking investment and tax revenues with them, and the local government started to allow for the construction of low- and mixed-income apartments in the southeastern corner of the town.[33] These developments fit a general pattern of spatial polarisation and local homogenisation, as segregation has occurred between blocks of increasing size — town and suburb rather than neighbourhood.[34] Through such dynamics, the population of Ferguson has become increasingly black over recent decades: from 1% in 1970, to 25% in 1990, to 67% in 2010. But the local state ruling over this population has lagged significantly behind its rapidly shifting racial profile: in 2014 only about 7.5% of police officers were African-American, and almost all elected officials white. Meanwhile the gender balance has changed just as rapidly, with Ferguson displaying the highest number of "missing black men" in the US: only 60 black men for every 100 women; thus more than 1 in 3 black men absent, presumed either dead or behind bars.[35]

A further influx to Ferguson — and specifically Canfield Green, the apartment complex in the southeast where Michael Brown lived and died — came from another mass demolition of housing stock: neighbouring Kinloch, a much older African American neighbourhood, had also been suffering from the general dynamics of declining population and high crime until much of the area was razed to make way for an expansion of Lambert-St. Louis International Airport. While Kinloch and Ferguson may together form a continuous picture of racialisation, urban decay and brutalisation at the hands of planners and developers, viewed at other scales it is the polarisations that start to appear: a couple of kilometers from Ferguson's southern perimeter lies the small townlet of Bellerive. Bordering on the campus

32 See Anthony Flint, 'A Failed Public-Housing Project Could Be a Key to St. Louis' Future', *Citylab*, 25 August 2014; R.L. 'Inextinguishable Fire: Ferguson And Beyond', *Mute*, 17 November 2014.

33 See Chris Wright, 'Its Own Peculiar Decor', in this issue for an analysis of such dynamics.

34 See Daniel Lichter et al., 'Toward a New Macro-Segregation? Decomposing Segregation within and between Metropolitan Cities and Suburbs', *American Sociological Review*, vol. 80, no. 4, August 2015.

35 The national average for whites is 99 men for 100 women, 83 for blacks. Wolfers et al, '1.5 Million Missing Black Men', *New York Times*, 20 April 2015.

of the University of Missouri-St. Louis, Bellerive has a median family income of around $100,000.

Indeed, Ferguson itself remains relatively integrated by the standards of St. Louis County, with a quite prosperous white island around South Florissant Road. Thus both crime and poverty are lower than in neighbouring suburbs like Jennings and Berkeley. But it is a suburb in transition. If in the 1960s and 70s the racial divisions of St. Louis County were largely carved out by public policy, as well as semi-public restrictive covenants, in the 1990s and 2000s they tended to follow a more discrete and spontaneous pattern of real estate valuations. Ferguson, like Sanford, Florida, was impacted heavily by the recent foreclosure crisis. More than half the new mortgages in North St. Louis County from 2004 to 2007 were subprime, and in Ferguson by 2010 one in 11 homes were in foreclosure. Between 2009 and 2013 North County homes lost a third of their value.[36] Landlords and investment companies bought up underwater properties and rented to minorities. White flight was now turning into a stampede.

36 Jim Gallagher, 'Blame poverty, age for weak North County home market', *St. Louis Post Dispatch*, 18 August 2013.

Because property taxes are linked to valuations, the Ferguson city government had to look elsewhere for funding. Between 2004 and 2011 court fines netted $1.2 million, or around 10% of the city's revenue. By 2013 this figure had doubled to $2.6 million, or a fifth of all revenues. The city's annual budget report attributed this to a "more concentrated focus on traffic enforcement". In that year the Ferguson Municipal Court disposed of 24,532 warrants and 12,018 cases, or about 3 warrants and 1.5 cases per household. A Department of Justice report would soon reveal that these had been far from evenly distributed across the population:

> African Americans account for 85% of vehicle stops, 90% of citations, and 93% of arrests made by FPD

> officers, despite comprising only 67% of Ferguson's population. [They] are 68% less likely than others to have their cases dismissed by the court [and] 50% more likely to have their cases lead to an arrest warrant.[37]

In high poverty areas like Canfield Green, non-payment of fines can easily lead to further fines as well as jail time, and the report found that "arrest warrants were used almost exclusively for the purpose of compelling payment through the threat of incarceration". Here the disappearance of white wealth and the destruction of black had led to a mutation in the form of the local state: revenue collected not through consensual taxation but by outright violent plunder.

37 'Investigation of the Ferguson Police Department', United States Department of Justice, Civil Rights Division, 4 March 2015. The very existence of a DoJ report taking notice of these issues in Ferguson is itself an outcome of the struggles that happened in large part because of them.

MIKE BROWN'S BODY

For four and a half hours Mike Brown's body lay mouldering on the hot tarmac. By the time the cops finally dragged it away—not even into an ambulance but merely the back of an SUV—the pool of blood had turned from red to black. They left the body on the street for so long because they were busy "securing the crime scene", which meant dispersing the large angry crowd that was gathering as residents poured out of surrounding apartments. As local news reporters arrived on the scene, shaky cellphone footage of Brown's body was already beginning to circulate. Dorian Johnson, a friend of Brown's who was with him at the time of the fatal incident, told interviewers that he had been "shot like an animal". Cops reported gunfire and chants of "kill the police". "Hands up, don't shoot" and "We are Michael Brown" would soon be added to the chorus, while someone set a dumpster on fire; signs already that an anti-police riot was in the offing. The exposed body, doubled over, blood flowing down the street, had seemed to say: you matter this much. As if to reinforce the point, more cops arriving on the scene drove over a makeshift memorial of rose petals where Brown's body had lain; a police dog may also have been allowed to urinate on it.

At a daytime vigil the next day, 10 August 2014, a black leader of the County government tried to calm the mounting unrest, but was shouted down. Members of the New Black Panther Party chanted "Black Power" and "rambled nonsensically about that devil rap music, the Moors, etc".[38] As day tilted into evening, the large, restive crowd met with massive police presence—a conventional proto-riot scenario. Confrontations ensued: a cop car and a TV van attacked; shops looted; a QuikTrip gas station the first thing aflame. This acted as a beacon, drawing more people out.[39] And rather than the mythically random object of "mob rage", it was a deliberately selected target: rumour had it that staff had called the cops on Brown, accusing him of shoplifting. The QuickTrip was followed by some riot standards: parked vehicles set alight; looting on West Florissant Avenue—plus a little festivity, music playing, people handing out hotdogs. The cops backed off for hours, leaving that odd sort of pseudo-liberated space that can appear in the midst of a riot.

As the eyes of the nation turned to watch, people joined in on social media with the #IfTheyGunnedMeDown hashtag, mocking the media selection of the most gangsta possible victim portraits. Activists from St. Louis, some of whom had been involved in a spontaneous march the year before through the city's downtown in response to the Zimmerman verdict, began to descend on the suburb. Meanwhile standard mechanisms sprung into action: on 11 August the FBI opened a civil rights investigation into Brown's shooting, while NAACP President Cornell William Brooks flew into Ferguson, calling for an end to violence. Obama intervened the next day with a statement offering condolences to the Brown family and asking for people to calm down.

38 Anonymous testimony posted on Dialectical Delinquents website.

39 The scorched forecourt of this place would become a central gathering point for protests over the coming weeks.

Faced with an immediate wave of rioting, it was predictable which way the constitutive tension would now be resolved: Obama eschewed any racial identification with Brown or his family, in favour of "the broader American community".

But the rioting rolled on over days; action necessarily diffuse in this suburban landscape, police lines straining to span subdivisions.[40] Away from the front lines strip malls were looted while carnivalesque refrains lingered in the air: protesters piling onto slow driving cars, blasting hip-hop, an odd sort of ghost riding. In altercations between cops and protesters the latter sometimes threw rocks or molotovs. But they were also often hands-up, shouting "don't shoot". In retrospect, this may look like an early instance of the theatrics of this wave of struggle, and it would soon become a familiar meme. But it was also apparently a spontaneous response to the immediate situation, right after Brown's shooting, before the media-savvy activists rolled into town at the end of the month — for it had an immediate referent, not only symbolically, in Brown himself, but also practically, as protesters confronted the diverse toolkit of the American state: SWAT teams, tear gas, rubber bullets, pepper balls, flash grenades, bean bag rounds, smoke bombs, armoured trucks. The nation was aghast as images scrolled across screens of this military hardware, of a cop saying "Bring it you fucking animals" — coverage which police attempted at points to shut down.

Social contestation in the US has long faced much greater threat of physical violence than in other comparable countries — indeed, those protesting in Ferguson would also at points be shot at with live ammunition by unidentified gunmen, and sometimes get hit. (This is surely one reason why such contestation often seems markedly muted, given conditions.) Police violence against unarmed black people was thus not a simple

40 Phil A. Neel, 'New Ghettos Burning', *Ultra*, 17 Aug 2014.

content of these protests, an issue for them to merely carry along, like any other demand. It was also implicated in the nature of the protests themselves, where everyone out on the streets those days was a potential Mike Brown. There was, we might say, a peculiar possibility for movement unification presenting itself here; a unity one step from the graveyard, given by the equality that the latter offers; a unity of the potentially killable: hands up, don't shoot. And as the country looked on, this performance of absolute vulnerability communicated something powerful; something with which police were ill-equipped to deal: Will you even deny that I am a living body?

Such messages, broadcast on the national stage, seemed to pose a threat to police legitimacy, and raised practical questions about the continuing management of the Ferguson unrest. Criticism of the militarised policing came even from the midst of the state — albeit its libertarian wing.[41] On the 14th the Highway Patrol — a state police force, less implicated in the immediate locality, with a much higher ratio of black officers and distinctly non-militaristic style — was ordered in as an alternative, softer approach with a view to easing tensions, apparently with some success. In the evening hours, a captain even walked with a large peaceful demonstration. At "an emotional meeting at a church", clergy members were despairing at "the seemingly uncontrollable nature of the protest movement and the flare-ups of violence that older people in the group abhorred."[42] Meanwhile, Canfield Green turned into a block party.

After 5 days of protests often violently dispersed, the name of Brown's killer, Darren Wilson, was finally announced, along with a report that Brown had stolen a pack of cigarillos from Ferguson Market & Liquor — not the QuickTrip gas station — the morning of his death. The timing of this identification of criminality was probably tactical; it was soon followed by an admission

41 Senator Rand Paul, 'We Must Demilitarize the Police', *Time*, 14 August 2014.

42 Julie Bosman, 'Lack of Leadership and a Generational Split Hinder Protests in Ferguson', *New York Times*, 16 August 2014.

that Wilson had not stopped Brown for this reason. That night, Ferguson Market & Liquor received similarly pointed treatment to the QuickTrip: it was looted. The next day a state of emergency and curfew was declared. There were now a small but significant number of guns on the streets, often fired into the air, and police were getting increasingly nervous. On 12 August Mya Aaten-White, great-granddaughter of local jazz singer Mae Wheeler, was shot whilst leaving a protest; the bullet pierced her skull but missed her brain, lodging in her sinus cavity. On 17 August an anarchist from St. Louis was shot in the kidney, the bullet grazing his heart. Both survived and refused to cooperate with police investigations.

While some came in from neighbouring areas, those out on the streets in the early days remained predominantly local residents.[43] But a mass of creepers was already climbing over Ferguson's surface, forming vegetal tangles, trying to grasp some masonry: Christian mimes, prayer and rap circles, wingnut preachers, the Revolutionary Communist Party, "people who would walk between the riot cops and the crowd just saying 'Jesus' over and over again"; a generalised recruitment fair.[44] Bloods and Crips were out, participating in confrontations with cops as well as apparently protecting some stores from looters. Nation of Islam members too took to the streets attempting to guard shops, arguing that women should leave; others called for peace in the name of a new Civil Rights Movement; Jesse Jackson was booed and asked to leave a local community demonstration when he took the opportunity to ask for donations to his church; "African-American civic leaders" in St. Louis were said to be "frustrated by their inability to guide the protesters": a rift seemed to be opening.[45]

This riot could easily have remained a local affair like those in Cincinnati 2001, Oakland 2009 or Flatbush

43 Solid statistics on participation seem to be unavailable at present, but arrest figures chime with logical readings of the events: in its first phase, Ferguson was clearly a community anti-police riot, and its social character may thus be judged in part by using the place itself as a proxy. Ann O'Neill, 'Who was arrested in Ferguson?', *CNN*, 23 August 2015.

44 Various, 'Reflections on the Ferguson Uprising', *Rolling Thunder #12*, spring 2015.

45 Bosman, 'Lack of Leadership and a Generational Split'.

the year before. Yet it happened to coincide with a high point in a national wave of activism, and it managed to shake free of local mediators, opening up a space for others to interpret and represent it at will. Soon social media-organised busloads of activists descended on Missouri from around the country — Occupy and Anonymous apparently identities at play here, plus a scattering of anarchists. In the following month "Freedom Rides" — another Civil Rights reference — were organised under the Black Lives Matter banner: it was at this point that this really emerged in its own right as a prominent identity within these movements. Ferguson was mutating from a terrain of community riots into a national centre for activism. Key figures began to emerge, often identified by their number of Twitter followers: some local, like Johnetta Elzie ("Netta") and Ashley Yates, others who had made the pilgrimage, like DeRay McKesson from Minneapolis.[46]

46 For profiles of the new activists, see 'The Disruptors', *CNN*, 4 August 2015.

THE NEW RACE LEADERS

> It's more than a hashtag — it's a civil rights movement.
> — *YES! Magazine,* 1 May 2015

All the pieces were now in place. What appeared as one movement was actually two: media-savvy activists and proletarian rioters, for the most part divided both socially and geographically.[47] But in Ferguson's aftermath this divide was spanned by a shared sense of urgency; by the diverse resonances of a hashtag; by developing institutional bridges; and perhaps above all by the legacy of the Civil Rights Movement itself, with its ability to conjure black unity. The similarities were many: "black lives matter" evoking the older slogan "I am a man";[48] the faith and religious rhetoric of many activists; the tactics of nonviolent civil disobedience and media visibility — contrasted with the far more opaque riots; not to mention the direct involvement of Civil Rights organisations and veterans themselves.

47 Special thanks to Chino for help on this section.

48 The iconic photo of men carrying signs reading 'I am a man' is of striking garbage workers in Memphis, 1968. That slogan can in turn be linked back to the 18th century abolitionist slogan 'am I not a man and a brother?', which was echoed by Sojourner Truth's 'ain't I a woman?'.

The key to this encounter is the simple fact that the historic gains of the Civil Rights Movement failed to improve the lives of most black Americans. Today racial disparities in income, wealth, schooling, unemployment and infant mortality are as high as ever. Segregation persists. Lynching and second class citizenship have been replaced by mass incarceration. The fight against a New Jim Crow would thus seem to require the kind of movement that overthrew the Old. But something fundamental has changed and therefore troubles this project: a small fraction of African Americans reaped significant benefits from the end of *de jure* discrimination. In 1960, 1 in 17 black Americans were in the top quintile of earners; today that number is 1 in 10 (for whites it is 1 in 6). Inequality in wealth and income has risen significantly among African Americans, such that today it is much higher than among whites.[49]

For some Marxists, the participation of the black middle class in anti-racist movements is seen as a sign of their limited, class-collaborationist character. When such people become leaders it is often assumed they will attend only to their own interests, and betray the black proletariat.[50] It is true, as such critics point out, that the institutional and political legacy of Civil Rights has more or less been monopolised by wealthier blacks.[51] However, these critiques tend to run up against notorious problems with defining the middle class, problems that are particularly acute when it comes to the black middle class. In American political ideology "the middle class" consists of everyone except the poorest members of society. For mainstream sociology it is the centre of a spectrum of income or wealth, a variously wider or narrower range around the median. Weberians add certain status markers to the definition, such as supervisory roles in the workplace, "white collar" professions, or college education. Finally, Marxists tend to simply add, in an *ad hoc* manner, the mainstream or Weberian definitions to a two-class model based on ownership

49 A simple measure is the ratio of top to bottom income quintiles within the black population. In 1966 this was 8.4 (the richest 20% blacks had about 8 times the income of the bottom 20%); by 1996 it had doubled to 17. The corresponding figures for whites were 6.2 and 10. Cecilia Conrad et al., *African Americans in the* US *Economy* (Rowman and Littlefield 2006), pp. 120–124.

50 See, e.g., Adolph Reed Jr., 'Black Particularity Reconsidered', *Telos* 39, 1979; Keeanga-Yamahtta Taylor, 'Race, class and Marxism', *Socialist Worker,* 4 January 2011.

51 For example, affirmative action has been largely restricted to white collar professions and elite universities. C.f. the 1978 'Bakke' struggle over quotas in medical schools.

or non-ownership of the means of production. None of these approaches provide us with a consistent class subject bearing a coherent set of interests.

These problems of definition are amplified with the black middle class. We know that there has been an influx of black people, women in particular, into "white collar" professions, but this occurred just when much of the higher status associated with this work was being stripped away.[52] We know that many more black people today have a college education, but also that the value of a college education has fallen sharply in recent decades. (One might reasonably surmise that these things may be connected...) The transformation in the income distribution, both between blacks and whites and among blacks, thus seems more revealing than these Weberian measures. However, the rising incomes experienced by certain families since the 1960s have not always been durable. The intergenerational transmission of wealth is less assured for African Americans, whose historical exclusion from real estate markets has meant that middle income earners typically possess much less wealth than white households in the same income range. As a result, those born into middle income families are more likely than whites to make less money than their parents.[53] Downward mobility was amplified by the recent crisis, which negatively affected black wealth much more than white.[54]

Partly because available measures of social structure are so shaped by this notion, partly because there really are strata whose most salient structural trait is their falling — however vaguely — between true elites and those unambiguously identifiable as poor, it is impossible to do away with the concept of the "middle class". Here, and in what follows, we use "middle class" in the mainstream sense, to mean middle income earners. But one must remain on guard about the ambiguities and potential traps lurking in this term. In the case of the

52 13% of black employees were 'white collar' in 1967, 40% in 1984 and 51% in 2010 (compared to 62% of whites). Bart Landry, 'The Evolution of the New Black Middle Class', *Annual Review of Sociology* 37, no. 1, 2011.

53 Of those born into the bottom quintile, over 90% of both blacks and whites earned more than their parents, but only 66% of blacks born in the second quintile surpass their parents' income, compared with 89% of whites. Pew Trusts, 'Pursuing the American Dream: Economic mobility across generations', 9 July 2012

54 From 2005 to 2009, the average black household's wealth fell by more than half, to $5,677, while white household wealth fell only 16% to $113,149. Rakesh Kochhar et al, '20 to 1: Wealth Gaps Rise to Record

"black middle class" the fundamental problem is that it tends to conflate two different layers: (1) those who made it into stable blue-collar or public sector professions, and who thus achieved a little housing equity, but who generally live close to the ghetto, are a paycheck away from bankruptcy, and got fucked by the subprime crisis; and (2) a smaller petit-bourgeois and bourgeois layer that made it into middle-management positions or operated their own companies, who moved into their own elite suburbs, and who are now able to reproduce their class position.

Many of the new activist leaders fall into one or another of these layers.[55] This in itself is nothing new. The old Civil Rights leaders also tended to come from the "black elite". Yet that elite was relatively closer to the black proletariat in income and wealth, and was condemned by Jim Crow to live alongside them and share their fate. It consisted of religious and political leaders, as well as professionals, shopkeepers, and manufacturers who monopolised racially segmented markets — the "ghetto bourgeoisie". Although many helped to build Jim Crow segregation, acting as "race managers", they also had an interest in overcoming the barriers that denied them and their children access to the best schools and careers, and thus in the Civil Rights Movement they adopted the role of "race leaders", taking it as their task to "raise up" the race as a whole.[56]

The new activists distinguish themselves from the previous generation along technological, intersectional and organisational lines. They are suspicious of top-down organising models and charismatic male leaders. But this is less a rejection of leadership per se than a reflection of the fact that — in an age of social media niches — almost anyone can now stake a claim to race leadership, to broker some imaginary constituency. They strain against the hierarchical structures of traditional NGOs, although many are staff members thereof.

Highs Between Whites, Blacks and Hispanics', Pew Social & Demographic Trends 2011.

55 Alicia Garza, co-founder of the Black Lives Matter network, grew up in predominantly white Marin County, CA, where the median household income is over $100,000. DeRay McKesson, by contrast, grew up in a poor neighbourhood of Baltimore. Yet he earnt a six-figure salary as the director of human capital for the Minneapolis School District, where he developed a reputation for ruthlessness in firing teachers. Jay Caspian Kang, 'Our Demand Is Simple: Stop Killing Us', *New York Times*, 4 May 2015.

56 On the history of 'race management', see Kenneth W. Warren, 'Race to Nowhere', *Jacobin* 18, summer 2015.

They identify more with the inspiring prison break of Assata Shakur than with the careful behind-the-scenes coalition-building of Bayard Ruskin. They want to shake off these stultifying mediations in a way that aligns them with the younger, more dynamic Ferguson rioters, and social media seems to give them that chance.

But despite their good intentions and radical self-image, and despite the real unity that Ferguson seemed to offer, differences between the new generation of race leaders and the previous one only reinforce the gap between the activists and those they hope to represent. Those differences can be described along three axes:

1 Firstly, most of the activists are college-educated. And unlike the previous generation they have not been restricted to all-black colleges.[57] This doesn't mean they are guaranteed well-paid jobs, far from it. But it does mean that they have a cultural experience to which very few people from poor neighbourhoods in Ferguson or Baltimore have access: they have interacted with many white people who are not paid to control them, and they will typically have had some experience of the trepid, cautious dance of campus-based identity politics, as well as the (often unwanted) advances of "white allies". Thus although their activism isn't always directed at white liberals, their social and technical abilities in this respect often exceed those of skilled media-manipulators like Sharpton.

2 Secondly, unlike the previous generation, many of them did not themselves grow up in the ghetto. This is perhaps the single biggest legacy of the Civil Rights Movement: the ability to move to the suburbs, for those who could afford it. In 1970, 58% of the black middle class lived in poor majority-black neighbourhoods; today the same percentage live in wealthier majority-white neighbourhoods, mostly in the suburbs.[58] This means that they have much less personal experience of

57 Many are from elite universities, including Nyle Fort at Princeton, and the Black Ivy Coalition. DeRay McKesson, alum of an elite Maine liberal arts college, was recently hired by Yale.

58 Patrick Sharkey, 'Spatial segmentation and the black middle class', *American Journal of Sociology* 119, no. 4, 2014.

59 Karyn Lacy describes the 'exclusionary boundary work' with which the black middle class distinguishes itself from the black poor in the eyes of white authority figures. *Blue Chip Black: Race, Class, and Status in the New Black Middle Class* (UC Press 2007).

60 Today white men with no highschool education are incarcerated at three times the rate of black men with a college education. Western, *Punishment and Inequality.*

crime. Of course, they still experience racist policing, are stopped by cops far more than whites and are subject to all manner of humiliations and indignities, but they are much less likely to be thrown in jail or killed.[59] Indeed the likelihood of ending up in jail has fallen steadily for the black middle class since the 1970s even as it has skyrocketed for the poor, both black and white.[60]

3 Finally, and perhaps most significantly, activism is for them, unlike the previous generation, in many cases a professional option. Today an expectation of "race leadership" is no longer part of the upbringing of the black elite. Identification with the victims of police violence is generally a matter of elective sympathy among those who choose to become activists, and of course many do not make that choice.[61] But for those who do, traditional civil service jobs and voluntary work have been replaced by career opportunities in a professionalised non-profit sector. These jobs are often temporary, allowing college graduates to "give back" before moving on to better things.[62] DeRay McKesson, before he became the face of the new activism, had been an ambassador for Teach for America, an organisation that recruits elite college graduates to spend two years teaching in poor inner-city schools, often as part of a strategy to promote charter schools and bust local teacher's unions.[63] In general the "community organising" NGOs, whether they are primarily religious or political, are often funded by large foundations such as Ford, Rockefeller and George Soros' Open Society. An integral aspect of the privatisation of the American welfare state, they can also function as "astroturf": supposedly grassroots political movements that are actually fronts for lobby groups (e.g. school reform) and the Democrats.

Thus, in the aftermath of Ferguson, along with the influx of activists from around the country there came an influx of dollars. Whilst existing non-profits competed to recruit local activists, foundations competed to fund

61 On the growing gap between proletarian and middle class black identity, see Ytasha L. Womack, *Post Black: How a New Generation Is Redefining African American Identity* (Chicago Review Press 2010); Touré, *Who's Afraid of Post-Blackness?: What It Means to Be Black Now* (Free Press 2011).

62 See e.g., Obama's stint in a church-based community organisation on Chicago's South Side.

63 DeRay is not the only Teach for America (TFA) leader involved. CEO Matt Kramer showed up at the Ferguson protests, and Brittany Packnett, executive director of St. Louis TFA, launched Campaign Zero along with DeRay and Netta. Anya Kamenetz, 'A #BlackLivesMatter Leader At Teach For America', *NPR*, 12 May 2015.

new non-profits, picking winners.[64] Netta was initially recruited by Amnesty International, and she and DeRay would set up Campaign Zero with backing from Open Society.[65] Subsequently DeRay gave up his six-figure salary to "focus on activism full time".[66] Some local activists were not so lucky. Many lost their jobs and became dependent on small, crowd-funded donations. In January 2015 Bassem Masri, who livestreamed many of the original protests, was outed by a rival livestreamer as an ex-junkie.[67]

REFORM RIOTS

On 18 August Missouri Governor Jay Nixon called in the National Guard to enforce the curfew. Two days later Attorney General Eric Holder traveled to Ferguson, where he met with residents and Brown's family. In nearby Clayton, a grand jury began hearing evidence to determine whether Wilson should be charged. On 23 August at least 2,500 turned out for a Staten Island Garner demonstration, led by Sharpton, with chants of "I can't breathe", and "hands up, don't shoot", picking up the meme from Ferguson. A group called Justice League NYC, affiliated with Harry Belafonte, demanded the firing of Officer Pantaleo and the appointment of a special prosecutor. The next day, Brown's funeral in St. Louis was attended by 4,500, including not only the ubiquitous Sharpton and Jackson, and Trayvon Martin's family, but also White House representatives, Martin Luther King III, and a helping of celebrities: Spike Lee, Diddy, and Snoop Dogg. In the name of Brown's parents, Sharpton's eulogy disparaged rioting:

> Michael Brown does not want to be remembered for a riot. He wants to be remembered as the one who made America deal with how we are going to police in the United States.

64 The Open Society Foundation claimed to have 'invested $2.5 million to support frontline community groups in Ferguson' including Organization for Black Struggle and Missourians Organizing for Reform and Empowerment. See 'Healing the Wounds in Ferguson and Staten Island', Open Society Foundations blog, 19 December 2014.

65 Darren Sands, 'The Success And Controversy Of #CampaignZero And Its Successful, Controversial Leader, DeRay Mckesson', *Buzzfeed*, 14 Sept 2015.

66 DeRay also sits on the board of Justice Together, a new non-profit dedicated to 'ending police brutality', along with a director of the Rockefeller Foundation and several Silicon Valley liberal-libertarians. See Tarzie, 'Meet The New Police Reform

But these were, of course, not mutually exclusive, as the history of riot-driven reform testifies. While riots generally consolidate reaction against a movement — with the usual pundits baying for punitive measures, while others jostle to conjure from the events a more reasonable, law-abiding "community" with themselves at its head — they also tend to shake the state into remedial action. Only days later the Justice Department announced an enquiry into policing in Ferguson. Shortly after, large-scale reforms to Ferguson's political and legal institutions were announced. By the end of September the Ferguson police chief had publicly apologised to the Brown family, who were also invited to the Congressional Black Caucus convention, where Obama spoke on race. From the single national community invoked against the immediate impact of rioting, he again ceded significant ground to the particularity of racial questions, speaking of the "unfinished work" of Civil Rights, while simultaneously presenting this as an issue for "most Americans".

Unrest was still ongoing through September, overstretching Ferguson's police force, who would soon be replaced again, this time by St. Louis County police. With the thickets of organisations and professional activists on the ground, other, more theatrical and non-violent forms of action were now tending to replace the community riot, such as the 6 October interruption of a St. Louis classical concert with the old Depression-era class struggle hymn "Which side are you on?". On the same day a federal judge ruled on the side of peaceful activists and against police, over whether demonstrations could be required to "keep moving". Meanwhile, Eric Holder announced a general Department of Justice review of police tactics, and from 9 October Senate hearings began on the question of militarised policing. Ferguson actions stretched on through October, under the aegis of many different groups, including "Hands Up United", which had been formed locally after Brown's death, while more protesters rolled in from around the country.

Bosses', *The Rancid Honeytrap,* 25 June 2015.

67 This appears to have been motivated by competition over potential funders. Sarah Kenzior, 'Ferguson Inc.', *Politico Magazine,* 4 March 2015.

Elsewhere, demonstrations for John Crawford were ongoing, with the occupation of the police station in Beavercreek, Ohio, and rallies at the Ohio statehouse. Out of these, a draft "John Crawford Law" was to emerge, a bold bit of legislation requiring toy guns sold in Ohio to be identifiably marked as toys. After all, Ohio police did seem to have a peculiar difficulty with differentiating toys from real weapons — at least when in the hands of black people — for another name was soon to be added to the list: Tamir Rice, 12, shot and killed in Cleveland, Ohio on 23 November 2014 by police officer Timothy A. Loehmann while playing with what the 911 caller had already identified as a toy. Two days later, Tamir Rice protesters would bring gridlock to downtown Cleveland.

In mid-November, as the Grand Jury decision on Brown's killer drew near, Missouri Governor Jay Nixon had once again declared a state of emergency, bringing in the National Guard in anticipation of the usual non-indictment and a new round of rioting.[68] On 24 November these expectations were fulfilled. As the non-indictment was announced, Michael Brown's mother was caught on camera yelling "They're wrong! Everybody wants me to be calm. Do you know how those bullets hit my son?". As she broke down in grief, her partner, wearing a shirt with "I am Mike Brown" written down the back, hugged and supported her for a while, before turning to the crowd, clearly boiling over with anger, to yell repeatedly "burn this bitch down!"; if Mike Brown's life mattered little to the state, it might at least be made to. As looting and gunshots rattled around the Ferguson and St. Louis area, protests ignited in New York, Sanford, Cleveland, Los Angeles, Seattle, Washington and on — reportedly 170 cities, many using the tactic of obstructing traffic. After a "die-in" and roving traffic-blocking in the perennial activist hotspot of

68 In the US, a Grand Jury plays a filtering role in relation to normal court proceedings, determining in secret whether criminal charges should be brought. They are led by a prosecutor, and the defence presents no case. The lack of accountability here makes them a preferred option in these sorts of circumstances. Although under normal circumstances the absence of defence typically increases the likelihood of indictment, if the prosecutor who leads the jury is himself reluctant to indict (due to institutional ties with the police), then non-indictments are more or less guaranteed, and can always be blamed on the Grand Jury itself.

69 See, e.g., 'Presbyterian Church Stated Clerk responds to Ferguson grand jury decision', pcusa.org,

Oakland, riots spread, with looting, fires set, windows smashed. In the midst of the national unrest, church groups made interventions criticising the Grand Jury decision and supporting peaceful demonstrations. Ferguson churches brought a newly religious twist to activist "safe spaces" discourses, offering themselves as "sacred spaces" for the protection of demonstrators.[69]

In the following days, as the National Guard presence in Ferguson swelled, demonstrations were ongoing across the country—and beyond. Outside a thoroughly bulwarked US Embassy in London, around 5,000 assembled in the dank autumn evening of 27 November for a Black Lives Matter demonstration, before this precipitated in a roving "hands up, don't shoot" action down Oxford Street and confrontations with cops in Parliament Square—an event that drew links between Brown and Tottenham's Mark Duggan, whose own death had ignited England's 2011 riot wave.[70] In cities across Canada, too, there were Ferguson solidarity actions.[71] On 1 December Obama invited "civil rights activists" to the White House to talk, while the St. Louis Rams associated themselves with the Brown cause, walking onto the field hands-up.

Then on 3 December 2014 came the second Grand Jury non-indictment in just over a week: the officer whose chokehold had killed Eric Garner, in full vision of the country at large, predictably cleared of wrongdoing. Cops, of course, are almost never charged for such things, and are even less likely to be convicted, in the US or elsewhere; the executors of state violence cannot literally be held to the same standards as the citizenry they police, even though their credibility depends upon the impression that they are. Due process will be performed, stretched out if possible until anger has subsided, until the inevitable exoneration; only in the most blatant or extreme cases will individual officers be sacrificed on the altar of the police force's general

24 Nov 2014: 'We call the church to pray that God will give us the courage and strength to have honest conversations about race where we live, work, and worship. We pray for safe spaces in Ferguson and in all communities for people to voice their views.'

70 For an account of the Duggan case, and the riot wave that followed it, see 'A Rising Tide Lifts All Boats', *Endnotes* 3, September 2013.

71 Early on, Palestinians had sent messages of solidarity with Ferguson, including tips for dealing with riot police – an echo of the international linkages that had once characterised the Black Power movement. In April, as Baltimore was recovering from its own riot wave, Ethiopian Israelis would also draw connections between their own

legitimacy. Nonetheless, it seems in some ways remarkable that such petrol would be poured with such timing, on fires that were already raging.[72]

The following day thousands protested in New York City, with roving demonstrations blocking roads, around the Staten Island site of the killing, along the length of Manhattan, chanting "I can't breathe. I can't breathe". Die-ins happened in Grand Central Station, mirrored on the other side of the country in the Bay Area. Significant actions were happening almost every day now, typically called on Facebook or Twitter, with groups blocking traffic in one corner of a city receiving live updates of groups in many other areas, sometimes running into them with great delight. In the coastal cities the recent experience of Occupy lent a certain facility to spontaneous demonstration. Police appeared overwhelmed, but in many cases they had been instructed to hold back for fear of fanning the flames.

Then on 13 December large scale demonstrations were called in various cities: New York, Washington, Oakland, Chicago. The Washington demo was lead by the inevitable Sharpton, and the Garner and Brown families, though speakers were disrupted by young Ferguson activists — further sign of a rift. Tens of thousands came out in New York, but this was a traditional stewarded march, the energy of the previous weeks either contained or spent. A few days later, two Brooklyn cops were executed by Ismaaiyl Brinsley ostensibly in revenge for Garner and Brown, with the police union blaming the left-leaning Mayor, Bill de Blasio, for taking a soft line on the protestors.[73] Meanwhile Obama announced a further institutional response: a commission on police reform, "Task Force on 21st Century Policing" to "examine how to strengthen public trust and foster strong relationships between local law enforcement and the communities that they protect, while also promoting effective crime reduction."

struggles against police violence and the Black Lives Matter movement, using the 'hands up, don't shoot' meme. See Ben Norton, 'Baltimore Is Here': Ethiopian Israelis protest police brutality in Jerusalem', *Mondoweiss*, 1 May 2015.

72 The prosecutor who supervised the grand jury investigation, Daniel Donovan, was subsequently elected to represent Staten Island, a borough heavily populated with police officers, in the United States Congress. The city later settled a wrongful-death claim by paying $5.9 million to Garner's family.

73 This, as well as the subsequent 'police strike', turned out to be an opening gambit in contractual negotiations between the city and the Patrolmen's Benevolent Association.

While unrest simmered down in the cold winter months, it was not extinguished. In early January 2015 a small camp was formed outside the LAPD headquarters, publicised with both #OccupyLAPD and #BlackLivesMatter hashtags, to protest the killing of Ezell Ford, a mentally-ill 25-year-old who had been shot by LA police in 2014, and whose death had already formed the focus of several demonstrations. In February Black Lives Matter memes were going strong in celebrity circles, with Beyoncé's and Common's backing dancers and Pharrell Williams all performing "hands up, don't shoot" gestures at the Grammys. Such celebrity involvement has been another remarkable aspect of a wave of struggles characterised by some forms of action that must horrify polite American society — from the November 2013 Trayvon fundraiser that Jamie Foxx threw in his own home, to Snoop Dogg's associations with the Brown and Davis families, to Beyoncé and Jay-Z's bailing-out of Ferguson and Baltimore protesters, to Prince's 2015 "rally4peace" and protest song, "Baltimore".

In early March came the Department of Justice announcement that Darren Wilson would not be charged at the federal level for civil rights violations in the shooting of Brown, citing a lack of evidence. But this was in concert with more carrot proffering, presumably in anticipation of further unrest: on the same day, the same department issued a damning report on the racial bias of policing in Ferguson, evidenced in emails containing racist abuse and a systematic use of traffic violations to boost state coffers. The local police chief would resign within days. The initial findings of the "Task Force on 21st Century Policing" were also released the same day, to further underline prospects for reform — and, by implication, the efficacy of riot in achieving this. But the next day riotless Cleveland's legal filings managed to blame 12-year-old Tamir Rice for his own shooting, something on which the city was quickly to backtrack after the scandal broke. In

Ferguson, protests continued, in the context of which a further two cops were shot, though not killed, leading to demonstrations of support for police and confrontations between pro- and anti-police actions.

ROUGH RIDE

Then the beginning of April added another name to the list: Walter Scott, 50, shot and killed while fleeing, by police officer Michael Slager, in North Charleston, South Carolina. This was another case caught on camera—footage soon released with the assistance of a Black Lives Matter activist. When Anthony Scott saw the video he echoed Brown's friend Dorian Johnson in remarking "I thought that my brother was gunned down like an animal." Murder charges were brought against Slager within days, as activists arrived on the scene and small Walter Scott demonstrations kicked in at North Charleston's City Hall. Like Renisha McBride's, Scott's family seem to have initially resisted his incorporation into the chain of deceased and the associated media spectacle. Nonetheless, the story had soon made the cover of *Time* magazine, photos of Scott's blatant murder deployed on a blacked-out cover under a large bold type "BLACK LIVES MATTER". And another blast of oxygen would soon hit the movement's still smouldering embers: the day after Scott's funeral, Baltimore police arrested Freddie Gray, 25, and took him for a "rough ride" in the back of a police van, in the course of which his neck was broken.[74]

During Gray's subsequent days of coma, before his 19 April death, demonstrations had already started in front of the Western District police station. On 25 April Black Lives Matter protests hit downtown Baltimore, bringing the first signs of the unrest to come.[75] The 27 April funeral, like Brown's, was attended by thousands, including White House representatives, the Garner family, "civil rights leaders" etc. A confrontation between

74 'Rough ride': a police technique for inflicting violence on arrestees indirectly, through the movements of a vehicle, thus removing them from the culpability of more direct aggression. Manny Fernandez, 'Freddie Gray's Injury and the Police "Rough Ride"', *New York Times*, 30 April 2015.

75 White Orioles' fans partying outside the stadium clashed with demonstrators, police intervened violently, and a 7-11 was looted.

cops and teenagers outside Baltimore's Mondawmin Mall was the trigger event for the massive rioting that would now engulf Baltimore for days, causing an estimated $9m of damage to property.[76] Tweets declared "all out war between kids and police" and "straight communist savage".[77] A familiar riot-script followed: calls for calm and condemnations of "thugs", allocating blame to a selfish minority and upholding peaceful protest in contrast; the National Guard called in; a curfew announced, mass gatherings to clean up the riot area; a disciplinarian parent puffed up into a national heroine after being caught on camera giving her rioting child a clip round the ear; suggestions that gangs were behind it all; some people spying an influx of outside agitators...

But the archetypes thrown by the light of the flames must of course not blind us to each riot-wave's specificities. In the English riots early claims about gang involvement later proved unfounded. In Baltimore, gangs seem to have performed the exact opposite function to that claimed early on. Police had issued warnings of a truce between Bloods, Crips and the Black Guerilla Family with the intention of "teaming up" against them. But it was soon revealed that the truce, brokered by the Nation of Islam, was in fact to suppress the riot. Bloods and Crips leaders released a video statement asking for calm and peaceful protest in the area, and joined with police and clergy to enforce the curfew. On 28 April news cameras recorded gang members dispersing "would-be troublemakers" at the Security Square Mall.[78]

76 Police shut down the mall in response to a flyer circulating on social media calling for a 'purge' – a horror-movie reference to a day of lawlessness. Dozens of high school students showed up for this, but many more were trapped in front of the mall by police who shut down the buses that were supposed to take them home, and fired tear gas into the gathering crowd. Justin Fenton, 'Baltimore rioting kicked off with rumors of "purge"', *The Baltimore Sun*, 27 April 2015.

77 *The 2015 Baltimore Uprising: A Teen Epistolary* (Research and Destroy, New York City 2015).

78 'Gangs call for calm in Baltimore', *Baltimore Sun*, 27 April 2015; Garrett Haake, 'Gang members help prevent riot at Baltimore mall', *WUSA9*, 28 April 2015.

HARD TIMES IN THE CITY

> The best image to sum up the unconscious is Baltimore in the early morning.—Jacques Lacan

The similarities between Baltimore and St. Louis are striking. Both have been shrinking for decades as a result of deindustrialisation, with roughly half the inner city below the poverty line. Both were epicenters of state-mandated segregation up to the 1970s, and sub-prime lending in the 2000s.[79] And while in most US cities crime rates have fallen sharply since their 1990s peak, in St. Louis and Baltimore they have stayed high, with both consistently in the top ten for violent crime and homicide.[80] Yet while traditional black suburbs of St. Louis, such as Kinloch, have been gutted, those in Baltimore have thrived and proliferated.[81] Situated at the nexus of the wealthy tri-state sprawl of Maryland, Virginia and DC, Baltimore's suburbs contain the largest concentration of the black middle class in the US. Prince George's County is the wealthiest majority black county in the country, often cited as the quintessential black middle class suburb, and its police force has a special reputation for brutality.[82] In his most recent memoir Ta-Nehisi Coates cites his discovery of this fact as the source of his disillusionment with black nationalism. Coates' fellow student at Howard University, Prince Jones, was killed by a black P.G. County officer who mistook him for a burglary suspect. At the time Coates devoted an article to the questions of race and class raised by this killing:

> Usually, police brutality is framed as a racial issue: Rodney King suffering at the hands of a racist white Los Angeles Police Department or more recently, an unarmed Timothy Thomas, gunned down by a white Cincinnati cop. But in more and more communities, the police doing the brutalising are African Americans, supervised by African-American police chiefs, and answerable to African-American mayors and city councils.

In trying to explain why so few showed up for a Sharpton-led march in the wake of the Jones shooting, Coates pointed out that "affluent black residents are just as likely as white ones to think the victims of police brutality have it coming".[83]

79 Baltimore was the first city to adopt a residential segregation ordinance (in 1910). Richard Rothstein, 'From Ferguson to Baltimore', *Economic Policy Institute*, 29 April 2015.

80 They also share a distinctive history: both were border state cities where slavery had a tenuous foothold. See Barbara Fields, *Slavery and Freedom on the Middle Ground* (Yale 1985).

81 In 1970 there were 7 census tracts in the Baltimore area that were majority black, relatively wealthy, and far from the concentrated poverty of the inner city. In 2000 there were 17. Sharkey, 'Spatial segmentation and the black middle class'.

82 P.G. County police were among the first to descend on Baltimore in response to the riots.

For decades these suburbs have incubated a black political establishment: federal representatives, state senators, lieutenant governors, aldermen, police commissioners. This is another legacy of Civil Rights.[84] It meant, as several commentators have noted, that Baltimore was the first American riot to be waged against a largely black power structure.[85] This was in marked contrast to Ferguson, and it raised a significant problem for simplistic attempts to attribute black deaths to police racism: after all, three of the six cops accused of killing Grey were black.[86] It seemed, that is, that events were starting to force issues of class back onto the agenda. Blackness had for a while presented itself as the solution to a previous composition problem, supplanting the weakly indeterminate class politics of the 99% with something that seemed to possess all the social actuality that Occupy did not. But just as descending compositional modulations had produced that change of key, they now raised the question of whether the new black unity could hold along its hitherto extremely vertical lines. Was class the rock on which race was to be wrecked, or its social root, by which it might be radicalised? At this point, the former prospect seemed the more likely.

83 Ta-Nehisi Coates, 'Black and Blue: Why does America's richest black suburb have some of the country's most brutal cops?', *Washington Monthly*, June 2001.

84 In 1970 there were 54 black legislators in the US. By 2000 there were 610. Most are in state houses, but the Black Caucus has become a powerful force in Congress, with over 40 members.

85 Curtis Price, 'Baltimore's "Fire Next Time"', *Brooklyn Rail: Field Notes*, 3 June 2015.

LOOKING DOWN

On 28 April, as FBI drones circled the skies over Baltimore, Obama gave his statement, interrupting a summit with Shinzo Abe. This seemed markedly less scripted than those hitherto, stepping gingerly from phrase to phrase, balancing statements of support for police with those for the Gray family; noting that peaceful demonstrations never get as much attention as riots; fumbling a description of rioters as "protesters"—before recognising the faux pas and quickly swapping in "criminals", then escalating and overcompensating with a racialising "thugs"; linking Baltimore to Ferguson and locating the ongoing chain of events in "a slow-rolling crisis"

86 44% of Baltimore's police are black, compared to 60% of its population, but the wider metropolitan area from which police are recruited is 30% black. See Jeremy Ashkenas, 'The Race Gap in America's Police Departments', *New York Times*, 8 April 2015.

that had been "going on for decades"; calling on police unions not to close ranks and to acknowledge that "this is not good for police".

But most notably, the race contradiction which had described the polar tensions of Obama's rhetoric now receded into the background, while the problem over which "we as a country have to do some soul searching" became specifically one of *poor* blacks, impoverished communities, the absence of formal employment and its replacement with the illicit economy, cops called in merely to contain the problems of the ghetto; this was the *real* problem, though a hard one to solve politically.[87] Hillary Clinton too was falling over herself to express an understanding of core social issues at play in these struggles.[88] The conservative *Washington Times* declared Baltimore's problem to be a matter of class, not race, and spoke sympathetically of how "residents in poorer neighbourhoods feel targeted by a police force that treats them unfairly".[89] Mainstream opinion seemed to be shifting, with Democrats and Republicans trading shots over Baltimore, while often tacitly sharing the premise that the problem was inner-city poverty. The contrast with the 1960s was striking: where ultra-liberal Johnson once saw black riots as a communist plot, now the entire political class seemed to agree with the rioters' grievances: black lives did indeed matter, and yes, ghetto conditions and incarceration were problems.[90]

As well as the relatively low level of property destruction in comparison to 60s riots (see table), the surprising degree of elite acceptance here might perhaps be attributed to the very different possibilities facing these two Civil Rights Movements, old and new. Where the first threatened substantially transformative social and political effects, challenging structures of racial oppression that dated back to Reconstruction's defeat, and brought the prospect of dethroning some racist elites along the way, the new politics of black unity seemed to

87 'Remarks by President Obama and Prime Minister Abe of Japan in Joint Press Conference', White House, 28 April 2015.

88 'It's time to end the era of mass incarceration', 29 April 2015, speech available on hillaryclinton.com. Even Tea Party Republican Ted Cruz has joined the anti-incarceration chorus.

89 Kellan Howell, 'Baltimore riots sparked not by race but by class tensions between police, poor', *Washington Times*, 29 April 2015.

90 Similarly striking is the contrast to the reaction of the British state and media to the 2011 English riots, which was uniformly authoritarian and uncomprehending.

91 See 'A Statement from a Comrade and Baltimore Native About the Uprising' on *SIC* website.

	LA 1965	Detroit 1967	Baltimore 1968	LA 1992	Baltimore 2015
Days or rioting	6	4	6	6	3
Buildings looted/burnt	977	2,509	1,200	3,767	285
People killed	34	43	6	53	0
Arrests	3,438	7,200	5,800	11,000	486
Damage (millions of $)	40	60	13.5	100	9.2

Table: Impact of selected US riots (source: Wikipedia)

be kicking at an open door that led nowhere. Where the first could offer the prospect of incorporation of at least some parts of the black population into a growing economy, the new movement faced a stagnant economy with diminishing opportunities even for many of those lucky enough to have already avoided the ghetto, let alone those stuck in it.[91] Aspirations to solve these problems were good American pipe dreams, easily acceptable precisely because it was hard to see what reform might actually be addressed to them beyond anodyne steps such as requiring more police to wear bodycams.

The existing black elite is willing to embrace the "New Jim Crow" rhetoric as long as it funnels activists into NGOs and helps to consolidate votes — but always within a frame of paternalism and respectability, sprinkled with Moynihan-style invocations of the dysfunctional black family. Here lame initiatives focus on such things as mentoring to improve individual prospects, thus sidestepping social problems.[92] Meanwhile churches function both as substitutes for the welfare state and as organs of community representation — roles they have proved willing to embrace and affirm in the context of this movement.[93] Elites in Baltimore have capitalised on the mood, for example by indicting all the cops in the Grey case — something that will win State's Attorney Marilyn J. Mosby accolades whatever the outcome. But it is probably significant that the word "thug" was first deployed here by those same elites — and Obama.[94] While people across the spectrum of black American

92 For example, 'Big Brothers Big Sisters', and Obama's 'My Brother's Keeper' initiatives.

93 See Antonia Blumberg and Carol Kuruvilla, 'How The Black Lives Matter Movement Changed The Church', *Huffington Post*, 8 August 2015.

94 Also this time it was the NAACP, headquartered in Baltimore, that blamed 'outside agitators'. Aaron Morrison, 'NAACP condemns looting and violence in Baltimore', *International Business Times*, 28 April 2015.

society and beyond could easily affirm that all those lives from Trayvon Martin onwards certainly did matter, what could they say to rioters from Baltimore's ghettos? Could the thin unity of black identity still hold when the stigma of criminality pushed itself to the fore?

GRACE

On 8 June a police officer on one of the most prominent cases was indicted: Michael Slager, for the murder of Walter Scott. We might reasonably anticipate that, here, finally, a cop is likely to be sacrificed to the greater legitimacy of the police. Surely they can hardly do otherwise: this case seems as clear-cut as they come, and any other outcome would be an outright admission of double standards. But, as we've recently seen with Randall Kerrick — killer of Jonathan Ferrell — even clear-cut cases typically fail to produce convictions; much like with civilian Stand Your Ground cases, the police officer needs only to say that they felt "threatened"— even if the victim was unarmed.

The cell neighbouring Slager's would soon be occupied by another South Carolina man: Dylann Roof, 21, executioner, on 17 June, of 9 black churchgoers in Charleston. His was a white supremacist's reaction to the post-Trayvon events. With the demand for indictment of cops finally met (more were to be indicted over the next month, in Cincinnati), the reaction to the massacre appeared muted. No angry protests, only shock and grief. At Roof's pre-trial hearing family members of his victims showed up and publicly forgave him. It was this Christian "grace" that gave Obama the opportunity to finally present himself as a Civil Rights president, at the funeral of state senator Reverend Pinckney, who had died in the massacre. The lamblike innocence of the victims and the civil response of the community allowed him to invoke an image of blackness clothed in that most American tradition: Christian faith.

Appropriating the rhetorical vernacular of the black church, he could finally put aside his equivocations over race and racism: "we're guarding against not just racial slurs but we're also guarding against the subtle impulse to call Johnny back for a job interview but not Jamal." Cue uproarious cheers: "Hallelujah!" Roof's revanchist Southern nationalism meant that righteous black rage could now be targeted not at killer cops but at a symbol: the Confederate flag, which had flown from the statehouses of Alabama and South Carolina ever since George Wallace led a white backlash against Civil Rights in the 1960s. On 27 June Bree Newsome, a black Christian activist, tore down the flag from the South Carolina statehouse. By the following week the Republican governors of both states had ordered the flag removed from official buildings.[95] For a while videos of attacks on people, cars and buildings flying the flag became a popular internet meme.[96]

With summer came the interventions of Black Lives Matter activists into the Democratic primaries: interruptions of surprise leftist contender Bernie Sanders' speeches that would be construed as confrontations between "race first" and "class first" leftisms; an impromptu meeting with Hillary Clinton, followed by a denunciation of "her and her family's part in perpetuating white supremacist violence in this country and abroad". Tensions began to emerge at this point between Campaign Zero, identified with DeRay, and the Black Lives Matter Network, led by Garza, Tometi and Cullors, in large part over the question of whether they should accept the tender embrace of the Democrats.[97] This guardedness is not without justification: after all, as American leftists are fond of saying, the Democratic Party is where social movements go to die. In August the Democratic National Committee passed a "Black Lives Matter" resolution, only to be rebuffed in a statement by the Black Lives Matter Network; senior Democrats competed to endorse the more obedient pupil, Campaign Zero.

95 No other states fly it, but it is incorporated in Mississippi's state flag, supported by a recent 2-1 popular vote.

96 At the end of June a more ancient and anonymous meme was revived in response: eight Southern black churches were burnt in one week.

97 Darren Sands, 'The Success And Controversy of #CampaignZero'.

Receiving less coverage, but perhaps more significant, the summer also saw an open confrontation with the Civil Rights old guard at the NAACP. A large part of the rift here is defined by the issue of "black-on-black" crime: according to the Bureau of Justice Statistics, 93% of murders of black people are at the hands of other black people — as Rudy Giuliani was keen to point out at the peak of the Ferguson unrest. For NAACP figures such as Roslyn Brock, the pressing question is thus: "How do we give life to the narrative that Black Lives Matter when we are doing the killing?"[98] For the new activists, such discourses let "white supremacy" off the hook, placing the blame on black people themselves, and amount to black leaders "policing" their own communities as part of a generalised "respectability politics".

98 Darren Sands, 'The NAACP And Black Lives Matter Are Talking Past Each Other', *BuzzFeed*, 17 July 2015.

CRIMING WHILE BLACK

The question of "black criminality" is overdetermined by decades of liberal vs. conservative acrimony, dating back to Moynihan's 1965 lament over the state of the "negro family".[99] Approximately three distinct sets of diagnoses and prescriptions stake out the rhetorical perimeter of this triangular debate. Conservatives condemn cultural pathologies and a lack of stable two-parent families, seeing this as the source of high crime in black neighbourhoods; the solutions thus become promotion of religious observance and black fatherhood, paired with condemnation of rap music. Liberals defend rappers and single mothers from patriarchal conservatives, and condemn racist cops who exaggerate black criminality by over-policing black neighbourhoods; thus the solution becomes police reform and fighting racism. Finally, social democrats will agree with conservatives that black crime is real but point to structural factors such as high unemployment and poverty, themselves driven in part by present and past racism; the solution thus becomes a Marshall Plan for the ghetto.

99 For a summary of the report and subsequent debates, see Stephen Steinberg, 'The Moynihan Report at Fifty', *Boston Review*, 24 June 2015.

Many in the black middle class are sceptical of liberal denials of black criminality; many have family members or friends who have been affected by crime. Often open to structural arguments, they are also tired of waiting for social democratic panaceas which seem ever less likely. Noting their own capacities for relative advancement, it's easy for them to contrast the condition of the black poor to the supposed success of other racialised immigrant groups. They are thus drawn to conservative conclusions: there must be something wrong with their culture, their sexual mores, and so on. This is not just a matter of the Bill Cosbys and Ben Carsons. It is the position of influential liberal academics like William Julius Wilson and Orlando Patterson. It has also increasingly become the position of many supposed radicals: Al Sharpton raging against sagging pants, Cornel West decrying the "nihilism" within black culture and identifying religion as a solution.[100] This is what Black Lives Matter activists mean when they object to "the politics of respectability".

Such objections are, of course, essentially correct: it is stupid to blame crime on culture.[101] Michelle Alexander's *The New Jim Crow* is a key reference point for these activists. Alexander points to racial disparities in drug-related incarceration: blacks and whites use drugs at similar rates, but blacks are arrested far more often, and sometimes receive longer sentences for the same offence, with the implication that these disparities are the work of racist cops and judges. Such liberal responses to conservative arguments tend, however, to come with a blind spot. By concentrating on low level drug offenders—who even many conservatives agree shouldn't be serving time—Alexander avoids some thorny issues. Among inmates, violent offenders outnumber drug offenders by more than 2-to-1, and the racial disproportion among these prisoners is as high as among drug offenders.[102] But with these crimes it

100 Stephen Steinberg, 'The Liberal Retreat From Race', *New Politics*, vol. 5, no. 1, summer 1994.

101 For contemporary evidence of the structural determinants of crime see Ruth Peterson and Krivo Lauren, 'Segregated Spatial Locations, Race-Ethnic Composition, and Neighborhood Violent Crime', *Annals of the American Academy*, no. 623, 2009.

102 Drug offenders make up a much higher proportion of federal prisoners, but only 6% of prisoners are in federal prisons. See Forman Jr., 'Racial Critiques of Mass Incarceration'.

is hard to deny that black people are both victims and perpetrators at much higher rates.[103] Here the explanation of the structuralists is basically right, even if their solutions look implausible: black people are much more likely to live in urban ghettos, faced with far higher levels of material deprivation than whites.

With their endemic violence, these places are the real basis for the high "black-on-black crime" statistics that conservatives like to trot out as evidence that responsibility for the violence to which black people are subjected lies with black communities themselves. Understandably reacting against such arguments, liberals have pointed out similarities between intra-racial murder rates: 84% for whites and 93% for blacks.[104] This seems a polemically effective point: shouldn't white communities thus take more responsibility for "white-on-white crime" too? But again, something is being obscured: according to the Bureau of Justice Statistics, black people kill each other 8 times more often. It is not necessary to accept the rhetorical logic by which acknowledging this appears a concession to conservative moralising. Aren't high crime rates to be expected in the most unequal society in the developed world? And isn't it entirely predictable that violent crime should be concentrated in urban areas where forms of employment are prevalent that do not enjoy legal protections, and which therefore must often be backed up with a capacity for direct force? Arguments that avoid such things often involve implicit appeals to an unrealistic notion of innocence, and therefore seem to have the perverse effect of reinforcing the stigma of crime; here the critics of "respectability politics" reproduce its founding premise.[105] While the prospect of the underlying problem being solved through a gigantic Marshall Plan for the ghetto looks like the most forlorn of hopes, many policy proposals from Black Lives Matter activists merely amount to some version of "more black cops".[106] The history of police reform in places

103 If we look only at homicides (generally the most reliable data), from 1980 to 2008 blacks have been 6–10 times more likely than whites to be victims and perpetrators. Cooper and Smith, 'Homicide Trends in the United States'.

104 Jamelle Bouie, 'The Trayvon Martin Killing and the Myth of Black-on-Black Crime', *Daily Beast*, 15 July 2013.

105 Indeed, in questioning the reality of crime, liberals suggest that the most dispossessed are obediently acquiescing to their condition.

106 For example, Michael Mcdowell, of Black Lives Matter Minneapolis, has advocated making 'community leaders' police officers. Waleed Shahid, 'The Interrupters', *Colorlines*, 14 August 2015.

like Baltimore, where the police and "civilian review boards" have long mirrored the faces of the wider population, clearly demonstrates the insufficiency of these responses. But those who make the more radical claim that the demand should be *less* rather than *better* policing, are in some ways just as out of touch.[107] The troubling fact—often cited by the conservative right, but no less true for that reason—is that it is precisely in the poorest black neighbourhoods that we often find the strongest support for tougher policing. When Sharpton, in his eulogy for Brown, railed against the abject blackness of the gangster and the thug, some of the activists were horrified, but his message was warmly received by many of the Ferguson residents present. This is because Sharpton was appealing to a version of "respectability politics" that has roots in the ghetto. Ta-Nahesi Coates, who grew up in West Baltimore, has acknowledged that many residents "were more likely to ask for police support than to complain about brutality". This is not because they especially loved cops, but because they had no other recourse: while the "safety" of white America was in "schools, portfolios, and skyscrapers", theirs was in "men with guns who could only view us with the same contempt as the society that sent them".[108]

107 See Alex Vitale, 'We Don't Just Need Nicer Cops: We Need Fewer Cops', *The Nation*, 4 December 2014.

108 Coates, *Between the World and Me* (Spiegel & Grau 2015), p. 85. Coates further describes this as 'raging against the crime in your ghetto, because you are powerless before the great crime of history that brought the ghettos to be.'

POLICING SURPLUS POPULATIONS

At the most abstract level, capital is colour-blind: surplus value produced by white labour is no different to that produced by black, and when racist laws interfere with the buying and selling of labour, as they ultimately did in the Jim Crow South, capitalists will tend to support the overturning of those laws. Yet when the demand for labour falls and the question arises of who must go without, workers can generally be relied upon to discover the requisite divisions amongst themselves, typically along lines of kinship, ethnicity and race. Capitalists thus benefit from racism even if they don't create it, for in periods of growth these divisions undermine any collective bargaining power that workers might otherwise be able to achieve. Historically, rigid racial hierarchies have been the work not of capital, but of the state — especially, though not exclusively, white-settler and other colonial states. State racism is epitomised by anti-miscegenation laws, which aim to realise racial difference by outlawing racial mixing; the nation-state became a racial state. During times of economic crisis, racial states could be counted on to intervene in labour markets — which contingently assign workers to the employed and the unemployed — in order to assign these determinations methodically, along racial lines.

In the mid-twentieth century this state-orchestrated project of race-making broke down at a global level. On the one hand, exposure of the Nazi genocide and the success of decolonisation movements de-legitimated explicit state racism. On the other, rapid post-war growth led to tight labour markets, reducing competition for jobs between racialised groups. This was thus an era of assimilation, evinced by the partial victories of the Civil Rights Movement. What put this process into reverse was the reassertion of capitalist crisis tendencies in the 1970s. Falling profits led to a fall in the demand for labour. Recently achieved formal equality did nothing to stop real economic inequalities being reinforced by heightened competition for jobs. Here the state would find for itself a new race-making role, this time not as arbiter of legal separation, but rather as manager of racialised surplus populations.[109]

As the regulation of social relations by the labour market began to break down with the slowing of the economy, proletarians were ejected from the industrial sector, leading to rising unemployment and under-employment, and growth in low-wage services. Populations fled towards suburbs, leaving behind decaying inner cities. This brought a fraying of the social fabric, alongside

109 See Chris Chen, 'The Limit Point of Capitalist Equality' in *Endnotes 3*, September 2013.

a fiscal crisis of the state. Across bipartisan divides, governments from Reagan onwards took this as an opportunity to force the end of a whole range of already meagre social programmes. Previously existing communities began to break down. This had a cultural dimension: private in-home consumption of media, growing atomisation and so on. But most of all, existing solidarities had been premised on a growing economy. Communities that were supposed to achieve autonomy in the context of the Black Power Movement found themselves riven with crime and desperation. Here the police stepped in as a last resort form of social mediation, managing a growing social disorder, becoming ubiquitous across the social fabric. When people entered altered mental states through some breakdown or another, for example, the state increasingly dispatched not "mental health professionals" but cops, who would subdue by force and frequently kill in the process.

In this precarious world one must survive with little help, and any accident or run of bad luck can result in losing everything. It is no surprise that people get sick or turn to crime when they fall down and can't get back up. The police are there to ensure that those who have fallen don't create further disturbances, and to haul them away to prison if they do. People who are thereby snared are not just those nabbed by the cops, but people — not angels — caught in the vectors of a spreading social disintegration. At the same time, broader populations — fearful of looking down — develop their own cop mentalities. This gives the lie to anti-police slogans that present the police as an imposition on the community, that hinge on assumptions that these communities would do just fine if the police stopped interfering: where community and society are themselves in states of decay, the police offers itself as a stand-in; bringing a semblance of order to lives that no longer matter to capital.

For much the same reason, it is more or less impossible for the state to resolve the problem by changing the fundamental character of the police. A full-scale reform that did away with the present function of the police as repressive, last-resort social mediation, would require a revival of the social democratic project. But with its diminished economic resources, the state lacks the key to that door. Meanwhile the softer reforms around which Black Lives Matter activists can unite with a bipartisan political elite — things like decarceration for low-level drug offenders and "justice reinvestment" in community policing — only raise the prospect of a more surgically targeted version of the carceral state. The brutal policing of black America is a forewarning about the global future of surplus humanity. Escaping from that future will require the discovery of new modes of unified action, beyond the separations.

CODA

Drawing in people from across a vast span of American society under the heading of "black", to protest over issues deeply entwined with racialising structures, this wave of struggles has displayed a peculiar vertical integration. The content of this unifying term has suggested a certain weightiness when set against the orientationless groping towards unity of other recent movements such as Occupy. It is a rare movement that can seem to unite the ghetto-dweller, the multi-millionaire star and the political power-broker behind a substantive social cause. But there's the rub. Stretched across such an unequal span, it was inevitable that the unity at play here would be correspondingly thin. If the content of identity is null without it, at extremes of difference the positing of identity reverts to the merest formality, while the content escapes.

That blackness can seem to offer something more substantial is an effect of its peculiar construction: a social content forcefully given by its role as marker of subordinate class, but also an identitarian unity enabled by its ultimate non-correspondence with class. These poles in tension have long identified the specificity of black struggles: proletarian insurgency or "race leadership"; blackness as socio-economic curse or as culture. But as the divide between rich and poor gapes ever wider, and as the latter sink further into misery and crime, gestures at holding the two poles together must become ever emptier. To reach towards the social content one must loosen one's hold on the identity; to embrace the identity one must let go of the content. It is practically impossible to hold both at once. Is the core demand to be about police reform? Or is it to be about ameliorating ghetto conditions in which police violence is more or less the only check on other kinds? If blackness seems to offer itself as a space in which these demands might not actually be at odds, this is only by the indistinct light from the gloam of older capacities for solidarity, when the black middle class too lived in the ghetto and shared its fate; when the black working class could reasonably hope to see better days.

Though it is clear that blackness has been in large part evacuated of consistent social content, from its evident capacity to induce such large-scale dynamic mobilisations in the American population it is equally clear that it would be premature to announce its demise. And in its tensions there still lies an unstable if unaffirmable moment, at the social root of racialising logics, where capitalist social relations are rotting into nothing, and where the most pressing problems of surplus humanity lie. If race could present itself as the solution to one compositional riddle, conjuring a new unity through descending modulations, that unity itself issues in another compositional impasse as a further descent threatens to undo it. Now the ghetto has rediscovered its capacity to riot, and to force change by doing so, will other, larger components of America's poor—white and latino — stand idly by? And what role, in such moments, will the new race leaders play? One must bend one's ear to pick out the new compositions into which these modulations are resolving.

EPILOGUE

The bodies have not ceased to pile up. On 16 July 2015, Black Lives Matter activist Sandra Bland, 28, was found hanged in a police cell in Waller County, Texas — an event ruled suicide, but with many of course suspecting foul play. Those who enter the macabre pantheon of this movement are the tip of an iceberg. As we laid down these words, 891 people had been killed so far this year by US police, of which 217 were identified as black, more than double the rates for whites and hispanics.[110] Though exact figures aren't available, in the years since this wave of struggles began, tens of thousands of black people will have been murdered in the US.[111] Though the total would be only slightly less for whites, they represent 63% of the US population, while black people are only 13%.

110 These figures from the Guardian's 'The Counted' project, started in response to this wave of struggles, which aims of keep track of those killed by US police. A similar count by the Washington Post, restricted to shootings, reports 759 deaths, of which 190 were black. Accessed 9 October 2015.

On 9 August, the anniversary of Brown's shooting, 250 people gathered in Ferguson during the day. In the evening there was some shooting at police, looting, and a journalist was robbed, whilst armed men guarded Ferguson Market & Liquor. Tyrone Harris Jr., 18 — apparently a close friend of Mike Brown's — was shot by four plain-clothed police officers, after supposedly being involved in a gunfight between looters. On 19 August another St. Louis teenager, Mansur Ball-Bey, 18, was shot in the back by police after running from a search of his home. Large crowds gathered in North St. Louis, to be tear-gassed by police; rocks thrown, cars burned, looting... A video went viral of Peggy Hubbard, a black grandmother who grew up in Ferguson, attacking Black Lives Matter for supporting "thugs" like Ball-Bey — and her brother and son, who were in

111 For 2000–2010 the figure was over 78,000, more that the total number of US military casualties during the Vietnam War.

jail — whilst ignoring the tragic death of Jamyla Bolden, 9, killed by a stray bullet from a drive-by as she lay in her mother's bed. On 24 August a newly appointed Ferguson judge announced that all arrest warrants issued prior to 2015 would be cancelled, and the Missouri legislature capped court fees in St. Louis County at 12.5% of municipal revenues. Although the slaughter shows no sign of abating, collective bargaining by riot is once again leveraging concessions.

A HISTORY OF SEPARATION

The rise and fall of the workers' movement, 1883–1982

> We have no models. The history of past experiences serves only to free us of those experiences.
>
> —Mario Tronti, "Lenin in England", 1964

PREFACE: BETRAYAL AND THE WILL

What should we be doing today, if we are "for" the revolution? Should we build up our resources now, or wait patiently for the next rupture? Should we act on invariant revolutionary principles, or remain flexible, so we can adapt to new situations as they arise? Any response to these questions inevitably tarries with the history of revolutions in the twentieth century. The failure of those revolutions accounts for the fact that we are still here asking ourselves these questions. All attempts to account for our agency, today, are haunted by the debacles of the past. That is true even, or perhaps especially, for those who never mention the past in the first place. The reason for this is plain to see.

The history of communism is not only the history of defeats: taking risks, coming up against a stronger force and losing. It is also a history of treachery, or of what the Left has typically called "betrayal". In the course of the traditional labour movement, there were many famous examples: of the Social Democrats and the trade union leadership at the start of World War I, of Ebert and Noske in the course of the German Revolution, of Trotsky in the midst of the Kronstadt Rebellion, of Stalin when he assumed power, of the CNT in Spain, when it ordered revolutionaries to tear down the barricades, and so on. In the anti-colonial movements of the mid-twentieth century, Chairman Mao, the Viet Minh, and Kwame Nkrumah were all called betrayers. Meanwhile, in the last major upsurge in Europe, it was the CGT in 1968 and the PCI in 1977, among others, who are said to have betrayed. The counter-revolution comes not only from the outside, but apparently also from the heart of the revolution itself.

That defeat is ultimately attributed to the moral failings of Left organisations and individuals, at least in leftist histories, is essential. If revolutions were defeated for some other reason (for example, as a result of the exigencies of unique situations), then there would be little for us to learn with respect to our own militancy. It is because the project of communism seemed to be blocked — not by chance, but by betrayal — that communist theory has come to revolve, as if neurotically, around the question of betrayal and the will that prevents it. The link between these two is key: at first glance, the theory of betrayal appears to be the inverse of a heroic conception of history. But betrayal delineates the negative space of the hero and thus of the figure of the militant. It is the militant, with her or his correct revolutionary line and authentic revolutionary will — as well as their vehicle: the party — who is supposed to stop the betrayal from taking place, and thus to bring the revolution to fruition.[1]

The origins of this thought-form are easy to identify: on 4th August 1914, German Social Democrats voted to support the war effort; the trade unions vowed to manage labour. The Great War thus commenced with the approval of socialism's earthly representatives. A year after the war began, dissident anti-war socialists convened at Zimmerwald, under the pretence of organising a bird-watching convention, in order to reconstruct the tattered communist project. But even here, splits quickly emerged. The Left of that dissident group — which included both Lenin and representatives of the currents that would become the Dutch-German left communists — broke away from the main contingent, since the latter refused to denounce the Social Democrats outright. In their own draft proposal, the Left did not hold back: "Prejudiced by nationalism, rotten with opportunism, at the beginning of the World War [the Social Democrats] betrayed the proletariat to imperialism."[2] They were now "a more dangerous enemy to the proletariat than the bourgeois apostles of imperialism."[3]

1 To give just one example, in 1920 at the Second Congress of the Communist International, Grigory Zinoviev asserted that: 'A whole series of old social democratic parties have turned in front of our eyes ... into parties that betray the cause of the working class. We say to our comrades that the sign of the times does not consist in the fact that we should negate the Party. The sign of the epoch in which we live … consists in the fact that we must say: "The old parties have been shipwrecked; down with them. Long live the new Communist Party that must be built under new conditions."' He goes on to add: 'We need a party. But what kind of party? We do not need parties that have the simple principle of gathering as many members as possible around themselves ... [We

But this denunciation was only one instance of a trope repeated a thousand times thereafter. The organisations created for the purpose of defending working class interests — often doing so on the basis of their own notions of betrayal and the will — betrayed the class, time and again, in the course of the twentieth century.

Whether they call themselves communists or anarchists, those who identify as "revolutionaries" spend much of their time examining past betrayals, often in minute detail, to determine exactly how those betrayals occurred.[4] Many of these examinations try to recover the *red thread* of history: the succession of individuals or groups who expressed a heroic fidelity to the revolution. Their very existence supposedly proves that it was possible not to betray and, therefore, that the revolution could have succeeded — if only the right groups had been at the helm, or if the wrong ones had been pushed away from the helm at the right moment. One becomes a communist or an anarchist on the basis of the particular thread out of which one weaves one's banner (and today one often flies these flags, not on the basis of a heartfelt identity, but rather due to the contingencies of friendship). However, in raising whatever banner, revolutionaries fail to see the limits to which the groups they revere were actually responding — that is, precisely what made them a minority formation. Revolutionaries get lost in history, defining themselves by reference to a context of struggle that has no present-day correlate. They draw lines in sand which is no longer there.

THE PERIODISING BREAK

We might be tempted to read the runes again, to try to solve the riddle of the history definitively: what was the right thing to do in 1917, 1936, 1968? However, the purpose here is not to come up with new answers to old questions. Instead, our intervention is therapeutic: we aim to confront the questioners, to challenge

need] a centralised party with iron discipline.' It is impossible to read these lines without remembering that, fifteen years later, Zinoviev would stand accused in the first Moscow show trial. He would be executed by the same party he had stalwartly defended. By then Trotsky, who stood by him in the second congress, had already been run out of the country and would soon be murdered.

2 Draft Resolution Proposed by the Left Wing at Zimmerwald, 1915.

3 Ibid.

4 'This was a political milieu where the minute study of the month-to-month history of the Russian revolution and the Comintern from 1917 to 1928 seemed the key to the universe as a whole. If someone said they believed

their motivating assumptions. Any strategic orientation towards the past must base itself, at least, on the assumption that the present is essentially like it. If the present is not like the past, then no matter how we solve the riddle of history, it will tell us very little about what we should be doing today.

Our goal is therefore to introduce a break, to cleave off the present from the past (and so, too, to sever the relation between betrayal and the will). If placed successfully, this periodising break will allow us to relate to the past as past, and the present as something else. Of course, this periodisation cannot be absolute. The present is not wholly unlike the past. The capitalist mode of production remains. Indeed, the capital–labour relation defines the shape of our lives more than it ever did those of our ancestors, and it does so in at least two fundamental ways.

First, compared to the past, a greater share of the world's population today consists of proletarians and semi-proletarians: they must sell their labour-power in order to buy at least some of what they need. Second, this "some of what they need" has expanded massively so that today, people's lives are deeply submerged within market relations: in the high income countries, and also in parts of the low-income world, workers not only pay rent and buy groceries. They purchase ready-made meals, talk to their families on cell phones, put their parents in nursing homes, and pop pills in order live, or live better. They must continue to work in order to afford these things, that is, in order to maintain their social ties.

Many revolutionaries take this ever-deepening imbrication within market relations as a sufficient proof that the present is like the past, in whatever senses are relevant. The result is that they relate to the past through a screen. The past becomes a fantasy projection of the present. Often enough, that screen is called "the Left".

that the Russian Revolution had been defeated in 1919, 1921, 1923, 1927, or 1936, or 1953, one had a pretty good sense of what they would think on just about every other political question in the world: the nature of the Soviet Union, of China, the nature of the world CPs, the nature of Social Democracy, the nature of trade unions, the United Front, the Popular Front, national liberation movements, aesthetics and philosophy, the relationship of party and class, the significance of soviets and workers' councils, and whether Luxemburg or Bukharin was right about imperialism.' Loren Goldner, 'Communism is the Material Human Community: Amadeo Bordiga Today', *Critique* 23, 1991.

Debates about history become debates about the Left: what it was, what it should have done (and there are some who, on that same basis, come to see themselves as "post-Left"). What escapes notice, thereby, is the absence, in our own times, of the context that shaped the world in which the Left acted in the course of the twentieth century, namely, the workers' movement and its cycles of struggle.

The workers' movement provided the setting in which the drama of "the Left" took place. That movement was not simply *the proletariat in fighting form*, as if any struggle today would have to replicate its essential features. It was a particular fighting form, which took shape in an era that is not our own. For us, there is only the "latecomers' melancholy reverence".[5] It is our goal, in this essay, to explore this totality as past and to explain its dissociation from the present.

Our contention is that, if the historical workers' movement is today alien to us, it is because the *form* of the capital–labour relation that sustained the workers' movement no longer obtains: in the high-income countries since the 1970s and in the low-income countries since the 1980s (late workers' movements appeared in South Africa, South Korea and Brazil, but all now present the same form: social democracy in retreat). Indeed, the social foundations on which the workers' movement was built have been torn out: the factory system no longer appears as the kernel of a new society in formation; the industrial workers who labour there no longer appear as the vanguard of a class in the process of becoming revolutionary. All that remains of this past-world are certain *logics of disintegration*, and not only of the workers' movement, but also of the capital–labour relation itself. To say so is not to suggest that, by some metric, all workers are "really" unemployed, or to deny that there is an emergent industrial proletariat in countries like India and China.

5 'The more we seek to persuade ourselves of the fidelity of our own projects and values with respect to the past, the more obsessively do we find ourselves exploring the latter and its projects and values, which slowly begin to form into a kind of totality and to dissociate themselves from our own present.' Fredric Jameson, *A Singular Modernity: Essay on the Ontology of the Present* (Verso 2002), p. 24.

It is rather to point out that the following. The world economy is growing more and more slowly, on a decade by decade basis, due to a long period of overproduction and low profit rates. That sluggish growth has been associated, in most countries of the world, with deindustrialisation: industrial output continues to swell, but is no longer associated with rapid increases in industrial employment. Semi-skilled factory workers can thus no longer present themselves as the leading edge of a class-in-formation. In this context, masses of proletarians, particularly in countries with young workforces, are not finding steady work; many of them have been shunted from the labour market, surviving only by means of informal economic activity. The resulting low demand for labour has led to a worldwide fall in the labour-share of income, or in other words, to immiseration. Meanwhile, the state, in an attempt to manage this situation, has taken on massive amounts of debt, and has periodically been forced to undertake "reforms"—a term which in our era has come to mean a falling away of social protections—leaving a larger portion of the population in a tenuous position.

The social links that hold people together in the modern world, even if in positions of subjugation, are fraying, and in some places, have broken entirely. All of this is taking place on a planet that is heating up, with concentrations of greenhouse gases rising rapidly since 1950. The connection between global warming and swelling industrial output is clear. The factory system is not the kernel of a future society, but a machine producing no-future.

These are not merely political consequences of neoliberalism; they are structural features of the capitalist mode of production in our time. Struggles within and against this world are just beginning to take on a greater global significance, but they have not found a coherence comparable to that which pertained in an earlier era. A key feature of struggles today is precisely that, although they remain the struggles of *workers*, they present themselves as such only when they remain at the level of sectional struggles, that is, struggles of particular fractions of the class, which are almost always defensive struggles against ongoing "reforms" and "restructurings". When struggles take on a wider significance, that is, for the class as a whole, then the unity they present, both to themselves and to others, goes beyond a class identity. Workers find a shared basis for struggle, not by means of the class belonging they have in common, but rather, as citizens, as participants in a "real democracy", as the 99 percent, and so on. Such forms of identification sharply distinguish these workers' struggles from the core struggles of the era of the workers movement. They have also made it difficult to see the way forward, to a communist future.

It is this context — that of the disintegration of the capital–labour relation, and of the unrealised potential for struggles to generate new sorts of social relations — that distinguishes the epoch in which we find ourselves from the past.

THEIR PERIODS AND OURS

In the first issue of *Endnotes* we published a series of texts that we called "preliminary materials for a balance sheet of the twentieth century". In this issue we draw up that balance sheet as it presents itself to us today. But before we do so it will be useful to contrast our approach with that of *Théorie Communiste* (TC), whose texts featured prominently in that first issue, and have continued to influence our thinking over the years.

The periodising break we present in this article has much in common with TC's.[6] Our perspective emerged, in part, out of an attempt to measure TC's theory against the global history of the workers movement in the course of the twentieth century. One difference between our account and theirs is that TC try to ground their

6 See *Endnotes 1*, October 2008.

periodisation in Marx's categories of formal and real subsumption. For Marx, these terms referred specifically to the transformation of the labour process; TC apply them to the capital–labour relation as a whole, and even to capitalist society.[7] They place the break between formal and real subsumption around WWI, then divide the latter into two distinct phases. They then overlay this structural periodisation — of the "form" of the "capital–labour relation"— with a second periodisation — of communism, or what they call "cycles of struggle"— where the current phase, beginning in the 1970s, corresponds to a second phase of real subsumption:

However, somewhat strangely, the key break in one sequence does not match up with the key break in the other: a complete transformation in the "cycle of struggle" (the 1970s) corresponds to a minor transformation in the form of the "capital-labour relation". This

	1910s		1970s
cycle of struggle:	programmatism		communisation
capital-labour relation:	formal subsumption	real subsumption I & II	

gives TC's periodisation the tripartite form of a narrative structure, with beginning, middle and end. As usual in such structures, the middle term tends to dominate the others: TC define the first and last phases negatively in relation to the height of "programmatism" from the 1910s to the 1970s.[8] Thus in their texts the ghost of programmatism, supposedly long slain, has a tendency to hang around and haunt the present moment. A more serious problem is that the schematism fits neatly, if at all, only in France (at best, it might apply to Western Europe).[9] It can only with great difficulty be extended to the rest of the world, and is particularly inapposite to poor and late-developing countries.

7 TC were not the first to do so: Jacques Camatte, Negation, and Antonio Negri did the same. See 'The History of Subsumption', *Endnotes* 2, April 2010, for our critique of these attempts.

8 For this thought, see 'Error' in the next issue of *Endnotes*.

9 Perhaps this is because TC seem to derive their structural periodisation from the work of Michel Aglietta, the Regulation School economist who sees French history mirrored in the US (Aglietta, *A Theory of Capitalist Regulation: The US Experience*,

In this article, we begin from what we consider to be the grain of truth in TC's distinction between formal and real subsumption. Rather than two phases, we argue that their distinction roughly corresponds to two aspects of the world in which the workers movement unfolded. The first "formal" aspect had to do with the persistence of the peasantry — extended here to include the persistence of old regime elites whose power was based in the countryside — as a kind of outside to the capitalist mode of production. This outside was in the process of being incorporated into capitalist social relations, but this incorporation took a long time. The second, "real" aspect was the "development of the productive forces", that is, cumulative increases in labour productivity and the accompanying transformations, both of the productive apparatus and of the infrastructure of capitalist society, on which it relies.

These two aspects in turn gave rise to the two imperatives of the workers movement: on the one hand, to fight against the old regime elites, who sought to deny workers the freedoms of liberal capitalist society (e.g., the right to vote, the freedom to choose one's employer), and on the other hand, to set loose the development of the productive forces from the fetters that they encountered, particularly in late developing countries (those fetters often resulting, in part, from the persistence of the old regime).[10] In each case our focus will be on the divergence between the *expected* and the *actual* consequences of capitalist development.

The concepts of formal and real subsumption are inadequate to the task of explaining the history of the workers' movement. The two aspects of the movement that these concepts vaguely describe are not distinct periods, which could be precisely dated, but rather unfold simultaneously, much like the formal and real subsumption of the labour process itself. Nonetheless TC's periodisation of communism remains close to our own. The key

Verso, 1976). Aglietta ignores the growth of labour productivity and wages in the late 19th century, and imagines that 'Fordism' in the US had a state-led form similar to post-war France. See Robert Brenner and Mark Glick, 'The Regulation Approach: Theory and History', *NLR* I/188, July 1991.

10 TC touch on these two tendencies with their notion of a conflict between the demands for 'autonomy' and a 'rising strength of the working class within capitalism', but they fail to draw the connection with their categories of formal and real subsumption, as if the former were purely 'subjective' whilst the latter purely 'objective' features of the class struggle.

periodising break, for us as for TC, begins in the mid 1970s. The two aspects of the workers movement which we have described were both radically transformed in the last quarter of the twentieth century. Instead of a break between two "phases" of real subsumption, marked by "revolution" and "counter-revolution", we see this transition in terms of the ongoing transformation of the labour process, the end of the peasantry, the slowing down of capitalist accumulation on a global scale, and the corresponding onset of a long period of deindustrialisation, all of which have transformed the conditions of workers' struggles, for reasons explored in detail below. A *communist horizon* broke apart and dissolved in this moment, enclosing us, for a time, within a capitalist world seemingly without a vanishing point.

HORIZONS OF COMMUNISM

There is another distinction between our periodisation and TC's, one more concerned with content than form. TC often refer to the workers' movement (the era of "programmatism") as a "cycle of struggle". They thus fail to clearly distinguish between, on the one hand, cycles or waves of struggle, and on the other, the horizon of communism, within which cycles unfold. Both of these concepts are necessary to our balance sheet of the twentieth century.[11]

11 On communist horizons see 'Crisis in the Class Relation', *Endnotes* 2, April 2010.

The concept of a cycle of struggle describes how the class clash takes place. The latter typically unfolds neither in long marches nor in short outbursts, but rather, in waves. There are times of reaction, when revolutionary forces are weak and episodic, but not entirely absent. These reactionary eras may last for decades, but they do end, at a moment that is extremely difficult to predict in advance. Revolt then breaks out, more and more frequently. Militants, who formerly made little impression on their fellows, now find their numbers swelling. Meanwhile, struggles take on a new content, evolve new tactics, and discover new forms of organisation (all three are won only through the frightening melée of suffering and retribution). Over time, struggles coalesce — but never in a linear way — in waves that ebb and flow over years. That is what makes revolution possible. Insofar as revolutions fail or counter-revolutions succeed, the cycle comes to an end, and a new period of reaction begins.

Revolutionary strategists have mostly concerned themselves with the high points of various cycles of struggle: 1917, 1936, 1949, 1968, 1977, and so on. In so doing, they usually ignore the context in which those cycles unfold. The workers' movement was that context: it provided the setting in which distinct cycles unfolded: e.g. (in Europe) 1905–1921, 1934–1947, 1968–77. It was because each cycle of struggle unfolded in the context of the workers' movement that we can say of their high points: *these were not just ruptures within the capitalist class relation but ruptures produced within a particular horizon of communism.*[12] It is worth examining such ruptures in detail, although that is not the task we set for ourselves in this text.[13] Our contention is that it is only by looking at the workers movement as a whole, rather than at distinct high points, that we can see what made these points distinct, or even, *exceptional.* The revolutions of the era of the workers' movement emerged in spite of rather than in concert with overall trends, and did so in a manner that went wholly against the revolutionary theory of that era, with all its sense of inevitability.

Thus, for us, the workers' movement was not itself a cycle of struggle. It made for a definite communist horizon, which imparted a certain dynamic to struggles and also established their limits. To say that the workers' movement was *a* horizon of communism is to say that it was not *the* invariant horizon. It is necessary to reject the idea that communism could become possible again only on the

12 On the idea of a 'produced rupture', see Théorie Communiste, 'Sur la critique de l'objectivisme', TC 15 Feb 1999.

13 See 'Spontaneity, Mediation, Rupture', *Endnotes* 3, September 2013, for a discussion of the concept of cycles of struggle and revolutionary strategy.

basis of a renewal of the workers' movement (which is not the same thing as organised workers' struggle). We will here try to understand the conditions that, between the late 19th century and the 1970s, opened up the era of the workers' movement, made for several cycles of struggle, and then irreversibly collapsed. We focus, in other words, on the *longue durée* of the movement.

TWO FALLACIES

The essential thing to understand about the workers' movement is that it represented the horizon of communism during the era of the long *rise* of the capitalist mode of production, that is, an era in which "all fixed, fast frozen relations, with their train of ancient and venerable prejudices and opinions" were "swept away". Marxists have often drawn the wrong conclusions from this passage in the *Communist Manifesto*. Thus, before we begin it will be helpful to first disabuse ourselves of two common fallacies.

The first fallacy is that *capitalism is an inevitable or evolutionary stage of history*. Marxists in the late 19th century often imagined that capitalist social relations were relentlessly spreading across the globe. They thought the city, the factory, and wage labour would soon absorb everyone. In actual fact by 1950, some two-thirds of the world's population remained in agriculture, the vast majority self-sufficient peasants or herdsmen. Even in the high-income countries, some 40 percent of the workforce was in agriculture. It was not until the late 1970s and early 1980s that a tipping point was reached: the agricultural population of the high-income countries shrank to a vanishing point, and globally, for the first time in thousands of years, the majority of the world's workers were no longer working in the fields. Thus, the global peasantry, and the "fast-frozen relations" with which it was associated, were not so quickly "swept away". This house cleaning took longer than expected because — in contrast to what historical materialists imagined — there was no natural or automatic tendency for the global peasantry to fold into the proletariat, whether by the corrosion of market forces or by some tendency of capitalists to expropriate peasants *en masse*.

Indeed, capital did not inevitably draw peasants into its orbit. Whenever possible, peasants fought to secure their non-market access to land. In the 19th and most of the 20th century, peasants' eviction from the land was necessarily a political act. But then, such acts were rarely undertaken by capitalists, who preferred to employ non-free or semi-free labour wherever it was available, in order to produce for world markets (where levels of inequality were high, domestic markets were tiny). In fact, when expropriation was undertaken, it was often by representatives of the labour movement, or at least, with their support.

Proletarians could support the project of de-peasantisation because peasants were embedded in pre-capitalist class relations with landlords. These patriarchal social forms, stratified into castes or estates, offered little opportunity for change or mobility. Old-regime elites, oriented towards military affairs, were to some degree interested in pursuing alliances with capitalists (often the children of those elites, facing up to a changing world); however, this amalgamated elite-class saw nothing to gain by extending the franchise. Elites often did not even consider workers to be of the same species, that is, human beings *capable* of managing the affairs of the polity, let alone *deserving* of doing so. Such elites did not give up their privileges without a fight. Observers in the nineteenth century — or for that matter, in the twenty-first — can be forgiven for imagining that "free labour" was the inevitable accompaniment of capitalist accumulation. The history of the twentieth century showed that "free labour" had to be won.

The second fallacy is that *the development of capitalism tends to unify the workers.* The labour market may be singular, but the workers who enter it to sell their labour power are not. They are divided by language, religion, nation, race, gender, skill, etc. Some of these differences were preserved and transformed by the rise of capitalism, while others were newly created. Such remixing had ambivalent consequences. Most divisions proved to be obstacles to organising along lines of class solidarity. However, some pre-existing forms of collectivity proved to be their own sources of solidarity, an impetus to mass direct-action.

Champions of the workers' movement declared that the development of the forces of production would get rid of divisions among the workers. The dispersed masses, the "class in itself", would be formed by factory discipline into a compact mass, which might then be capable of becoming the "class for itself". Thus if the workers would only give up on their attempts to preserve the old ways, if they would only give in to the scientific (and constant) reorganisation of the workplace, they would soon find themselves positively transformed: they would be unified by the factory system into a "collective worker". For a while, in the early part of the twentieth century, this vision seemed to be coming true.

But in fact, these transformations led to the integration of workers (for the most part, former peasants) into market society, not only at the point of production, but also in exchange and in consumption, where workers were atomised. It was this atomising feature of the new world, not the cooperative aspects of work in the factory, that would prove dominant. That was true not only in consumer markets, where workers exchanged wages for goods, but also in labour markets, where they exchanged their promise to work for a promised wage—and even in the factories themselves, since divisions among workers were retained and made anew. The resulting intra-class competition was only partly mitigated by unions, which acted as rival salesmen's associations, attempting to corner the market in labour power.

Here is the unity-in-separation of market society. People become ever more interdependent through the market, but this power comes at the expense of their capacities for collective action. Capitalist society reduces workers to petty commodity sellers, providing them with some autonomy, but always within limits. In hindsight, it is clear that the dream of the workers' movement—that an "actual unity" of workers, as opposed to their unity-in-separation, would be realised in the factories through the further development of the productive forces—was not true. *Such an actual unity can come about only by means of a communist transcendence of capitalist social relations.*

1 THE CONSTRUCTION OF THE WORKERS MOVEMENT

Both of the above-mentioned fallacies were elements in the story that the workers movement told about itself, via its leaders and theoreticians. The first fallacy, the stagist, progressivist view of history, was a staple of 19th century bourgeois thought, from Ranke to Comte to Spencer, and one that proved particularly attractive to the workers' movement's official scribes. Kautsky, Bernstein and Plekhanov, as well as Lenin, Luxemburg and Lukács, all took heart from the idea that their revolution inherited the baton from a previous one, the so-called "bourgeois revolution", which they saw as the inevitable result of the development of the forces of production and the rising power of an urban bourgeoisie. In early writings Marx himself subscribed to this view of inevitable stages, but as we shall see in the postface, "The Idea of the Workers Movement", he rejected it in his later writings on the Russian Mir.

In this section we show that the "final" Marx was right in repudiating the stagist perspective that he himself had promulgated. Except in England, capitalism did not develop *in nuce* within the old regime; the European bourgeois revolutions, when and where they took place, were not really bourgeois at all.[1] Instead, they largely found their basis in the internal tensions of the old regime, that is to say, first of all, in an ongoing contest between peasants and the elites who extracted an income from their labours, and second, in contests among elite factions, vying for dominance. As we will see, these old regimes tried to modernise themselves in response to the onset of capitalist development in the UK, and the military expansionism with which it was associated. That eventually led to attempts to institute capitalist social relations, by decree, on the continent.

We do not claim that capitalist development failed to take place outside of the UK and US. It's just that *the*

1 Neil Davidson has recently attempted to save the notion of the bourgeois revolution by dropping the (now widely rejected) claim that these revolutions were led by a bourgeoisie intent on spreading liberal democracy. He claims instead that, without necessarily intending it, they gave rise to states that 'promoted capitalist development'. That may be true of the 'passive revolutions' (Italy, Germany, Japan), but it is not true of the classic case, the French revolution, which consolidated peasant land rights and the tax-office state. See Davidson, *How Revolutionary Were the Bourgeois Revolutions?* (Haymarket 2012).

2 The stalling out of what Théorie Communiste has called the 'formal subsumption' of

political revolution which was supposed to accompany the economic revolution did not take place on European soil. Thus, the establishment of liberal norms — with assurances of universal (male) suffrage, individual freedoms, and government by laws debated in parliament — was not guaranteed. Instead, the old regime, with its system of privileges, largely preserved itself alongside an ongoing capitalist development. Elite privileges would be abolished only where the working class completed the political tasks that the bourgeoisie had not. Such was the social setting for the emergence of the labour movement, and also for the development of socialist and anarchist perspectives. The labour movement had to fight its way into existence in a world where both the peasantry and the old regime elites remained powerful forces.[2]

society played a key role in determining what shape the workers' movement took. However, unlike TC, we do not think this phase ended with the conclusion of WWI. Even in Europe, the restructuring of social relations along capitalist lines carried on into the post-WWII era.

A NON-TRANSITION

According to the formerly prevailing stagist view of history, the rise of the absolutist state was already a symptom of the transition to capitalism, which was supposedly going on all across Europe in the early modern period. Towns were swelling with the commercial activity of the bourgeoisie; the revolutions of 1789 and 1848 were supposed to mark its rise to political power. But in fact, the peasant revolts at the heart of modern revolutions — which spanned the centuries from 1789 all the way down to the 1960s — did not usher in the political rule of capital; rather, they largely continued class struggle within the context of the old regime. Peasant communities were fighting to free themselves from the domination of feudal lords. However, the upshot of doing so "would not be the transition to capitalism, but the strengthening of precapitalist social property relations".[3] Peasant revolts had as their goal to strengthen the resistance of their communities to all forms of exploitation — both capitalist and non-capitalist.

3 Robert Brenner, 'Property and Progress: Where Adam Smith Went Wrong', in Chris Wickham, ed., *Marxist History-Writing for the Twenty-First Century* (British Academy 2007), p. 89. We are heavily indebted to Brenner's thesis concerning the historical origins of the capitalist mode of production. See T. H. Aston and C. H. E. Philpin, eds, *The Brenner Debate: Agrarian Class Structure and Economic Development in Pre-industrial Europe* (Cambridge 1987).

The peasants could carry on without the lords for they were already constituted as a community: they had "direct access to factors of production — land, tools, and labour — sufficient to enable them to maintain themselves without recourse to the market".[4] Under these conditions, the removal of external domination by lords would not release peasants into capitalist social relations. For that to happen, their communities would have to be dissolved. But it was difficult to make that happen. On the one hand, peasant communities did not dissolve themselves. On the other hand, they fought tenaciously against attempts to separate them from the land. Therefore, peasants — like every other non-capitalist social formation — do not *necessarily* become imbricated in markets. There is no historically inevitable tendency to proletarianise the world's population.

While it was important as a step towards the formation of the modern state, the emergence of absolutism in continental Europe was only indirectly related to the transition to the capitalist mode of production. Absolutism arose because, in the aftermath of the Black Death, peasant communities in that region were stronger. It was difficult for feudal lords to extract rent from the peasants: "suffering from reduced revenues, local lords were often too weak to stand up to the expansionist designs of those great lordly competitors, monarchs and princes, who extended their territorial jurisdiction at [the local lords] expense."[5] On that basis, the absolutist state was able to centralise lords' rent-extracting activity as state taxation (though only in a highly conflictual process, which pitted elites against one another). Thus, the wealth of absolutist states was won by squeezing the peasants more severely. What commercial development took place in this context merely reflected age-old cycles of urban growth and decline. While this process laid bases for what would become the modern *state*, there was no transition to the specifically capitalist *mode of production* necessarily implied in these developments.

4 Brenner, 'Property and Progress', p. 63.

5 ibid., p. 92.

Likewise, elsewhere in Europe, the strength of old regimes remained a constant feature of the landscape. But outside of Western Europe, that was not because peasants were growing stronger. Rather, it was because their communities were weak. In Eastern Europe, where territories were more recently colonised, lords retained a tight grip on the peasants. Even in the aftermath of the Black Death, lords were able to keep peasants in conditions of servitude, in some cases into the twentieth century, without having to centralise lordly extraction.

And beyond Europe? Marx had expected European colonialism to bring capitalism to the rest of the world.[6] However, colonial administrations, even as late as the 1920s and 30s, only ended up reinforcing the power of the local elites, who ruled, in different ways, over various agrarian societies. Where those elites did not exist, for example, in parts of sub-Saharan Africa, colonial powers designated certain individuals as "chieftains", sometimes inventing this role out of whole cloth. The point of colonialism was not to proletarianise the population, initiating a transition to fully capitalist social relations. On the contrary, the point was to reinforce existing social relations in the countryside — pinning "natives" down and then partially proletarianising them — in order to secure the space and the labour needed for limited projects of resource extraction.

6 'England, it is true, in causing a social revolution in [India], was actuated only by the vilest interests', but 'whatever may have been the crimes of England she was the unconscious tool of history in bringing about that revolution.' Marx, 'The British Rule in India', *New-York Daily Tribune*, 25 June 1853.

DEVELOPMENT AND LATE DEVELOPMENT

It was only in England that capitalist social relations emerged as an unanticipated development out of the old regime. Here, class struggle in that context had a novel result. After the Black Death, strong peasant communities won formal freedom, but well-organised lords secured the right to charge rent on the land peasants farmed. The latter became market-dependent for the first time. There followed a veritable agricultural revolution, marked by the consolidation of land-holdings and an adoption of new techniques, as well as the growth of the division of labour in the countryside. Agricultural productivity rose, and that, in turn, fostered demographic growth and urbanisation. It was unlike what was happening anywhere else in Europe, or anywhere else in the world.

This capitalist pattern of development swelled the military power of the state in Britain. The resulting European power imbalance drove a logic of territorial conquest through which the British Empire would eventually cover a quarter of the Earth's landmass. In response, the absolutist states of continental Europe tried (and failed) to rationalise their empires, leading to fiscal and social crises, the most famous of which was the one that led to the French Revolution. For elites outside of Britain, regime change thus appeared a political necessity. Otherwise, they were going to fall further behind it militarily, as was proven in the course of the Napoleonic wars. Elites had to figure out how to introduce capitalist social relations by political design — and as fast as possible: "while Britain did not have a policy to 'industrialise', most countries since have had a strategy to emulate its success."[7] That strategy came to be known, at least in the economics literature, as "late development".

The key point is that, in the mid-nineteenth century, late development was based on alliances between a capitalist class and old regime elites: "Iron and Rye". In fact, it was often unclear whether there was any separation in the first place between these classes, from which alliances might be concluded: the emergence of a bourgeoisie was often merely a partial embourgeoisement of a section of the aristocracy. In regard to late development, "the decade of the 1860s was a fundamental conjuncture. It saw the US Civil War, the unification of Germany, the unification of Italy, the Russian serf emancipation and the Meiji Restoration in Japan."[8] While wars and internal conflicts in the 1860s

7 Robert Allen, *Global Economic History: A Very Short Introduction* (OUP 2011), p. 41 – a much more important book than its title suggests.

8 Goldner, 'Communism is the Material Human Community'.

served to consolidate the power of elites over territories, protectionism in the 1870s created a space for national industry. It also preserved peasantries against grain imports from the United States and Eastern Europe.

Some of the countries where elites made power plays on this basis were able to catch up with Britain, and thus to join the club of rich countries: "not only did continental Europe and North America overtake Britain in industrial output between 1870 and 1913, but they manifestly joined it in technological competence."[9] However, the nature of late development ensured that old regime elites and the peasantry persisted. On the continent, "industrialisation proved to be compatible with the preservation of a firmly entrenched agrarian ruling class and a dynastic state of a conservative and militaristic stamp. It took place without the destruction of the peasantry as a class and gave opportunities for the emergence of prosperous peasant strata producing for the market."[10] The old regime went into decline in Europe only following the First World War. Then, after limping back onto the scene, it was decimated in the Second: old regime elites were finally liquidated only by the Red Army, which — having already eradicated the Czar and the Russian aristocracy in the Civil War — now opened up a path of slaughter that marched all the way into Prussia, the heart of the old regime in Central Europe.

Yet even then, the old regime persisted in the rest of the world, strengthening itself by allying with other classes in the anti-colonial movements of the middle twentieth century. Without an international war (on the scale of the World Wars), which might have unified nations and strengthened the hands of developmentalists, it proved difficult to dislodge such elites. The task of doing so was made even more difficult in the global context of imperialist interventions: the US feared that any attempt at real land reform would lead inevitably to communist revolution and regional contagion. And indeed, where

9 Allen, *Global Economic History*, p. 43. As we will see, Russia and Japan were unsuccessful in their attempts to catch up with Britain by means of late development. For them, catch up would come only via 'big-push' industrialisation, and only in the middle decades of the twentieth century.

10 Tom Kemp, *Industrialisation in Nineteenth Century Europe* (Routledge 2014), p. 104.

elites were not defeated by communist revolution, they managed to retain much of their control, both of politics and of the economy. It is still the case, even today, that many national economies in low-income countries are overseen by a few extended families and their retinues.

THE PERSISTENCE OF THE PEASANTRY

It was in the context of "the persistence of the old regime" that the new industrial cities first materialised in continental Europe, in the second half of the nineteenth century.[11] In some places, cities emerged from the transformation of medieval towns; elsewhere, conurbations sprung up where only villages had been. In any case, by the end of the nineteenth century, the speed of urbanisation was unprecedented. That was true in spite of the fact that, throughout this period, there remained a substantial number of peasants. From great reservoirs in the countryside, peasants streamed into the towns — in a slow trickle or in a torrent — either because they had lost their land due to expropriation, or else because, on account of demographic growth, their parents did not have enough land to divide among all of their descendants.[12]

11 For the best account of this phenomenon, see Arno Mayer, *The Persistence of the Old Regime* (Pantheon 1981).

12 It is important to note that it was not until the public health interventions and medical innovations of the last quarter of the 19th century and the beginning of the 20th that demographic growth within the cities displaced migration as the main source of urban growth.

Nevertheless, individuals were not only pushed into the cities; they were also drawn to them. Cities offered a real if partial emancipation from rural patriarchy, from the law of the father as well as the lord. The total dependence of children on their fathers was grounded in the fact that land — not labour — was the limiting productive factor in rural areas, and so also the real source of social wealth. Men had to inherit land from their parents, or to acquire it with their parents' resources; likewise, in order to marry, women needed dowries, which only parents could provide. That was the source of an overbearing paternal power: children couldn't make decisions about their own lives. They couldn't afford to upset their fathers. The prospect of finding work in a nearby city disrupted that age-old relation: the autonomy of the young was won via the wage. In that sense, capitalist social relations extended an existing feature of medieval cities, delimiting a zone of relative freedom in a world of strictures.

However, that freedom was secured only in a situation of immense danger. The facilities where proletarians worked were hastily constructed. Their jobs required them to handle lethal machinery, with little fresh air or daylight. Capitalists found that they did not have to worry about the working conditions they offered. For no matter how bad those conditions were, young proletarians, often fresh from the countryside, still lined up for work; they even fought over it. Internecine conflicts emerged between peasants arriving from different villages, speaking mutually unintelligible dialects of a national language, or different languages altogether. Capitalists played workers off one another to secure low wages and a docile workforce. The same sorts of conflicts and in-fighting then emerged in proletarian residences.

In this strange new world, laden with suffering, proletarian freedoms created openings for self-destruction: "if at the end of the week the worker had enough left to enable him to forget the hell he lived in for a few hours by getting drunk on bad liquor, it was the most he could achieve. The inevitable consequence of such a state of affairs was an enormous increase in prostitution, drunkenness, and crime."[13] Households were always one step away from penury, and thus could be pushed into begging, petty crime, or sex work when one of their members became an alcoholic.[14] In the new industrial city *it was easy to fall down and difficult to get up.* That was all the more true, insofar as moving to the cities meant cutting the ties of support that existed in rural communities. Nor were capitalists going to help workers survive: under conditions of capitalist competition and an oversupply of labour, employers couldn't afford to care whether any individual worker or family survived.

13 Rocker, *Anarcho-Syndicalism: Theory and Practice – An Introduction to a Subject Which the Spanish War Has Brought Into Overwhelming Prominence* [1937] (AK Press 2004).

14 The notion that poverty was pushing proletarian women, against their will, into sex work, was a major theme of the socialist literature of the late nineteenth and early 20th century.

That was to be expected: after all, the working class would be emancipated only by the workers themselves.[15] And yet, contrary to the narrative of the workers' movement, the development of the productive forces was not tending to strengthen the working class by giving birth to the collective worker. The workers' movement supposed that this collective worker would be a byproduct of the factory: it would stamp its universal form on its victims, annihilating their relationships to the past (which remained all around them, in the form of villages outside the city limits); the class in-itself would then become the class for-itself. But that did not happen automatically. Most workers were not even factory workers. And in any case, those who did work in factories were often divided, not only by skill, or position within the division of labour, but also by religion and customs. Many did not even speak the same language! Lacking a basis for solidarity, proletarians found it difficult to convince their co-workers to risk their jobs for the greater good by going on strike. The working class was a class that tended to express itself not by striking, but by rioting.

15 Although, in fact, early labour legislation was not won by workers, but rather, by teams of factory inspectors and their supporters in government.

THE PERSISTENCE OF OLD REGIME ELITES

Periodic explosions of urban riots gave rise to what was known as the "social question". What did the workers want? And what would it take to pacify them? In fact, it seemed, at first, that there was no need to pacify workers: as capitalists expanded production, their power over them only grew. Moreover, when proletarians did revolt, the ownership class found that it could call on the army and the police to beat or shoot them for disturbing the peace. Against these repressive interventions, proletarians had few resources on which to draw.

They needed to organise themselves. According to what became the prevailing revolutionary theory, workers needed to organise themselves to win rights that would help them in their further struggle. They needed the right to assemble and the freedom of the press. They needed to force the army and the police to remain neutral in the class struggle.[16] To get all that — so the theory went — workers needed power at the political level: they needed to win the right to vote. On that basis, they could form a class party which would compete for power in national elections. This political perspective was reinforced almost everywhere by the failure of alternatives: "While strikes oriented toward extensions of suffrage were successful in Belgium and Sweden, the use of mass strikes for economic goals invariably resulted in political disasters: in Belgium in 1902 ... Sweden in 1909 ... France in 1920 ... Norway in 1921 ... and Great Britain in 1926 ... All these strikes were defeated; in the aftermath, trade-unions were decimated and repressive legislation was passed."[17]

The problem for workers, in trying the parliamentary route, was that the old regime controlled politics. The lower classes were "not supposed to share ... the prerogatives of full-fledged human beings", who made up the elite.[18] There was a material basis underlying this perspective: elites feared that recognising the lower classes as equals, even formally, would undermine the basis of their power in the countryside: that power was based not on success in free markets, but rather, on strictly controlling access to limited resources — including the rights to own land, and the rights to mine, log, or graze animals on that land — all of which was determined by elite privileges.[19]

As it turned out, the bourgeoisie in Europe did not displace those elites as the workers' movement had expected. Instead, factory owners grew up within the old regime, often taking on noble titles. In defending their interests, the ownership class appealed to privilege as much as liberal economics. There was a material basis underlying that perspective as well: capitalists benefited from workers' lack of freedom. Particularly in agriculture

16 These reforms had nothing to do with 'reformism' –the belief that the working classes could become full and equal members of the capitalist polity, thus making revolution unnecessary. On the contrary, such reforms were seen as essential weapons for the coming class war.

17 Adam Przeworski, *Capitalism and Social Democracy* (Cambridge 1985), p. 12.

18 G.M. Tamás, 'Telling the Truth about Class' in *Socialist Register*, vol. 42, 2006; available on grundrisse.net.

19 'No landlord-dominated government will happily vote itself out of landowning status and various other privileges without strong pressure from other socio-political groups.' Russell King, *Land Reform: A World Survey* (Westview 1977), pp. 9–10.

and in resource extraction, aimed at international markets, employers did not need workers to be fully free in order to make a profit. Plantation owners, engaged in the production of all sorts of raw materials and agricultural products, profited handsomely from the employment of slaves. On the Russian steppes, exported grain was produced by quasi-serfs. Thus, capitalist development did not automatically lead to the double freedom that Marx described as its foundation: workers were not transformed into formally free commodity sellers who also happened to be free of access to means of production. Only some workers obtained the economic right to sell their labour-power; fewer achieved the political rights of equal citizens.

The old regime had only contempt for workers' calls for full economic and political equality, arguing that they didn't deserve it, for they lacked the self-control and independence that comes with owning property. Instead, proletarian neighbourhoods were rife with unconventional and ecstatic forms of religious belief. Drunks begged in the street, while in ports and public parks proletarian prostitution and male homosexuality disturbed refined sensibilities. These indecencies became the subject matter of newspaper exposés; elites gawked and laughed at the lawlessness and penury of proletarian life. Politically-minded workers could see that these were problems, not just for their image, but also for their capacity to organise: how were workers going to win the vote — let alone abolish class society — if they could not even keep their own houses in order?

THE AFFIRMATION OF A CLASS IDENTITY

In order to abolish class society, workers needed to win reforms, and in order to do that, they first needed to present themselves as capable and worthy of power. The difficulty they faced was twofold. In the cities, workers had to acclimatise to dangerous conditions of life.

Coming from different villages (and having such diverse experiences), they had to figure out how to organise together. Meanwhile, in newly-constructed liberal states, workers faced the hatred of their social betters, who were looking for any excuse to exclude them from civil society. In response to these problems, the workers' movement constituted itself as a project: proletarians would fight for their right to exist. They would show that there was dignity and pride in being a worker; the workers' culture was superior to that of other social classes. Eric Hobsbawm suggests that "no term is harder to analyse than 'respectability' in the mid-nineteenth century working class, for it expressed simultaneously the penetration of middle-class values and standards, and also the attitudes without which working class self-respect would have been difficult to achieve, and a movement of collective struggle impossible to build: sobriety, sacrifice, the postponement of gratification".[20] This mid-century notion of respectability then matured into the more developed programs and projects of the late-nineteenth and early-twentieth century workers movement in all its forms: as socialist and communist parties, as anarchist unions, and as assorted other revolutionary forces.

20 Hobsbawm, *The Age of Capital, 1848–1875* (Penguin 1984), p. 224.

Supporting workers' claims to respectability was a vision of their destiny, with five tenets:

(1) Workers were building a new world with their own hands. (2) In this new world, workers were the only social group that was expanding; whereas all other groups were contracting, including the bourgeoisie. (3) Workers were not only becoming the majority of the population; they were also becoming a compact mass, the collective worker, who was being drilled in the factories to act in concert with the machines. (4) They were thus the only group capable of managing the new world in accordance with its innermost logic: neither a hierarchy of order-givers and order-takers,

nor the irrationality of market fluctuations, but rather, an ever more finely-grained division of labour. (5) Workers were proving this vision to be true, since the class was realising what it was in a conquest of power, the achievement of which would make it possible to abolish class society, and thus to bring man's prehistory to a close.[21]

This vision wasn't something implanted from the outside, transforming a reformist movement into a revolutionary one. To muster the will to take risks and make sacrifices, workers needed to believe in a better world that was already in the process of realising itself. Their victory was supposedly guaranteed: it was a historical necessity but, paradoxically, also a political project. It is precisely the simplicity and self-evidence of these tenets, their immediate appeal, that explains the movement's exponential growth in the years between 1875 and 1921.

As mentioned above, at the heart of the workerist vision lay a mythic figure: the collective worker — the class in-and-for-itself, the class as unified and knowing its unity, born within the space of the factory. The collective worker was presupposed in workers' organising and posited through that organising effort. But, to a large extent, *the collective worker did not exist outside of the movement's attempts to construct it.*[22] The theorists of the labour movement could never have admitted that this was the case. They spoke of the factory system as if it came from the future: the development of the factory system was supposedly a consequence of the "progressive socialisation of the process of production", which created "the germs of the future social order".[23] It was expected that the socialised factory system would also prepare the workers for a socialist existence, transforming them from a disparate set of working *classes*, into a unified fighting force — the industrial proletariat — drilled on the factory floor.

21 This last tenet sometimes expressed a will to see the proletariat become the only class; at other times, it expressed a will to see all classes abolished and working time dramatically reduced (see afterword).

22 False consciousness supposedly hid the class from itself, but false-consciousness was a false concept.

23 Luxemburg, 'Reform or Revolution' (1900) in *The Essential Rosa Luxemburg* (Haymarket 2008), p. 45.

In reality, this transformation did not take place automatically. The factory system was not a time-traveler from the future. It was the form production took within developed capitalist societies. As such, it embodied not the "actual unity" of a world to come, but rather the unity-in-separation of this world. The factory system, in itself, did not tend to unify the workforce in a way that benefited workers engaged in struggle — or, at least, it did not do that exclusively. Capitalist development may have dissolved some pre-existing differences among workers, but it reinforced or created other divisions, especially as these emerged from the division of labour (that is, mostly around skill, but also around divisions of tasks by "race" and gender, as well as according to seniority, language, region of origin, etc).

Meanwhile, outside of the factory gates, workers continued to stand in conflict with one another. They had to look out for themselves, as well as their kin: "Similarity of class position does not necessarily result in solidarity since the interests which workers share are precisely those which put them in competition with one another, primarily as they bid down wages in quest of employment".[24] Given that there were never enough jobs for everyone (the existence of a surplus population was a structural feature of societies built around capitalist exploitation), allegiances of religion, "race", and "nation" made it possible for some workers to get ahead at the expense of others. As long as workers were not already organised on a class basis — and there was no pre-given, structural necessity for them to be so organised — they had a real interest in maintaining their individuality, as well as their extra-class allegiances.

This was the melée into which the workers' movement threw itself. The movement encouraged workers to forget their specificity and all that supposedly came from the past. Workers should turn their gaze towards

24 Przeworski, *Capitalism and Social Democracy*, p. 20.

the future; they should actively merge into the generality of the collective worker. Here was the essence of the workers' movement. Trade unions and chambers of labour, as well as social organisations, brought proletarians together on the basis of trades, neighbourhoods or hobbies. A general workers' interest was then cobbled together out of these local organisations. The Social Democratic and Communist parties and the Anarchist federations instantiated the collective worker at the national level.

These organisations could not have succeeded in their tasks without, at the same time, relying on an affirmable class identity. Insofar as they made sacrifices in the name of the labour movement, workers generally were not acting in their immediate interests. To say that they affirmed a shared identity is to say that the movement succeeded in convincing workers to suspend their interests as isolated sellers in a competitive labour market, and, instead, to act out of a *commitment* to the collective project of the labour movement.

To the extent that workers were willing to believe that having solidarity was morally necessary, they were able to realise — partially and fitfully — the slogan that "an injury to one is an injury to all". This phrase never described a preexisting truth about the working class; it was, instead, an ethical injunction. But insofar as workers accepted this injunction, their interests as *individuals* began to change: those interests were simplified, narrowed, or even wholly redefined, but also partially fulfilled.[25] By this means, competition between workers was muted, but only for as long as the shared ethic and identity could be preserved.

In that sense, the workers' movement was an apparatus, an urban machine, which bound workers together and kept them so bound.[26] Such binding did not only happen in the factories:

25 See the addendum to this part, p. 103 below.

26 The us presents only a partial exception to this story. Its distinguishing features are (1) the early achievement of universal manhood suffrage, and (2) the fact that it drew its industrial workforce not from its own agricultural periphery, but from that of Europe. Engels, in a letter to Weydemeyer, grasped the key to both phenomena, writing of the 'ease with which the surplus population [in the us] is drained off to the farms'. Free land on the frontier (ethnically cleansed of its initial inhabitants) stimulated the largest transoceanic migration in human history. States extended the franchise to all men in order to attract these immigrants (whilst women and free blacks were disenfranchised). Urban political machines

This remained one of the Left's most perduring misrecognitions: 'labour movements' implied a socialism beginning from the workplace, centred on strikes, and borne by militant working men; yet those movements were actually more broadly founded, also requiring women's efforts in households, neighbourhoods, and streets.[27]

The collective worker was cobbled together in towns, through an array of popular workers' organisations: workers' "savings banks, health and pension funds, newspapers, extramural popular academies, workingmen's clubs, libraries, choirs, brass bands, engagé intellectuals, songs, novels, philosophical treatises, learned journals, pamphlets, well-entrenched local governments, temperance societies – all with their own mores, manners and styles".[28] Through these means, proletarians were made to forget that they were Corsican or Lyonnais; they became workers. *The class came to exist* as an abstract identity that could be affirmed, dignified and proud.

This is how the workers' movement solved the problems of acclimatising the constant flow of new rural–urban migrants to the industrial cities, and of making them respectable. Respectability involved three operations. (1) The movement spread new behavioural codes, either appropriated from bourgeois culture, or directly opposed to it (heterosexual family norms, temperance). (2) The movement provided a sense of community, to help workers overcome the social dislocation involved in migrating to cities. Community organisations reinforced the new codes while providing for the spiritual needs of their members. And (3) the movement built up institutions that supported workers' struggles to transform their material situation — and to prevent individuals or families from falling into disrepute (unions and parties fought not only for better wages and conditions, but also for public health interventions, welfare schemes, provisions for the old and sick, and so on).

quickly arose in us cities to manage the white male vote along the lines of ethnic, religious and regional identity. These structures were only shaken in the 1920s, when the tap of immigration was turned off, and us industry for the first time began to draw on its own rural hinterland. It was only during this period of tight immigration, from 1932 to 1974, that the us came to approximate a European social democracy.

27 Geoff Eley, *Forging Democracy: The History of the Left in Europe, 1850–2000* (Oxford 2002), p. 58.

28 Tamás, 'Telling the Truth about Class'.

The first two of these operations supported the third, while it was the third that brought the class into conflict with the legal and political frameworks of the era. The workers were compelled to struggle "against throne and altar, for universal suffrage, for the right to organise and to strike".[29] It was necessary to take risks and make sacrifices, but both could now be justified through the movement's self-understanding — as a moral community, fighting to establish a better world, guided by the lights of rational production and equitable distribution.

29 Ibid.

THE PAST IN THE PRESENT

In truth this moral community was an ad hoc construction, supported by a beautiful dream. It was far from an ironclad reality: "what, from one point of view, looked like a concentration of men and women in a single 'working class', could be seen from another as a gigantic scattering of the fragments of societies, a diaspora of old and new communities."[30] Workers retained or preserved their links to the past, and did so in many different ways. Traditional artisan guilds shaded into the unions, ethnic and religious groups set themselves up in the new cities, and most new workers retained links to peasant families.

30 Hobsbawm, *Age of Empire*, p. 119.

31 Quoted in Geoff Eley, *Forging Democracy*, p. 78.

While workers did not so easily forget their links to the old communities, movement activists increasingly viewed those links as an obstacle: "world history cannot be turned back", proclaimed the German Metalworkers Union (DMV), "for the sake of the knife-grinders" and their craft mentality.[31] However, in many cases the culture of solidarity that activists were trying to build relied precisely on such holdovers, forged through the experiences of peasants and artisans. The idea that work was dignified — that one should identify with one's essence — was itself an inheritance from artisans. The movement tried to transfer the bonds of the craft workers over to the "mass workers", that is, the semi-skilled workers in the factories, who were supposed to identify with the class as a whole, while denying any attempt to preserve their specific trades.

32 Ibid., p. 78–79.

Resistance to the project of the workers' movement often took place on this basis; a conflict thus opened up between the class and its organisations. It was often workers resisting incorporation into the generality of the collective worker who undertook the most militant actions. In many places the most radical current of the workers' movement was associated — against the prevailing theory of the Social Democrats — with a defense of shopfloor autonomy, that is, with the right of workers to make decisions about the organisation of production, even when those decisions slowed the development of the productive forces. Conflict was apparent in rapidly growing cities like Solingen, in western Germany: "Where groups like the Solingen cutlery grinders clung to older ideals of a locally rooted cooperative commonwealth based on craft autonomy, the new DMV strategists [that is, the strategists at the German Metalworkers Union] celebrated technical progress, mass material improvement, and an industrial unionism proper to the structures of a continuously rationalising capitalism".[32] Socialists and communists did not see that it was only insofar as workers had a hand in determining how production took place that they were able to identify with their work as what defined who they really were. Once that right and its corresponding experience disappeared, so did the workers' identity.

ADDENDUM ON THE LUMPEN-PROLETARIAT

33 'Misery and Debt', *Endnotes* 2, April 2010.

We have referred elsewhere to the surplus population as the extreme embodiment of capital's contradictory dynamic.[33] What is the relationship between the surplus population and the lumpen-proletariat? Are they one and the same? Whereas Marx expounds on the surplus population, at length, in *Capital*, he does not refer to the lumpen-proletariat at all in that work; he uses the phrase only in his political writings. How did the "lumpen" become such a popular topic, among revolutionaries, in the course of the twentieth century?

As it turns out, "lumpen proletariat" was a key category for the workers' movement, and particularly for Marxists, in their Social Democratic and Bolshevik variants. Marxists were always hurling curses at perceived lumpen proletarians and anarchists alike, so much so that the two categories blended together. According to Rosa Luxemburg in *The Mass Strike*, "Anarchism has become in the [1905] Russian Revolution, not the theory of the struggling proletariat, but the ideological signboard of the counterrevolutionary lumpenproletariat, who, like a school of sharks, swarm in the wake of the battleship of the revolution."[34]

Who were these lumpen proletarians, preaching anarchy? Attempts to spell that out usually took the form not of structural analyses, but rather, of long lists of shady characters, lists which collapsed in on themselves in a frenzied incoherence. Here is Marx's paradigmatic discussion of the lumpen proletariat, from *The 18th Brumaire of Louis Bonaparte*: "On the pretext of founding a benevolent society, the lumpen proletariat of Paris had been organised into secret sections, each section led by Bonapartist agents". These lumpens supposedly consisted of "vagabonds, discharged soldiers and jailbirds, escaped galley slaves, swindlers, mountebanks, lazzaroni, pickpockets, tricksters, gamblers, pimps, brothel keepers, porters, literati, organ grinders, ragpickers, knife grinders, tinkers, beggars — in short, the whole indefinite, disintegrated mass, thrown hither and thither, which the French call *la bohème*."[35] Is there any truth in this paranoid fantasy? Do escaped convicts and organ grinders share a common, counter-revolutionary interest with beggars, which distinguishes them from the common mass of workers, who are apparently revolutionary by nature? To think so is insane.

34 Rosa Luxemburg, 'The Mass Strike' [1906] in *The Essential Rosa Luxemburg* (Haymarket 2008), p. 114.

35 Marx, 'The Eighteenth Brumaire of Louis Bonaparte' (MECW 10), p. 198.

The lumpen proletariat was a spectre, haunting the workers' movement. If that movement constituted itself as the movement for the dignity of workers, then the lumpen was the figure of the undignified worker (or more accurately, the lumpen was one of its figurations). All of the movement's efforts to give dignity to the class were supposedly undermined by these dissolute figures: drunks singing in the street, petty criminals and prostitutes. References to the lumpen proletariat registered what was a simple truth: it was difficult to convince workers to organise as workers, since mostly, they didn't care about socialism: "a great many of the poor, and especially the very poor, did not think of themselves or behave as 'proletarians,' or find the organisations and modes of action of the movement as applicable or relevant to them."[36] In their free time, they'd rather go to the pub than sing workers' songs.

In the figure of the lumpen, we discover the dark underside of the affirmation of the working class. It was an abiding class-hatred. Workers saw themselves as originating out of a stinking morass: "At the time of the beginning of modern industry the term proletariat implied absolute degeneracy. And there are persons who believe this is still the case."[37] Moreover, capitalism was trying to push workers back into the muck. Thus, the crisis tendencies of capitalism could only end in one of two ways: in the victory of the working class or in its becoming lumpen.

36 Hobsbawm, *Age of Empire*, p. 140.

37 Kautsky, *The Class Struggle* (1892), chapter 5, available on marxists.org.

2 THE INFRASTRUCTURE OF THE MODERN WORLD

The workers could have failed in their essay to defeat the old regime; we've certainly dwelled on the many obstacles that they faced. But in spite of all that, the movement was successful in achieving some of its goals. The labour movement shaped history (if not always as it had intended). That it did so, we argue, had everything to do with the emergence of *infrastructural industries*, that is, industries producing goods whose use depended on the construction of massive networked infrastructures: roads, electricity grids, plumbing, radio towers, etc.

If the persistence of the old regime set the scene or provided the stage on which the workers' movement was born, then these infrastructural industries supplied the dramatic action. It was in and through their growth that the drama of the workers' movement played out. These new industries came online just as those of the first industrial revolution — e.g., food processing, textiles, ironworks and railroads — were maturing. Taking their place at the leading edge, the infrastructural industries included, at first, everything to do with electrification and steel: safety razors, sliced bread, radios, and precision machines. There followed the heyday of so-called "Fordism": cars, refrigerators, washing machines, and all manner of consumer durables. Altogether, these industries employed huge masses of semi-skilled workers.

It was because they employed so many workers, and made their employment so central to the functioning of the wider economy, that the infrastructural industries determined the course of the workers' movement. The growth of these industries meant that, for a time, the development of the productive forces really did swell the size and power of the industrial workforce. Workers were also unified within massive factory complexes, which employed thousands of them at a time. Development therefore seemed to represent the growing strength of the proletariat and the shrinking relevance of its old-world enemies.

However, this growth in unity and power turned out to be a temporary phenomenon. Both were washed away in the 1970s, as industrialisation became deindustrialisation. Meanwhile, the expansion of infrastructural industries did not unify the wider class as expected. On the contrary, it deepened the imbrication of the proletariat within the unity-in-separation of capitalist social relations. Unity-in-separation was, at first, merely a formal feature of market exchange. But over time, this formal feature was "realised" in the transformation of the earth — a mess of steel and glass, concrete and asphalt, high-tension wires — taking place not only within the space of the factory, but also beyond the factory gates.

INFRASTRUCTURAL INDUSTRIES, SEMI-SKILLED WORKERS

Production in infrastructural industries was not tendentially automated. That made these industries unlike the ones Marx was thinking of in his famous fragment on machines: once chemical plants had been constructed, for example, they mostly needed to be maintained or monitored. Unlike chemicals production, the industries of the second industrial revolution required huge quantities of labour, not only for the construction of the plants, but also, once constructed, for the assembly of goods. The result was, from the standpoint of Marx's theory, a wholly unexpected support for the growth of labour demand.[1] On that basis, two waves of strong industrial employment growth took place in the 100 years after Marx's death: from the 1880s to 1914, then again from the 1950s to 1973. Both the fin-de-siècle upturn and the postwar boom seemed to confirm workers' sense that the fate of capital and of labour were tied together: accumulation of capital was multiplication of the proletariat.

1 On Marx's theory see 'Misery and Debt' *Endnotes* 2, April 2010.

This proletariat was, increasingly, a respectable class. It became respectable in the figure of the *male, semi-skilled, heavy industrial worker* (which is not to say that all such workers were male, only that they were imagined to be so, ideally). This figure became hegemonic in the course of the workers' movement: like the artisan, he really could define himself in relation to his work. That was because — at least until the 1960s, when the loss of shopfloor autonomy reached a tipping point — he was able to see his work as a source of growing collective power. He provided a model for the rest of the class: what it could be, what it was becoming.

Semi-skilled workers not only provided a model, they also had a measure of security denied to other members of the class. They were difficult to replace on a moment's notice, and they set in motion huge quantities of fixed capital, which were worthless when left idle. That security provided a firm basis from which to fight for freedoms for the class as a whole. The time of the workers' movement was simply the time of the rise and decline of the semi-skilled male worker and of the industries where he worked. Together they made it possible to imagine that capital was tendentially unifying the class by means of an affirmable workers' identity. But it was only insofar as those industries were expanding that the workers' movement could see the semi-skilled worker as its future being realised in the present. Once those industries went into decline, the glorious future declined as well.

THE ROLE OF THE STATE

But we will come to that later. For now, it is important to point out that, on the continent, the new industries emerging in this era did so only in the context of late development. As we saw above, late development was rooted in alliances between aristocratic and capitalist elites. Those alliances allowed European powers to institute "the American system".[2] The American system had four essential components. Late-developing regimes had to: (1) erect external tariffs to protect infant industries; (2) abolish internal tariffs and support infrastructure building, to unify the national market; (3) fund big banks, both to stabilise inflation and provide a boost to national capital formation; and (4) institute public education programmes, to consolidate allegiance to the state, standardise the national language, and promote literacy (literacy was a prerequisite for a lot of semi-skilled factory work, as well as office work).

Late development commenced in the 1860s and early 1870s. Then, in the course of the First Great Depression (1873–96), many states dropped pretenses to *Manchestertum*; they began to intervene extensively in national economies. That they did so made it possible to build a vast infrastructure, on which the new industries ran. Here were the canals, railroads and telegraph wires; here, too, the roads, telephone wires, gas lines, plumbing, and electrical grids. At first, this infrastructure was one dimensional: railroads and canals cut through the landscape. Then, it became increasingly two (or even three) dimensional: networks of roads, electrical grids and radio towers covered entire areas.

These latter necessitated some sort of urban planning. For example, the laying down of tram lines was associated with the separation out, on the one hand, of working class neighbourhoods, and on the other hand, of industrial zones (it was no longer the case that workers had to live within walking distance of their places of work).[3] Such residential and commercial districts had to be designated in advance, when the infrastructure was laid.

This sort of undertaking was often too difficult for capitalists, and not only because of the huge scale of investment required. To build a massive infrastructure requires an army of planners: to promote a wide reach,

2 Allen, *Global Economic History*, p. 80. The list that follows also comes from Allen's text.

3 See Wally Seccombe, *Weathering the Storm* (Verso 1993). Seccombe shows the extent to which capitalism really came into its own only with the 'second industrial revolution'. Until then, proletarian homes were not only located in the vicinity of factories, but also frequently functioned as extended sites of production for sale: families did 'finishing work' at home. The modern wage contract, which employed individuals rather than families to work *outside* the home, was generalised only at the end of the nineteenth century. Seccombe argues that, as a result, married women were increasingly relegated to non-income-earning activities.

to prevent wasteful duplication and to decide on industry standards. That meant a growing role for the state, as the only part of society capable of becoming adequate to this task — the task of planning society. Late development occurred alongside a burgeoning state apparatus, at once more centralised and more dispersed than ever before (although this apparatus remained relatively small until the World Wars spurred its growth).

The changed role of the state dramatically transformed proletarian visions of communism. In Marx's theory, there had been no role for the state to play, either before or after the revolution. Free-market capitalism was to be replaced by socialism: that is, the "conscious planning of production by associated producers (nowhere does Marx say: by the state)."[4] Marx's model of planning was not the state, but the workers' cooperative on the one hand, and the joint-stock company on the other. Likewise, Engels famously suggested in *Origins of the Family, Private Property and the State* that after the revolution, the state was to find its place in "a museum of antiquities, by the side of the spinning-wheel and the bronze axe."[5] Neither anticipated the massive role that states would play in the near future, in capitalist societies. Nor did they therefore anticipate the role the state would play in the socialist imaginary. Here's Kautsky:

> Among the social organisations in existence today there is but one that has the requisite dimensions, that can be used as the requisite field, for the establishment and development of the Socialist or Co-operative Commonwealth, and that is the modern state.[6]

State-led infrastructural development revealed the irrationality of capital, but in a particular way. It seemed irrational to consume commodities privately when they ran on an efficient public infrastructure. Why sell cars to individuals, when it was possible to build networks of collectively utilised trams? Why not just plan everything?

4 Ernest Mandel, 'Karl Marx' in John Eatwell et al., eds., *The New Palgrave Marxian Economics* (Norton 1990).

5 Friedrich Engels, *Origins of the Family, Private Property and the State*, 1884 (MECW 26) p. 272.

6 Kautsky, *The Class Struggle*. This was of course the thesis that Pannekoek and Lenin contested.

Socialism became a vision of the endless extension of the state—from partially to totally planned society.[7]

This new vision generated debates among revolutionaries: how would this total planner state come about, through nationalisation or socialisation? Would everything be directed from above, by national parliaments, or would it be necessary to wholly replace that bourgeois apparatus with one more appropriate to proletarians, for example, a federation of workers' unions? In either case, the problem was to figure out how separate units—still organised around economic activity, and thus surviving more or less intact from the capitalist era—would exchange their products with one another, while putting aside a portion of their output for the growth of the productive apparatus. Of course, automation would eventually solve these problems, but what about in the meantime? There were no easy answers:

> On the one hand, as Korsch ... Wigforss ... and others pointed out, direct control of particular firms by the immediate producers would not remove the antagonism between producers and consumers, that is, workers in other firms. On the other hand, transfer to centralised control of the state would have the effect of replacing the private authority of capital by the bureaucratic authority of the government.[8]

How one saw the future role of the state affected one's strategy in the present. Is the state a committee for managing the affairs of the bourgeoisie, or a neutral instrument, reflecting the balance of class forces? This question was not merely theoretical. Alliances between Iron and Rye seemed to suggest the state could strike a balance between classes. Would it be possible, then, for the working class to enter the fray, to reform capitalism on the way—or as the way—to socialism? Such debates gave rise to fundamental splits within the workers' movement, and later, to its fragmentation.

7 This vision of the total planning of society, as opposed to its partial planning, somehow mirrors the vision according to which the workers obtain not a portion, but the full value of the products of their labours.

8 Adam Przeworski, *Capitalism and Social Democracy*, p. 33.

The workers' movement was born not only in the context of a growing role of the state, but also of the nation: *late development was national development.* That explains why, when the Great War arrived, socialists were largely willing to jettison their internationalism. They justified their support for war by reference to the movement's success, following the wars of national consolidation in the 1860s and 70s.[9] Most assumed that the return of war merely presaged another wave of national consolidation, which would remix the interstate framework and set up the conditions for the further expansion of the industrial proletariat. By supporting the war effort, workers would prove themselves respectable. They would inch closer to power, or maybe even obtain it for the first time, during the next cycle of economic growth.

Luxemburg bemoaned this interpretation of the war in her *Junius Pamphlet.* She saw—almost uniquely among Social Democrats—that the 1914 war would be different: it would be a long one, and it would leave massive destruction in its wake. She scolded her comrades for their failure to understand the changing nature of war: "Today war does not function as a dynamic method of procuring for rising young capitalism the preconditions of its 'national' development. War has this character only in the isolated and fragmentary case of Serbia."[10] The implication was that war really had functioned that way in the past.

Indeed, in the 1860s and 70s wars of national consolidation had ushered in a period of rapid growth for the labour movement. Social Democratic parties and Anarchist federations were founded throughout Europe (and even beyond, e.g. in Argentina). Movement strategists knew their success was tied to the framework of the nation. If the accumulation of capital was the multiplication

9 Engels had written about those wars retrospectively: 'the irony of history had it that Bismarck overthrew Bonaparte, and King Wilhelm of Prussia not only established the little German Empire, but also the French Republic. The overall outcome, however, was that in Europe the independence and internal unity of the great nations had become a fact... on a scale large enough to allow the development of the working class to proceed.' Engels, 'Introduction to The Class Struggles in France, 1848–50', (MECW 27) p. 506.

10 Rosa Luxemburg, *The Junius Pamphlet*, 1915. Earlier than anyone else, she saw precisely what was coming: 'Another such world war and the outlook for socialism will be buried beneath the rubble.'

of the proletariat, then the strength of the nation was the degree of organisation of its working class: "the alternative to a 'national' political consciousness was not, in practice, 'working class internationalism', but a sub-political consciousness which still operated on a scale much smaller than, or irrelevant to, that of the nation-state".[11] The labour movement swelled with the consolidation of national languages and cultures, both of which were in large part effects of public education (and the associated growth in literacy), as well as of rail networks. The link between the fate of the nation and that of the class was clearest for those sections of the workers' movement that were able to contest national elections. Of course, these were the very same sections that patriotically voted for war credits in 1914.

11 Eric Hobsbawm, *Age of Capital* (Vintage 1996) p. 93.

12 Lenin, *State and Revolution.* (Haymarket 2015) p. 48.

Here is the point: in many ways, it was state-led infrastructure building, in the context of national development, that created a growing role for parliaments. Those parliaments had the power of the purse. They controlled taxation. It was because states were able to raise taxes regularly, via parliaments, that they were able to borrow on bond markets to fund their infrastructure projects: "The maintenance of the special public power standing above society requires taxes and state loans".[12] Thus, it was in the interest of the old regime to share power with national parliaments, in order to foster development. In return, the old regime got a massive boost to its military power. As a result the importance of parliament rose steadily (even though the levels of taxation involved remained low, compared to what would become possible in the course of the World Wars).

That was why it was worthwhile for the workers' movement to break into parliaments. From the perspective of the middle of the nineteenth century, that workers might have representatives in government was a fool's dream. However, by the century's end, Engels was publicly calling for a peaceful transition to socialism.

The ballot box replaced the barricade: "the two million voters whom [the SPD sends] to the ballot box, together with the young men and women who stand behind them as non-voters, form the most numerous, most compact mass, the decisive 'shock force' of the international proletarian army."[13] The peaceful victory of socialist electoral parties seemed all but assured (even if it might be necessary to rout the counter-revolution by force):

> It was only a question of time, according to systematic and statistically minded German socialists, before these parties would pass the magic figure of 51 percent of the votes, which in democratic states, must surely be the turning point.[14]

That hope survived down to the Great War. After the war, attempts to roll back constitutionalism and democracy proved successful (especially in Central, Eastern, and Southern Europe, where both were of recent vintage); by contrast, before the war, the expansion of the franchise through struggle had seemed inevitable. Social Democracy became the dominant form of the workers' movement in countries where workers had been enfranchised. In states where workers had not won the vote, they could look to those where workers had, in order to see their own future emerging in the present. In that way, stagism extended itself: Russia looked to Germany as a model, both economically and politically.

As it turned out, the trajectories of late-late developing countries did not actually replicate those of the late developing ones. Outside of Western Europe, movements had to have a more revolutionary orientation, since the old regime was more resistant to recognising workers' interests. Anarchism was strongest in Southern and Eastern Europe for that reason (and also because, there, advance was impossible without the peasantry). But stagism was also wrong for another reason: with the further advance of the technological frontier, catch-up

13 Friedrich Engels, 'Introduction to Karl Marx's The Class Struggles in France, 1848–50, 1895, (MECW 27) p. 522.

14 Hobsbawm, *Age of Empire*, p. 117.

was no longer possible on the basis of late development: "In the 20th century, the policies that had worked in Western Europe, especially in Germany, and the USA proved less effective in countries that had not yet developed."[15] The only way forward was through big push industrialisation. As we will see later, the latter required not alliances with the old regime, but rather its liquidation as the very precondition of catch-up growth.

15 Allen, *Global Economic History*, p. 2.

INTEGRATING WORKERS INTO THE POLITY

As the workers' movement developed within national zones of accumulation, it also fractured (that was true even before the Great War broke the movement apart). The movement became destabilised because — at least in the most "advanced" capitalist countries — it proved possible to ameliorate workers' conditions via national development in a way that dispelled workers' revolutionary energies. Reform and revolution split off from one another. Social Democrats had initially argued that such a split was impossible:

> The elevation of the working-class brought about by the class-struggle is more moral than economic. The industrial conditions of the proletariat improve but slowly, if at all. But the self-respect of the proletarians mounts higher, as does also the respect paid them by the other classes of society. They begin to regard themselves as the equals of the upper classes and to compare the conditions of the other strata of society with their own. They make greater demands on society [which society is unable to fill] … increasing discontent among the proletarians.[16]

According to Kautsky, it was a "children's disease" to think that reforms would make exploitation more palatable; reforms were necessary for the revolutionary effort — they afforded workers a little security, so they could focus on organising for the final battle.[17]

16 Kautsky, *The Class Struggle* (Norton 1971)

17 This is, of course, where Lenin gets his idea that left communism is an infantile disorder: he sees it as an early form of socialist consciousness, rather than a late one.

Kautsky could say so only because, like all Second Internationalists, he still believed in the *Kladderadatsch*, the coming collapse of the system, which was going to unfold regardless of what reforms were won. The onset of the First Great Depression, in 1873, seemed to confirm that belief. In the course of the Depression, capital centralised to an extreme degree; it concentrated in industrial combines, linked together through cartels. On that basis, socialists announced that proletarians — along with most capitalists, peasants, artisans and small-business owners — would soon find themselves thrown out onto the street.

The connection socialists perceived between industrial concentration and unemployment was the key to their revolutionary position: technical development would force capitalists to replace men with machines. In societies organised around the capitalist mode of production, that reduction necessarily issued in unemployment for many people. As it turned out, further technical development in the infrastructural industries did not generate unemployment, especially in large manufacturing combines. Instead, the growth of the productive forces created jobs — and even more so after the end of the First Great Depression in 1896.

Simplifying somewhat, we can explain this phenomenon as follows. Although there were huge technical advances in production in the course of the nineteenth century, few such advances took place in assembly. Here, human hands were still needed. As a result, infrastructural industries absorbed huge quantities of both capital and labour. They required a small army of engineers, but also a large army of hired hands, who actually put together all the precision-made parts. Moreover, the infrastructural industries were organised in such a way that whenever those hands obstructed the assembly process, they forced machines worth huge amounts of money to stand idle. Development thus created not impoverishment, but the possibility for some workers to win higher wages through work stoppages.

Under these changed economic-political conditions it was moreover the case that some workers were able to win dignity while remaining tethered to capital. Thus, the working class was no longer the class with radical chains—the class as a purely negative force which was going to rise up and negate society. Instead, the working class was integrated, slowly and haltingly (and, it should be added, far from completely), into society as a positive force for change. As Paul Mattick argued in 1939: "consciously and unconsciously, the old labour movement [came to see] in the capitalist expansion process its own road to greater welfare and recognition. The more capital flourished, the better were the working conditions."[18]

The consequences of this new situation were immense: the organisations of the workers' movement were able to gain recognition as part of society, and they won gains for their members on that basis. However, to accept social recognition required that they no longer promote revolution as their goal. It wasn't possible to accept the constitutional framework and simultaneously, to argue for its overthrow. That risked the possibility that the movement might lose its recognition and therefore also the gains that it had won: "the choice between 'legal' and 'extra-parliamentary' tactics had to be made."[19] This dilemma was clearest in the case of the unions, the key molecules that make up the collective worker.

LABOUR LEADERS AND THE RANK-AND-FILE

The main problem faced by unions was the same as that faced by every organisation of workers: "class interest is something attached to workers as a collectivity rather than as a collection of individuals, their 'group' rather than 'serial' interest."[20] Workers' class interest had to

18 Paul Mattick, 'Karl Kautsky: from Marx to Hitler' (1939), in *Anti-Bolshevik Communism* (Merlin 1978), p. 4. In this dark moment, Mattick claimed: 'Science for the workers, literature for the workers, schools for the workers, participation in all the institutions of capitalist society – this and nothing more was the real desire of the movement.'

19 Przeworski, *Capitalism and Social Democracy*, p. 15.

20 Przeworski, *Capitalism and Social Democracy*, p. 20.

be instantiated in some way. Towards that end, unions created organs to punish behaviours that maximised individual well-being (e.g. scabbing) at the expense of the collective. They then began to exert power by threatening to withdraw collective labour, and sometimes, by actually withdrawing it. Here was the crux of the issue: in a context where unions set out to improve workers' wages and conditions, *while remaining roughly within the bounds of legality*, unions needed to demonstrate not only a capacity to strike, but also a capacity not to strike, so long as their demands were met. Otherwise, they could not gain leverage.

For that reason, unions had to develop disciplinary mechanisms which, in addition to suppressing behaviour that maximised workers' serial interests, ensured that the collective acted in line with negotiated settlements. Developing such mechanisms did not necessitate a stable separation between an organisational leadership and the rank and file. However, that separation could be avoided only where rank and file militancy was continuously operating. Since struggles tended to ebb and flow, the only way for unions to remain effective, over time, was to build formal structures that allowed negotiators to appear as if they had the capacity to turn rank and file militancy on and off at will (when in fact, they could do neither).

At this point, the interests of leaders and of the rank and file diverged. Rank and file militancy became a liability, except when under the strict control of the leadership. Meanwhile, the leadership became a permanent staff paid from union dues, and no longer depended on employers for wages. Leaders' interests were increasingly identified, not with the defense of union members, but with the survival of the unions. Leaders thus tended to avoid confrontations with employers that put the future of the union at risk. In this way, substantive reform, let alone revolution, became an increasingly distant goal.

The very organisations that workers had built up to make the revolution possible—the organisations that instantiated the collective worker—became an impediment to revolution. For "a party oriented toward partial improvements, a party in which leader-representatives lead a petit-bourgeois lifestyle, a party that for years has shied away from the streets cannot 'pour through the hole in the trenches', as Gramsci put it, even when this opening is forged by a crisis."[21] From here on out, revolution emerged not as an internal tendency of capitalist development, but rather, as an external effect of geopolitics. Revolutions occurred only where capitalist development destabilised national frameworks of accumulation, pitting nation-states against one another.

21 Ibid, p. 15.

In the background was also this gnawing predicament: as the productive forces developed, it became increasingly difficult to know what it would mean to win, to run all these massive apparatuses in the interest of the workers. Just as the galaxy, when seen dimly, appears as a single point of light, but when seen up close turns out to consist mostly of empty space—so too the productive forces of capitalist society, when seen in miniature, appeared to give birth to the collective worker, but on a larger scale, gave birth only to the separated society.

ADDENDUM ON CLASS IDENTITY

The workers' movement promoted the development of the productive forces as a means of pressing the collective worker into being, as a compact mass. As it turned out, the extension and intensification of the factory system failed to have the desired effect; the collective worker really existed only in and through the activity of the workers' movement itself. But the mediations of the workers' movement did make workers' collective interest into something real. As we have argued, unions and parties constructed a working class identity as a key feature of their organising efforts. This is not to say that class unity, or the identity with which it was associated, was somehow merely imposed by union and party leaderships; that unity and identity were integral to the project of the labour movement itself, in which millions of workers participated.

Within the labour movement, workers claimed that the class identity they promoted and affirmed really was *universal* in character. It supposedly subsumed all workers, regardless of their specific qualities: as mothers, as recent immigrants, as oppressed nationalities, as unmarried men (and at the outermost limit: as disabled, as homosexuals, and so on). In fact, the supposedly universal identity that the worker's movement constructed turned out actually to be a particular one. It subsumed workers only insofar as they were stamped, or were willing to be stamped, with a very particular character. That is to say, it included workers not as they were in themselves, but only to the extent that they conformed to a certain image of respectability, dignity, hard work, family, organisation, sobriety, atheism, and so on.[22]

Earlier, we examined the historical genesis of this particular class identity — in the struggle against the old regime, and with the expansion of the infrastructural industries. It is possible to imagine that, in changed conditions, certain particular features of this identity may have turned out differently. To be sure, even within Europe, one would find many completely contradictory characteristics ascribed to workers as a class in different national and regional contexts. In that regard, however, we should exercise some caution. Even in the United States, where universal manhood suffrage was achieved early, and there was no old regime to defeat, a worker's identity was still constructed in the late nineteenth century around a similar set of markers: productivity, dignity, solidarity, personal responsibility. In a nation of immigrants, where African and Native Americans were at the bottom of the social hierarchy,

22 'It is always in the heart of the worker aristocracy that a hegemonic fraction forms, presenting itself as *the* proletariat and affirming the proletarian capacity to organise another social order, starting with the skills and values formed in its work and its struggle.' Jacques Ranciere, 'Les maillon de la chaine', *Les Revoltes Logiques* #2, Spring–Summer 1976, p. 5.

whiteness represented an additional marker, sometimes complimenting class identity and sometimes competing with it. The latter partly explains the weakness of a worker's identity in the US, and its earlier demise. But it also points to the deeper structural factors that gave rise to that identity, in spite of vast national and cultural differences.

There was something necessary, something spontaneous, in the narrowing of the class identity that took place in the workers' movement. The key point here is that the collective interests of workers cannot be determined simply by adding up their serial interests as individuals. This fact distinguishes workers from capitalists, and also puts the former at a disadvantage in negotiations. After all, the collective interests of capitalists are, to a large extent, simply a matter of arithmetic (or more accurately, a matter of solving complex systems of equations): costs must be kept as low as possible, while keeping profits as high as possible. There aren't, for example, environmentalist capitalists and feminist capitalists, who come to blows with other capitalists over the way a company should be run. Such considerations come into play only insofar as they do not affect a company's bottom line.[23]

Workers, by contrast, face much harder sorts of calculations: "how much in wages, for instance, can 'rationally' be given up in exchange for which amount of increase in job satisfaction? The answer to this question cannot be found by any calculus that could be objectively applied; it can only be found as the result of the collective deliberation of the members of the [workers'] organisation."[24] The answers that any particular workers might give to such a question depend on their individual preferences, as well as on the vagaries of their situations: young unmarried men have different interests from single mothers.

23 Capitalists can also express their particular interests in philanthropic settings: they damage or destroy in one moment that which they, with great fanfare, attempt to remedy in the next.

24 Claus Offe and Helmut Wiesenthal, 'Two Logics of Collective Action' in Offe, *Disorganized Capitalism* (MIT 1985), p. 179.

25 Offe and Wiesenthal, 'Two Logics of Collective Action', p. 183.

26 Offe and Wiesenthal, 'Two Logics of Collective Action', p. 184.

27 Anyone who participated in Occupy can see that: if unity of demands is to be obtained across diverse sections and then presented to the world – without a shared identity – that can be achieved only through an endless deliberation, and/or at the cost of many people not getting what they want.

28 Offe, 'Two Logics of Collective Action', p. 183.

29 For a development of this point in relation to a specific contemporary struggle, see 'Gather Us From Among the Nations', in this issue, pp. 210-14.

And yet, to deliberate every point, to reach some sort of consensus or compromise, which would ensure that every worker got at least something they wanted, would make workers' organisation difficult. The "costs" of organising would be too great. The solution is to be found in the formation of a collective identity: "only to the extent that associations of the relatively powerless succeed in the formation of a collective identity, according to the standards of which the costs of organisation are subjectively deflated, can they hope to change the original power relation."[25] That is precisely what the unions achieved, by promoting the workers' identity: by getting workers to perceive their interests through this identity-lens, the unions "simultaneously express[ed] and define[d] the interests of the members."[26]

Individual workers had to recognise the union as acting in their interests, in a broad sense, even when their own, particular interests were not being served by the union's bargaining strategies. This is a feature of all routinised, demand-based struggle: insofar as a collective wants to make demands, and in that sense, to engage in a sort of bargaining, the members of that collective must either share an immediate interest, or else they must be capable of forming an identity to plug gaps among their overlapping interests (paradoxically introducing a non-utilitarian element into a demands-based struggle).[27] It is because workers' organisations had to partly redefine interests in order to meet them that they were forced to rely on "non-utilitarian forms of collective action", based on "collective identities".[28] Indeed, the capacity for demand-making in a given struggle may be grasped as structurally linked with its capacity to draw upon an existing — or forge a new — collective identity; demand-making and composition are two sides of the same coin.[29]

In the context of the workers' movement, this point applies not only to negotiations with bosses, but also to the expansion of political parties, and to the growth of all other organisations existing in urban environments full of ex-peasants and/or recent immigrants. The sheer number and diversity of situations makes it hard to decide on common "intermediate" goals (that is, prior to the conquest of power). But even if this wasn't a problem, the costs of organising remain high in other ways. Workers have few monetary resources; they pay the costs of the class struggle mostly with their time and effort (joining a demo, attending a meeting, striking). If one has to work 12 hour days, or to look after children, as most women workers did, all of this is extremely difficult. Moreover, there is no way for workers to monitor each other's contributions. Together with the sheer size of the movement, that creates massive collective action problems. We see this in the moral centre of the workers' movement — cultivating a sense of duty, solidarity — but also in the means of discipline — the closed shop, attacks on scabs. Even with these assets, the attraction of workers' organisations varied greatly, as did their organisational capacities. It still usually took a tragedy, such an industrial fire or a massacre by company goons, to bring the majority of workers out onto the street.

3 THE FRACTURING OF THE WORKERS' MOVEMENT

Workers believed that if they partook in the terrifying march of progress, then the slaughter bench of history would cut down their enemies. The development of industrial civilisation would propel workers into a position of power. It was certainly true that in the decades before the Great War, trends seemed to be moving in the right direction. In the first decade of the 20th century, workers streamed *en masse* into organisations built around an affirmable workers' identity. Social Democratic parties went from netting thousands of votes — as a minority formation within the workers' movement — to acquiring millions, as that movement's main line.

Meanwhile, in some countries, union membership surged: "By 1913, British unions had added roughly 3.4 million, German unions just under 3.8 million, and French around 900,000 workers to their membership of the late 1880s. Unions finally invaded the factory floor, as against the building site, coal mine, and small workshop, where they already had a presence."[1] The class had become a force to be reckoned with, and knew it.

Revolutionaries' belief that trends would continue to move in their favour was enshrined in the policy of abstentionism. Social Democratic parties became the largest factions in parliaments, even if they remained in the minority; but those parties abstained from participating in government. They refused to rule alongside their enemies, choosing instead to wait patiently for their majority to arrive: "This policy of abstention implied enormous confidence in the future, a steadfast belief in the inevitable working-class majority and the ever-expanding power of socialism's working-class support."[2] But that inevitability never came to pass.

1 Eley, *Forging Democracy*, p. 75.

2 Ibid., p. 83.

THE EXTERNAL LIMITS OF THE WORKERS' MOVEMENT

The industrial workers never became the majority of society: "Even as industrial labour reached its furthest extent, long-term restructuring was already tipping employment toward white-collar and other jobs in services."[3] That was the movement's *external* limit: it was always too early for the workers' movement, and when it was not too early, it was already too late.

It was too early because the old regime persisted, in all its forms, despite the growing strength of the industrial working class. At the end of the 19th century, "it was undeniable that, except for Great Britain, the proletariat was not — socialists confidently claimed, 'not yet' — anything like a majority of the population."[4] The stalled growth of the working class was reflected in the obstinate continuance of peasants in the countryside, and in the tenacious holding-on of artisans and small shopkeepers in cities. It was also reflected in apparent quantitative limits to the movement's growth: the unions were far from organising the majority of the population; Social Democratic voting percentages remained below 51 percent. Looking over these numbers, the parties decided to wait. And wait they did, even during those moments when the class bucked and tried to trample its riders. Supposedly, history would take its course — this was guaranteed. However, history took an unexpected turn.

Almost as soon as the old regime was cleared away, the semi-skilled industrial working class stopped growing. It then went into an unarrested decline. At first it did so only relative to the total workforce. But then, in the 1980s and 90s, and in nearly every high-income country, it declined absolutely. As a result, *the industrial workers never made up more than, at most, 40–45 percent of the total workforce.*[5] A growing mass of private service workers expanded alongside the industrial workers

3 Ibid., p. 48.

4 Eric Hobsbawm, *Age of Capital*, p. 136.

5 In many countries, the peak was much lower, at around 30–35 percent of the workforce.

and then overtook them as the largest fraction of the workforce.[6] Likewise, many urban-dwellers came to find employment in the public sector — civil servants, teachers, etc — or else lived by neither wage nor salary: students, benefits claimants etc. All these groups were supposed to fall into the proletariat, but instead the proletariat fell into them.

That was the case, in spite of the fact that more and more of the world's population was made dependent on the wage. But for the most part, this wage-earning population did not find work in industry. The appearance of factories in some places did not presage their appearance everywhere: "Dynamism actually required backwardness in [a] dialectic of dependency."[7] The success of the workers' movement — in single-industry towns, or industrial cities — was not the realisation of the future in the present. The co-existence of massive factories and small shops was not a bug, but rather, a permanent feature of the system.

However, the deeper reasons for workers' abiding non-majority are to be found in the "laws of motion" of capital's dynamic. The key point, here, is that capital develops the productive forces in and through a massive increase in labour productivity. This has contradictory results with respect to the demand for labour: rising output causes employment to grow; rising productivity causes it to shrink. The balance between the two then determines the growth of the demand for labour. In the heyday of industrialisation, labour productivity rose quickly. However, industrial output rose more quickly, so industrial employment expanded. As we explore below, this overall relationship was reversed in the latter half of the twentieth century: output growth rates fell below rates of productivity growth; industrial employment growth steadily declined as a result. But even in the earlier period the balance between growth of output and growth of productivity presented real limits to the workers' power.

6 On the specificity of service labour, see section 5.2 below.

7 Geoff Eley, *Forging Democracy*, p. 48.

Employment in many of the leading-edge industries of the pre-WWI period — such as textiles and steel, where workers had achieved the most gains — ceased to keep pace with the growth of the labour force after WWI. Some industries even laid off more than they hired. Meanwhile, new sectors, like consumer goods and automobiles, picked up some of the burden of generating employment in industry, but it took time for unions to organise them. Moreover, *since they began at a high level of mechanisation, the expansion of these industries was less employment enhancing than the growth of earlier industries had been*, for example, in the mid and late nineteenth centuries. Here was the phenomenon of technological ratcheting, and relatively declining demand for labour, which Marx, in the first volume of *Capital,* termed the rising organic composition of capital.[8] In every country the industrial share of total employment remained resolutely below the 50 percent mark required to achieve a majority. Even in the most industrialised countries (the UK, Germany), it did not inch above 45 percent.

8 On this concept, see 'Misery and Debt' in *Endnotes* 2, April 2010.

THE INTERNAL LIMITS OF THE MOVEMENT

External limits set boundaries on the growth of the workers' movement by limiting the size of the movement's constituency. However, the movement faced internal limits as well: *only a portion of the proletariat ever identified with the programme of the workers' movement.* That was because many proletarians affirmed their non-class identities — organised primarily around race and nation, but secondarily around gender, skill and trade — above their class identity. They saw their interests as adding up differently, depending on which identity they favoured.

To speak of a "class identity" in this way would have seemed to the theorists of the workers' movement to be a sort of contradiction in terms. They saw identity and class as opposed concepts. Class was supposed to be the essence of what people were; to identify primarily with one's class was to have "class-consciousness". To identify oneself along some other line was to have "false consciousness". Non-class identities were seen as inessential traits which divided workers against one another, and so also as against their real interests (that is, their class interests). But it was only from inside the workers' movement that the horizontal struggle between political groups, organised around different identities, was perceived as a vertical struggle between a depth category — the class essence — and a variety of surface categories.

The worker's identity could function as a depth category because it seemed to be at the same time both a particular and universal identity. The particular identity was that of the semi-skilled, male industrial worker: "The working class was identified too easily with the wage relationship in a pure form: the authentic worker, the true proletarian, was the factory worker", and we might add, more specifically, the male factory worker.[9] Although it often held their needs to be secondary, the movement did not ignore women: among workers, Engel's *Origins of Private Property, the Family and the State*, and August Bebel's *Women and Socialism* were more popular than Marx's *Capital*. Of course, women did work in factories, particularly in light industry (textiles, electronics assembly), and were often important labour organisers.

Yet it remained the case that the particular identity of the semi-skilled, male industrial worker was seen as having a universal significance: it was only as the industrial working class that the class approximated the collective worker, the class in-and-for-itself. This significance was not just political. During the ascendency of the workers' movement it seemed that all non-class identities — even gender, insofar as it served to separate out certain tasks into male and female labours — were dissolving in the vast army of semi-skilled factory workers.

9 Geoff Eley, *Forging Democracy*, p. 51.

The theorists of the workers' movement saw the collective worker emerging from the bowels of the factory and envisaged the extension of this dynamic to society as a whole. Due to the division of labour and the deskilling of the worker, the sort of work that industrial workers did was expected to become ever more fungible. The workers themselves would become interchangeable, as they were shuffled from industry to industry, in accordance with an ever changing demand for labour and for goods. Moreover, in the factories, workers would be forced to work with many other members of their class, irrespective of "race", gender, nationality, etc. Capitalists were expected to pack all sorts of workers into their gigantic combines: the capitalist interest in turning a profit would overcome all unprofitable prejudices in hiring and firing, forcing the workers to do the same. As a result, workers' sectional interests would be short-circuited. Here were the solids melting into air, the holies profaned.

In reality, the homogenisation that seemed to be taking place in the factory was always partial. Workers became interchangeable parts in a giant machine; however, that machine turned out to be vastly complex. That in itself opened up many opportunities for pitting different groups against each other. In US auto plants, black workers were concentrated in the foundry, the dirtiest work. Southern Italians equally found themselves segregated from Northerners in the plants of Turin and Milan. Such segregation may appear inefficient, for employers, since it restricts the pool of potential workers for any given post. But as long as the relevant populations are large enough, employers are able to segment the labour market and drive down wages. If differential sets of interests among workers could be created by the internal divisions within the plant (as in Toyota-isation), so much the better. Capitalists were content for the labouring population to remain diverse and incommensurable in all sorts of ways, especially when it undermined workers' organising efforts.

Given that the expected homogeneity of the semi-skilled workforce failed to fully realise itself, it became part of the task of the workers' movement to realise that homogeneity by other means. As we saw above, organisation requires an *affirmable* identity, an image of working class respectability and dignity. When workers failed to fit this mold, the champions of the workers' movement became champions of self-transformation. The workers' movement was a sect — with DIY, straight-edge sensibilities, a particular style of dress, etc.[10] Yet the predicates of the dignified worker (male, disciplined, atheist, expressing a thirst for scientific knowledge and political education, etc.) were often drawn by analogy to the values of bourgeois society. "The party activists wanted to live worthy, upstanding, moral, moderate, and disciplined lives: on the one hand, to show the workers who were not yet organised a good example; on the other hand, to show bourgeois society that one was up to all tasks, that one deserved good standing and respect."[11] In other words, party activists were quite often killjoys.[12]

It is easy to point out that there were many workers to whom such a self-understanding could never appeal. The internal limit of the workers' movement was the limit of workers' capacity or desire to identify as workers, to affirm that identity as something positive, but more than that, as something essential, something that fundamentally defined who they were. That meant that the workers' movement came to include always only a fraction of the working class. On the outside there forever remained "the superstitious and religiously devout, the sexually transgressive, the frivolous young, the ethnically different and other marginalised minorities, and the rough working class of criminal subcultures, casualised labour markets and the migrant poor."[13] Political factions arose that tried to appeal to workers on the basis of some of these identities, which the workers' movement left out. Thus the movement found

10 See the importance of Methodism for the English labour movement. Prohibition was a key plank of Keir Hardie's original Labour party.

11 Eley, *Forging Democracy*, p. 82.

12 The movement opposed itself to all forms of mainstream popular culture, which were only just appearing at the time, since the latter kept proletarians at home, rather than out on the streets, where they were susceptible to soapbox sermons and entreaties to enter socialist or anarchist meetings. The success of mainstream forms of entertainment – above all the cinema, radio and television – goes a long way to explaining the eventual death of those forms of life on which the affirmation of a workers' identity was based.

itself competing with nationalist, Christian or Catholic parties. But it was nevertheless the case that, in the era of the workers' movement, all those factions found that they had to define themselves with respect to the workers' identity in order to matter at all. The workers' movement hegemonised the political field (even if from the sidelines of official politics).

13 Eley, *Forging Democracy*, p. 83.

STRATEGIES AROUND THE LIMITS

It was primarily in response to its external limit that the workers' movement developed divergent strategies. How were the workers going to overcome this limit and become the majority of society? In retrospect, we can see the external limit as an absolute barrier, but it was impossible to make that judgement during the era of industrialisation. For workers, it seemed likely that in one way or another industrialisation would take its course, or else that by various means the forces of production could be made to expand, thereby increasing the size and unity of the proletariat. Of course, those who believed that the project of the workers' movement would never realise itself under existing conditions simply left the movement, entering one or another utopian tendency lost to history, or giving up on politics.

For those who remained, the external limit presented itself as a set of strategic quandaries. These debates mostly concerned forms of struggle, as opposed to its content: (1) the form of revolution — insurrection or the ballot box? (2) the form of the organisation — direct action or parliamentary and union representation? and (3) the form of the state — tool of the ruling classes or a neutral instrument reflecting the balance of class forces?

In any case, the point for us is to see that the key strategic debates of the workers' movement emerged in relation to the specific limits that movement faced. Our own strategic debates, in our time, stand in relation to the limits we face or will face, which are rather different (this intuition should not be read as implying, pessimistically, that our limits will also turn out to have been insurmountable barriers). Any attempt to reactivate the strategic horizon of the workers' movement today is either based on a false reading of a similarity between eras, or else it is a delicate and difficult leap across the chasm of time, which knows itself to be such.[14]

14 This is not, of course, to say that all tactics and strategic devices of that movement are uniformly, absolutely moribund. Unions obviously still exist and identities and tactics forged in a previous era can be mobilised in particular cases. But it is clearly no longer the case that those particular instances can be inserted within a large-scale narrative at the other end of which lies some sort of workers' society, to be arrived at via either reform or revolution.

1) THE WAITING ROOM

On the right of the workers' movement, the social democrats were compelled to face the facts. They were waiting for their time to come, but everywhere they hit ceilings in terms of voting percentages, often significantly below 51 percent. They decided that they needed to prepare for the long road ahead. That meant, in particular, holding their membership in check when the latter tried to jump the gun by risking the organisation's gains too soon in a "test of strength".[15] Social democrats (and later, communist parties) were always motivated by this fear of the too soon. Instead of jumping the gun, they would bide their time and moderate their demands in alliance with other classes. In the past, social democratic parties had been strong enough to have a share in power but did not take it based on the policy of abstention. Now, they would begin to use the power they had: it was time to make compromises, to cut deals.

15 Anton Pannekoek discussed the debates around this phrase in 'Marxist Theory and Revolutionary Tactics,' 1912.

It was this compromising tendency that split the workers' movement. To many workers, giving up on abstentionism and making alliances was a "betrayal", signaling in particular the corroding influences of other classes (petit-bourgeois intellectuals), or of certain privileged, pro-imperialist sectors of the working class (the labour aristocracy). In fact, this turn within social democracy had more prosaic roots. In the first instance, it was the only way to give the voters something to celebrate, once voting percentages stopped rising so quickly. Second, and more importantly, once the social democrats could see that they couldn't reach the crucial numerical majority on the basis of workers alone, it made sense that they would begin to look for voters elsewhere: socialists had to "choose between a party homogeneous in its class appeal, but sentenced to perpetual electoral defeats, and a party that struggles for electoral success at the cost of diluting its class character."[16] Increasingly, all social democratic parties chose the latter. The "people" tended to be substituted for the working class (although social democratic rhetoric also tended to flip back, at crucial moments), with victory over the old regime within grasp, democracy became an end in itself. Socialists dropped any reference to violence, and then eventually, to revolution, in order to establish themselves in parliament, hunkering down for the long road ahead.

The problem is that appealing to the people requires diluting the programme.[17] Their expanded constituency of small shopkeepers, peasants, and so on experienced the problems of modernity in a number of different ways that were difficult to add up. The parties became containers for a set of sectional interests, tied together more by political maneuvering than by any internal coherence. The social democrats were forced to fight over the centre with other parties, nationalist and religious: "as class identification [became] less salient, socialist parties [lost] their unique appeal to workers."[18] Thus even with an expanded constituency, they still struggled to attain the elusive 51-percent majority.

The social democratic parties initially justified their reformism by saying the time was not yet ripe, but starting from the 1950s they gradually dropped the idea of socialisation of the means of production altogether. They had come to see this move as not necessarily a retreat. This is because, for many social democrats, a working class party at the helm of the state *is* socialism, or at

16 Adam Przeworski, 'Social Democracy as a Historical Phenomenon'. NLR I/122, July-August 1980

17 C.f. Amadeo Bordiga, 'The Revolutionary Programme of Communist Society Eliminates All Forms of Ownership of Land, the Instruments of Production and the Products of Labour' (*Partito Comunista Internazionale* 1957).

18 Przeworski, *Social Democracy as a Historical Phenomenon*. 'Social democratic parties are no longer qualitatively different from other parties; class loyalty is no longer the strongest base of self-identification. Workers see society as composed of individuals; they view themselves as members of collectivities other than class; they behave politically on the basis of religious, ethnic, regional, or some other affinity. They

least, all that is left of this idea: the state organises all the activities of the working class, not via their separate interests as workers in different factories or sectors, but rather, as a whole, as the collective worker, which then hands down orders to the different sectors. The workers' world, from this perspective, is not a far off dream, but an actually existing social democracy.

become Catholics, Southerners, Francophones, or simply "citizens".'

2) THE ROMANTIC REVOLUTIONARIES

In the centre of the workers' movement were the romantic revolutionaries. They argued that power should be seized now, precisely in order to complete the transition that capitalism failed to produce. Thus the Bolsheviks in Russia and the Maoists in China took it as their task to ensure that the working class became a majority, in spite of rather than in line with capitalist dynamics in their "backward" countries. In order to achieve this goal, the workers would have to complete the bourgeois revolution in place of a weak and servile bourgeoisie.

19 Robert Allen, *Global Economic History.*

In undertaking this task, the revolutionaries in the poor countries confronted a real problem. Due to ongoing capitalist development in the West, the technological frontier had continued to be driven outward. Catch up became much more difficult to achieve. It was no longer possible to catch up to the technological leaders in the West by means of the "American System". Allowing capitalist industries to develop on that basis would simply take too long: catch up would take hundreds of years, rather than decades.[19] Under these conditions, the only way to advance was to suspend the logic of the market completely. All the infrastructure and fixed capital had to be built at once. Prices had to be artificially deflated to their expected future level, a level that would not really be achieved until the whole interconnected industrial system had been more or less entirely built up. This very complex industrial strategy has been termed "big-push industrialisation".[20] It was only possible in countries where extreme forms of planning were permissible.

Yevgeni Preobrazhensky, in essence, discovered the possibility of big-push industrialisation, based on his analysis of Marx's reproduction schemes.[21] He developed his findings into a new sort of anti-Marxist Marxism: catch-up development via central planning. Thus, in an emerging "communist" bloc the figure of the technocrat-planner came into its own. However, setting up a technocratic planner state meant uprooting traditional agrarian relations, something old regime elites, as well as many peasants, would bitterly oppose. Marxism-developmentalism thus depended on getting rid of the old elites and reorganising life in the countryside; compromises were no longer an option.

In the end it was this aspect of the strategy that would pay off. In the twentieth century, only countries that wiped out the old regime elites were able to catch up: Russia, Japan, South Korea and Taiwan.[22] Of course, Japan, South Korea and Taiwan were able to achieve this result without turning communist, but their ability to do so had everything to do with a wave of revolutions that swept East and Southeast Asia (the main sites of victorious peasant wars), and also with assistance received from the US. Where romantic revolutionaries did not come to power, and old regime elites were not deposed, in India and Brazil, etc, developmentalism ran aground. They had to do it in the old way, via compromise and corruption, and that just wouldn't cut it.

We can see in this tendency the extreme form of the paradox of the workers' movement. Under the social democrats support for the development of the productive forces primarily meant constructing the image of the collective worker, calling for discipline, building the institutions to see workers through the long haul.

20 Ibid.

21 See Robert Allen, *From Farm to Factory: A Reinterpretation of the Soviet Industrial Revolution* (Princeton 2003).

22 One might also mention the settler-colonial state of Israel, which got rid of local elites in a different manner.

With the romantic revolutionaries we find the workers' movement not merely waiting for the development of the productive forces, having faith that they will develop, but *actively* developing them, with the iron discipline of a centralised state apparatus.[23]

3) THE COULD-HAVE-BEENS

Lastly, there was the left-wing: the anarcho-syndicalists and council communists. The left began from the fact that the working class was already a majority in the industrial towns, where the social democrats and unionists held power. In this narrow context, the external limit was invisible. To workers in these areas, it was clear that they were the ones building the new world. All that was left to do was seize control of the production process directly — not through the mediation of the state, but by means of their own organisations.

In this way, the left rejected the problem of adding up the class to get a 51 percent majority at the national level. There was no need for compromises with other parties, no need to appeal to the people instead of the class. That explains the increasingly anti-parliamentary character of a sizable fraction of the workers' movement after 1900: they rejected the parliament as the place where the entire country is added up and somehow the workers come up short. The left rejected the problem of the real majority — but they did so only in favour of so many local ones.

That was because the anarchists and the communist left, more than anyone else, really *believed* in the collective worker.[24] They saw the mass strike as the stirring of a sleeping giant, tugging at the ropes with which formal organisations had diligently bound it. The collective worker had to be encouraged to throw off the mediations that divided it, that trapped it in unions and parties,

23 Their support for the development of the productive forces involved a vision of communism as a world of plenty. Theoretically the dissolution of the state would take place alongside that of class. But to get there it had to be paradoxically enlarged and empowered.

24 The Italian left complicates this picture, for they didn't reject unions and parties in the same way as the anarcho-syndicalists and German/Dutch Communist Left. The mediations they opposed (mass party, united front, anti-fascism) were more particular, their dissent from the main line of worker's movement less pronounced. Yet Bordiga's critique of councilism would become the basis for a critical rupture with the ideology of the worker's movement (see Afterword).

with their fixed focus on this world and winning gains for workers qua commodity sellers.

In that sense, the left implicitly recognised that the development of the productive forces was leading to the separated society. They rightly saw this as, in part, the work of the workers' own organisations, their attempt to empower the class via integration with the state.[25] The left criticised the realities of the workers' movement in terms of its ideals, taking refuge or finding solace in the logic of Marx's purer, more revolutionary analyses. But in doing so, they sought mostly to turn back the clock. They didn't see that it couldn't have been otherwise: it was impossible to build the collective worker without, on the one hand, defeating the old regime, and on the other, building up class power through all these different mediations. They saw the mass strike as a revelation of the true essence of the proletariat. But what were those strikes for? Mostly, they either sought to secure political rights for workers' parties and unions, or else they sought to renegotiate, rather than overturn, the relationships between workers and their leaderships.

25 The left kept faith with the early period of the workers' movement, rejecting not only the parliament, but the state apparatus as a whole, advocating its replacement with the federation of workers. The collective worker would not constitute itself through organs of the state, handing down orders, but bottom up, in a direct democratic manner. However, the 'adding up' problem was thereby shifted to the relation between individual productive units. How would conflicts of interest between these units be resolved? The left imagined a magical resolution, through the direct exchange between productive units, money replaced by labour-chits – labour mediating itself. Instead of overcoming of alienation, they envisaged a lessening of its sphere.

4 THE STRANGE VICTORY OF THE WORKERS' MOVEMENT

The workers' movement survived WWII and even thrived in its aftermath. It did so by sticking to one safe strategy: to whatever extent possible, workers' organisations supported the war effort. They presided over a labour peace for the war's duration, hoping to gain power and recognition in the war's aftermath. Where fascists took power, no such peace was possible. All above-ground organisations of the workers' movement were annihilated. It was thus communists, rather than social democrats, who took the leading role, giving their lives in the Resistance. Following the war's conclusion, this Resistance served as a temporary irritation to the social democratic and communist leadership: armed revolutionary organisations, formed beyond the control of established parties and unions, had their own visions for post-war reconstruction. But these organisations were quickly disarmed, and then fell away. The same developmental strategy could then be pursued after the wars as before.

The postwar period was a triumph for communism in the East and social democracy in the West (although the latter often failed to obtain parliamentary majorities). The old regime was defeated on European soils, and in some cases, even in the wider world. Workers finally gained recognition as a power within society. And yet, in spite of these victories, it was becoming more difficult to see the way forward. The path from the development of the productive forces to the triumph of the class was becoming more obscure.

For the collective worker, product of the factory system, was ever more dispersed across a complex productive apparatus. As it turned out, the real links forged among workers were not found in their lived connection within workplaces. For the most part, their real links were formed outside of the factory gates: on the roads, in electricity lines, in the supermarket, on television. Instead of the "great evening" of the industrial worker triumphant, we got the groggy morning of the suburban commuter. *The atomised worker revealed itself as the truth of the collective worker.* Here was the unity-in-separation of capitalism, corroding the bases of workers' solidarity, not just in the factory, but also across the city. Instead of the Workers' Chorus there was Soul Train. Instead of the Thames Ironworks Football Club, there was West Ham on Match of the Day. Instead of neighbours filling up parks and seasides there were family holiday packages with Club Med. All this — it should go without saying — proved much more entertaining than a socialist meeting. Yet it wasn't to last. The strange victories of the postwar period turned out to be only a temporary respite from the ravages of capitalist society. Crisis tendencies re-emerged, already in the mid 1960s and early 1970s. The glorious advances in production became overproduction, and full employment became unemployment.

THE DEFEAT OF OLD-REGIME ELITES

World War II finally decapitated the European old regime. The Red Army marched through the central European blood-lands, making itself the inheritor of the opulent classes' wealth. Along the way, large landholdings — which still formed the material basis of elite power in countries where more than half the population was engaged in agriculture — were confiscated. Initially, some attempts were made to distribute this confiscated land to peasants, but these efforts were quickly abandoned in favour of large-scale agricultural collectivisation. Meanwhile, Prussia, historic stronghold of the old regime in Central Europe, was wiped off the map.

In Western Europe, too, the aristocracy went into an unarrested decline. Outside of Italy and Greece, this decline was not the result of land reform. Instead, the end of the old regime was a consequence of interwar and wartime turbulence. Stock market crashes, followed by rapid inflation, wiped out fortunes that had long ago been disinvested from the countryside and then invested in modern forms of wealth-accumulation (in particular, government bonds).[1] The loss of colonies and nationalisation of industries also wreaked havoc on upper class finances. This leveling down of wealth was then secured, politically, by high-rates of taxation.

Such material transformations were accompanied by cultural ones. Any lingering deference to established families was smashed in the war. The notables were no longer so notable, especially since so many had collaborated either with occupying forces or with discredited but home-grown Fascist regimes. From here on out, classes would no longer be distinguished by the head coverings (top hat, worker's cap) they wore. The wars thus completed one of the main tasks of the European workers' movement. They cleared the way for a further development of the productive forces, and, so too, for the expected triumph of the working class. In reality, Europe was now merely going to catch up to the United States, in terms of the commercialisation of life and the integration of all into the fully separated society.

It is true that, outside of Europe, old regimes remained in place, blocking the progress of such modernisation projects. However, precisely due to the war, colonial empires were significantly weaker, while socialist and capitalist models of development, within national zones of accumulation, were much stronger. By the 1950s, movements of national independence were sweeping through the world, extending the nation-state model to the edges of the earth (of course, there were holdouts: South Africa, the Portuguese colonies, etc). In the colonies, as in the metropoles, an attack was mounted against lingering economic backwardness.

1 Thomas Piketty, *Capital in the 21st Century* (Harvard 2013).

2 Two exceptional cases, which did not fly the red flag but still developed along these lines – and in fact, did so much more successfully, since they had the support of the us and access to its domestic market – followed a similar model of big-push industrialisation. South Korea and Taiwan were garrison states, meant to serve as models to East and Southeast Asian populations of what the latter could achieve with capitalist development. Here, too, successful big-push industrialisation was dependent on radical land reform programmes, which knocked out old regimes in the countryside early on in the postwar period. In these cases, radical land reform programmes were only implemented as

Yet, among the victorious independence movements—which unfolded alongside peasant insurgencies in Latin America—it was only the few that were led by romantic revolutionaries and inspired by Russia and then by China that were able to overturn the domination of rural elites decisively. Revolutionaries reabsorbed elites' landholdings into collective farms, creating the conditions for Russian-style big-push industrialisation (even if their success, in that regard, was usually rather limited): the removal of old regime elites freed technocratic communists to focus on the developmental tasks at hand—namely, breaking up peasant communities and displacing peasants to the cities, where they could be put to work in gigantic mills.[2]

last ditch, counter-revolutionary efforts, to stop the spread of communist revolution (the South Vietnamese regime refused to implement a similar programme of radical land reform, ensuring its defeat). As a result, state managers in these countries, like the romantic revolutionaries elsewhere, were able to institute barracks-style capitalist development.

Everywhere else, where the red flag was defeated—either because peasant insurgencies were too weak, or because peasants were drawn into anti-colonial alliances with local elites—movements for land reform either failed completely, or were so watered down as to become largely inconsequential.[3] As a result, old regime elites survived the transition to national-developmental capitalism, just as they had in the Europe of the nineteenth century, except that now, late development under "Iron and Rye" alliances was no longer viable.

3 Rehman Sobhan, *Agrarian Reform and Social Transformation* (Zed Books 1993).

Of course, the persistence of the old regime was not only a matter of elites: there was also a large remainder of the peasantry in the global countryside. Not only was this peasantry still a large minority in Western and Central Europe. In Southern and Eastern Europe, as well as in East Asia, the peasants accounted for the majority of the population. Where the old regime was cleared away, real domination unfolded rapidly in the countryside: within twenty to forty years (depending on the region), the peasantry had all but disappeared. That was partly a matter of reduced political protections for agricultural producers, and partly the result of new technologies that allowed the real subsumption of agricultural production to proceed rapidly. After the war, agriculture began to look more like a branch of industry.

Still, technical developments in agriculture could not have annihilated the heavy remainder of the peasantry worldwide by themselves. That task was left to demographic growth. Postwar developments in public health — including antibiotics, immunisation and DDT — led to an unprecedented drop in infant and child mortality levels. The resulting boost to population growth undermined the peasantry on a global scale. It was also associated with urbanisation. Today the majority of the world's population lives in cities. The urban proletariat, numbering more than three billion people (more than the global population at the end of WWII) is entirely dependent on market production and exchange to survive. We have yet to see *full communism* but, in the last hour, we are finally approaching *full capitalism*.

THE MOVEMENT TRIUMPHANT

With the old regime defeated in Europe — and at risk of revolutionary overthrow across the world — the workers' movement seemed to have triumphed, even where its parties were kept from power. By showing themselves to be valiant soldiers and capable co-managers of the war economy, the workers not only defeated the old regime: they also won recognition within national zones of accumulation. Workers' dignity was enshrined in law.[4] Not only were unions recognised as workers' official representatives; union bargaining was given legal support. Corporatism reigned, in the US from the 1930s, and then throughout Europe after the war.

4 The first article of the 1948 Italian constitution, co-written by the PCI, declares 'labour' the foundation of the Italian republic, the rock upon which the post-War state was built.

Meanwhile the very success of big-push industrialisation put the romantic revolutionaries in the East on the same footing as the social democrats, if always a few steps back. The 1950s were, according to some, the Golden Age of socialist planning; consumer goods finally became more widely available. Yet at the same time, any remaining appeal to a working class identity or class solidarity was reduced to a kitsch aesthetic, the source of many bitter jokes. The workers' movement thus tendentially completed (or participated in the completion of) the project of proletarianising the world's population, in "First", "Second" and "Third" world variants.

Paradoxically, at least from the perspective of the workers' movement, this same process depleted revolutionary energies, for two reasons. (1) The past, which the workers' movement set out to annihilate, turned out to be a fundamental support of its revolutionary vision. (2) The future, when it finally arrived in the form of a highly developed productive apparatus, turned out not to give birth to the collective worker; instead, it reinforced the unity-in-separation of capitalist society. The workers' movement persisted as a social force, but in a sclerotic form. It could probably have gone on forever had it not been defeated from an unexpected corner—that is to say, by the reactivation of capital's fundamental contradiction.

1) WITHOUT A PAST, THERE IS NO FUTURE

It was the lived experience of the transition—from peasant and artisan communities to capitalist society—that gave the workers the sense that another transition was possible—from capitalist society to the cooperative commonwealth. In some sense, this "transitional" perspective was simply about the visibility of ways of life that were not founded solely on the cash nexus.[5] But the transitional impulse was not just about the existence of alternatives.

It was also about the experience of history unfolding. The immediate obstacles to the arrival of that future—the persistence of the old regime—had provided a focal point around which to rally workers at the national level.

5 Fredric Jameson, *A Singular Modernity* (Verso 2002), p. 142.

Indeed, the privileges retained by lords reminded everyone of the failure of the bourgeoisie to stand up for its liberal values. That empowered workers to take the lead in a cross-class coalition: in defense of secularism, democracy and (formal) equality. The idea of "hegemony", made famous by Gramsci, extended the key question of 19th century French politics into the 20th century: which class can represent to other classes their true interest? And in the period in which social democrats and communists alike were running up against the impasse of the workers' movement, this interest appeared as a national one. As long as the "bourgeois revolution" appeared to be stalled, the workers could claim this mantle for themselves. That was their historic mission. Of course, it didn't hurt that it was easy to find hatred for the "high-born" among the lowest orders — and that the distinction between the aristocrat and the capitalist was often rather slim.

However, it was not only the myth of workers' historic destiny that had depended on the existence of the old regime. Many aspects of working-class culture were inherited from proletarians' direct experience of old-world forms of life. The workers' movement told former peasants to forget the past, but in spite of these entreaties, recent urban migrants found ways to build a new culture of resistance on the old foundations of face-to-face community and an uncompromising solidarity. Likewise, the workers' movement admonished the artisans — who knew the whole production process and really identified with their work — for their unwillingness to give up control over that process, which was the real basis of their pride in their work (and so also of their affirmation of their class identity). Spanish anarchism in particular drew on old world resources for its political intransigence. Once those resources were gone, so too was the most intransigent wing of the workers' movement.

2) THE PRESENT WAS NOT WHAT THEY HAD IMAGINED

In order to survive into the post-WWII era, the Social Democratic parties and the trade unions found themselves forced to disempower their own memberships as a means of steadying their course on the road to power. During the wars, the workers' organisations had become organisations for managing labour-power. Indeed, at key moments those organisations showed that they were willing to put down the radical wings of their own movements in order to demonstrate their capacity to rule within the bounds of capitalist society. But success in repressing memberships only tended to undermine the power of the leaderships in the long run.[6]

That was because the further development of the productive forces, in which the workers' movement put its faith, undermined the very basis of that movement. More and more workers were employed in industry, as the movement had hoped. However, the increasing fragmentation of the industrial labour process made it ever more difficult for workers to identify with their work as a source of dignity and pride. What each worker did was increasingly just one step in a large process, unfolding across multiple production sites, which individual workers could not possibly hope to understand. Factory work was both boring and unfulfilling, especially for young workers entering modern factories built in the 1950s and 60s.[7] *The falling away of an affirmable working-class identity did not need to wait for deindustrialisation to begin.* New anti-work, or at least, anti-factory-work sentiments within the factory led some theorists to question not only the form of the revolution (that is to say, the role of the party, or that of the state), but also "the content of socialism":[8] a better form of life had to be something else than the endless development of machinery and large-scale industry.

6 See Robert Brenner, 'The Paradox of Social Democracy: The American Case', in *The Year Left: an American Socialist Yearbook* (Verso 1985).

7 See Paul Romano and Ria Stone, *The American Worker* (Facing Reality 1969) and Bill Watson, 'Counter-Planning on the Shop Floor', *Radical America*, May-June 1971

8 Cornelius Castoriadis released three articles under the title 'On the Content of Socialism' between 1955 and 1958.

That workers would lose their ability to understand their work, and also their sense of fulfilment in work, had been anticipated by many movement strategists. Nevertheless, workers were expected to take pride in the fact that — even if they could no longer understand the entirety of the production process themselves — their understanding was still somehow embodied in the *savoir-faire* of the workforce as a whole, that is, the collective worker.[9]

In spite of the development of the productive forces, labour, it was insisted, remained the source of all wealth, its latent power and knowledge reflected precisely in that development. That turned out not to be true: knowledge of the production process was no longer located in the place of the collective worker, but rather (if anywhere), in the place of the collective technician. That was a key point because — while it upended the foundation-stone of the workers' movement — it also finally confirmed Marx's perspective in the "fragment on machines" (reproduced more soberly in *Capital*).

Here was the real obsolescence of the value form, of a social relation which measured wealth in terms of labour time. It was increasingly the case that human labour was no longer the main productive force; science — often applied to the worst ends of industrial "development" — took labour's place. That profoundly affected workers' self-understanding, their experience of what they did and their place in the world: workers could no longer see themselves as building the world in the name of modernity or a better, more rational way of living. On the contrary, that world was already built, and it was entirely out of their hands. Modernity presented itself as this imposing thing, which workers' confronted, not as subject, but rather, as an object to be regulated and controlled.

9 The concept of the 'collective labourer' was first outlined by Marx in his discussion of manufacture: 'The collective labourer possesses, in an equal degree of excellence, all the qualities requisite for production, and expends them in the most economical manner, by exclusively employing all his organs, consisting of particular labourers, or groups of labourers, in performing their special functions.' *Capital*, vol. 1 (MECW 35), p. 354.

The factory was only one part of this new reality. It was in the total transformation of the environment, both human and ecological, that the fully separated society really came into its own. Society is no longer just the means of production, a set of factories that can be taken over and self-managed by the workers who run them. Those factories, as well as everything else about modern life, rely on a massive infrastructure. One cannot hope that workers will storm the bosses' offices as if they were so many winter palaces. The bases of social power are now much more dispersed. They are located not just in the repressive apparatuses of the police, the jails and the armed forces and the so-called "ideological" apparatuses of schools, churches, and television. They include also power stations, water-treatment plants, gas stations, hospitals, sanitation, airports, ports, and so on. Just like the factories themselves, all of this infrastructure relies on a legion of engineers and technicians, who keep the whole things running from minute to minute. These technicians possess no collective workers' identity, nor were they ever included in the programmes of the workers' movements.[10]

10 These issues will be explored at greater length in 'Error', in *Endnotes* 5, forthcoming.

In this new context, the role of the socialist state could no longer be simply to add up the federated workers (a role it retained in the vision of council communists). The socialist state had to embody the technical rationality of the whole system, in all its complexity. It would have to become the central organ of coordination, handing down directives, but without replicating the authoritarianism of the USSR. Social democrats were at a loss in terms of figuring out how to achieve this new goal. Hence the growing identification of social democracy with a form of technocratic planning that would manipulate but not displace markets, in order to ensure full employment. This new vision owed much to military planning in the world wars and the (negative) example of the Soviet

Union. But it was possible because of the Keynesian Revolution. We will discuss the promises of that "new macroeconomics" shortly.

Before we do, however, it is worth reiterating this point. The postwar technocracy wasn't simply an ideological effect of an era that deified the scientist and engineer. It was a real problem of management that arises in a world that embodies the separation of each from each — and their reunification through markets — that is the value-form. This separation is first and foremost one between workers, a literal *division* of labour. This division means that workers can only come together on the basis of their prior separation, as so many operatives, as representatives of this or that workplace, in order to somehow decide what to do. In this context, getting rid of the state — without some degree of simplification of life — is extremely difficult to imagine.

LUMBERING ON

In the aftermath of WWII the socialists still expected that they would win. They imagined a glorious future would soon wash over them. But if they could deliver the goods in the meantime, by being better managers of capitalism than the capitalists themselves, then all the better. Indeed, for the workers' parties and unions in Europe, the post-war years were filled with promise. Having already (long before the war) diluted their class character to gain votes — embracing the bourgeois notions of "the people" and "the nation" — these parties (the British Labour Party, the SPD in Germany, the French SFIO) were in a position to capitalise on popular resentment for the old political establishment (and to draw on the apparent success of the planned war economies and the New Deal), to put forward a state-led reconstruction effort under the banner of Keynesian economics.

Keynesianism allowed socialists to maintain their ideological role as champions of the working class, but to shift away from the problems of power and autonomy on the shopfloor, towards policies that would affect wealth and income distribution at the national level. This move also coincided with a transfer of power and influence from union representatives to electoral representatives. Yet, in office, the latter were forced to behave like any other party — respecting the interests of those who control investment, and thereby their chances of re-election. Having abandoned all dreams of "revolution" in the name of "reform", the social democrats were increasingly forced to abandon all hope of "reform" in the name of "peace" and "stability".

The result was a hollowing out of the old workers' movement, the gutting of the collective identity that had undergirded it. There were two dimensions to this, prior to the revenge of the external limit in the 1970s. First of all, new forms of government stimulus to consumer demand were often taken directly from the workers' movement: unemployment benefits, pension schemes, collectively subsidised health care. When the state adopted these measures, workers could be forgiven for believing that they had won. But without these key elements of its programme — and having meanwhile abandoned the project of socialisation of the means of production — the social democrats were at a loss as to what to do. The same was true of the unions: "trade unionism lost its credentials as a progressive force," since "workers' well-being" now derived from "a wider public charge" (that is, the welfare state); consequently, "collective bargaining slid more easily into sectionalism, less attentive to a general working-class interest or to effects on other unions and categories of workers."[11] As wages were bolstered by post-war growth, unions were left to hash out the contractual fine print in each sector.

11 Eley, *Forging Democracy,* p. 402. The negative implications of this turn for class solidarity were soon apparent: 'poverty now became demonised into the pathologies of decaying regions and inner cities, from single mothers and ethnic minorities to violent and drug-abusing youth, in hidden economies of casualisation and permanent underemployment. In this racialised and criminalising discourse, movements shaped historically by appealing to white male workers in regular employment had less and less to say.'

However, in taking on this management role, the distance between union leaderships and the rank-and-file widened to a chasm. State recognition of unions ended up putting officials at yet another remove from their memberships, while simultaneously increasing their responsibilities as accepted co-managers of society. Under new conditions, the optimal size of unions increased; as a result formal grievance procedures were substituted for shop-floor militancy. At the same time, union officials had more and more functions to perform above and beyond the representation of workers to the employer: unions provided accident and unemployment protection, as well as pensions. While the partial de-commodification of labour power associated with government-recognised unions (and extensive labour regulations) gave workers more bargaining power, it simultaneously rendered union organisations more conservative in outlook. Management of ever more gigantic pension funds and insurance schemes turned unionists into bureaucratic functionaries, fearful of any disturbance that might hurt their — and they could reasonably claim, also the workers' — bottom line.

Whether they act as liaisons of state functionaries, or as quasi-state functionaries themselves, the pressure for union leaders to behave "responsibly" increased, and the distance from their base widened. Thus organisations formed in the defense of workers become organisations that co-manage labour markets on behalf of the regulated economy, ensuring labour peace on the one hand, and protecting wage gains on the other, all in the name of stabilising the business cycle. This move, on the part of unions, was not really a selling-out. Unions were pursuing the same course they always had, and to its logical conclusions: attempting 1) to preserve the organisations, and 2) to defend the membership, in a context in which most of the formal rights they had fought for had been won (the old elites had been destroyed) and the wage-earning population was less new, less unstable, and increasingly differentiated.

Combined with the fact that workers had much more difficulty identifying the world around them as "made" by them (rather than the machines, the engineers, or the state-planners), these transformations spelt the decline of a shared, affirmable workers' identity, even prior to the downfall of the workers' movement.

5 THE DEFEAT OF THE WORKERS' MOVEMENT

Left to its own devices, the workers' movement might have gone on indefinitely in a sclerotic form. Yet, as it turned out, the triumph of the workers' movement in the great post-war settlements was a Pyrrhic victory — and not because the workers, in '68, came to reject the best that capitalism had to offer. The end of the postwar compromise was the result of the re-emergence of capital's objective crisis tendencies after 1965. This is what we above called the "external limit" of the workers' movement, and it played out as 1) a global dynamic — in competition between regional blocs of capital, and 2) sectoral shifts within each bloc.

1) GLOBAL DYNAMIC

In the course of the twentieth century, the number of national zones of accumulation multiplied. Each zone developed its own factory system, and, moreover, the productive capacity of the factories was compounded exponentially over time. These were not automatic tendencies of an expanding world capitalism. As we have seen, late development was politically mediated; given prevailing class dynamics, in which old regime elites and colonial administrations played starring roles, ongoing industrial development was an uncertain prospect, even in parts of Europe. Moreover, late development became more difficult to pull off over time, since the technological frontier was always being driven outward and the necessary infrastructural support for industrial expansion became increasingly technically complex.

In the postwar period, new geopolitical realities helped some states overcome these impediments. During the war, Stalinism had expanded its sphere of influence; then the Chinese Revolution opened a new era of communist insurgencies, across the low-income world. Both encouraged the US and European powers (except Portugal) to relinquish strategies of isolationism and—after 1960—empire, and instead to promote industrial development within the bounds of the "free world". International trade was encouraged and industrialisation promoted (although programmes of radical land reform were crushed). The gap that had opened up between advanced capitalist countries and the rest of the world did not close; however, it was no longer expanding. Yet these changed global conditions were momentous only in Western Europe and in developing East Asia, where increasingly large, regional "blocs" of capital rapidly expanded their reach.

Twentieth century economists imagined that national zones of accumulation were the proper space for late development. In truth rapid economic expansion in the mid-nineteenth and early twentieth centuries was already predicated both on exporting industrial goods to foreign markets, and on importing raw materials and sources of energy, usually from other markets in the low-income world. Nevertheless, a qualitative transformation took place in the postwar period. The expanding industries of the second industrial revolution pushed against national boundaries, in search of new markets, to be sure, but also eventually in search of new sources of industrial parts production and sites for industrial assembly. The evisceration of old-world elites in the World Wars and the threat of a creeping Stalinism permitted the establishment of new regional zones of accumulation, as new containers for these industries, for it weakened protectionist interests.[1]

Thus much of the world was divided between an American bloc under US management, a European bloc under Franco-German management, an East Asian bloc under Japanese management, and a Soviet bloc under Russian management. Tying these together were transnational institutions like the UN, NATO, the GATT, etc. The brief triumph of the workers' movement was partly due to a

1 Also, the development of the atom bomb itself radically diminished, and perhaps even ended, the possibility of full-scale war between developed nation-states.

transnational component: in the influence of Russia on its opponents during the cold war, the military-industrial expansion of the state (enabling various experiments in social planning), and the extension of industrial firms into new regional markets without yet offshoring production itself. The workers could get a seat at the table both because of their strategic position in the heart of this growth machine, and because "state capitalism" was, for a brief moment, really on the cards.

Yet without the possibility of war between these regional blocs, their simultaneous growth inevitably led to a saturation of export markets. Competition between national blocs of capital — centered in the US, Western Europe and East Asia — intensified, in the mid-1960s. Global markets became increasingly oversupplied, eventually making it so that no one bloc could grow quickly unless it did so at the expense of the others.[2] The result was a decline in rates of industrial output growth, which fell below rates of labour productivity growth in the 1980s.

This point should be emphasised: de-industrialisation was not the result of a miraculous technological discovery, pushing productivity growth-rates to new heights. Rather, it was due to chronic overproduction, which pushed output growth-rates down, with less severe effects on productivity. The same trends of slowing global output growth, and mediocre productivity growth, have continued down to the present, even taking into account Chinese expansion. On this basis, industrial employment growth finally went into reverse, not only on a temporary, business cycle basis, but permanently, over crests as much as busts. De-industrialisation replaced industrialisation as a worldwide tendency, although like industrialisation, it was never a simple secular trend. Capital's trajectory was thus different from what the workers' expected. The development of the productive forces turned out to mean not the becoming majority of the industrial working class, but rather, its tendential dissolution.

2 For the best account of this phenomenon, see Robert Brenner, *The Economics of Global Turbulence* (Verso, 2006), especially the preface to the Spanish edition: 'What's Good for Goldman Sachs is Good for America'.

2) SECTORAL SHIFTS

Of course, this did not signal the end of the working class. Along with the above-mentioned technical and infrastructural innovations came the enormous growth of administrative, bookkeeping, logistical, service, communication and instructional labour: "white collar" jobs. These jobs grew even as industrial jobs were disappearing. Thus whilst the new industries (contra Marx's prediction) created jobs and temporarily saved the industrial working class from decline, it was this latter sector which absorbed most of the decline in the agricultural workforce. And whilst the old unions could organise this new sector, victories were far less consistent, for the hegemonic working class identity tended to dissolve on this new terrain. However, this is explained less by the nature of these jobs, and therefore not by their absolute growth, than by the fact of a sluggish demand for labour.

In part, service jobs grew because most services are not internationally tradable. There cannot be international overproduction in services, as there can be in both industry and agriculture. But the non-tradability of services is part and parcel of the fact that services, almost by definition, are only formally but not really subsumed. That is to say, the production process in services is resistant to the sort of capitalist transformation that would make those services amenable to regular increases in labour productivity. In other words, services aren't produced in factories (where direct human labour gives way to machine production).

It is the resistance of economic activities to real subsumption that makes them into lasting sources of employment growth. That was why, within industry, assembly processes saw the greatest increase in employment, in the course of the twentieth century. More rarely, whole industrial sectors resisted real subsumption, past a certain point. Those sectors saw massive employment growth, too: in the apparel industry, the sewing machine was the last great technological development. Clothing is still mostly sewn with those nineteenth-century machines in sweatshops across the world.

But most of what was resistant to real subsumption was not industry at all — but rather services. With notable exceptions, it has generally proven difficult to transform service-making processes, to make them amenable to constant increases in labour productivity. In fact, "services" is something of a false category. Services are precisely those economic activities that get left behind: they consist of all the activities that prove resistant to being transformed into goods (that is, self-service implements). To be transformed into a good is the typical way that an economic activity becomes really subsumed: carriage drivers are replaced with cars, washerwomen are replaced by washing machines. Because services are not really subsumed, productivity growth remains modest. Even if output grows more slowly in services than it had in industry (during the latter's heyday), it is nevertheless the case that the number of service jobs steadily increases. Here is the long-term tendency of capitalism: to produce a post-industrial wasteland, where employment grows slowly, and workers are very precarious.

The growing segment of the working class who occupied these not-yet-really-subsumed jobs had an experience of work and the capitalist mode of production that differed from the industrial workers who formed the core of the workers' movement:

1 Real subsumption is what makes workers' jobs alike, across industries. It is the process of mechanisation that reduces all workers to semi-skilled factory hands. Without mechanisation, labour processes retain their specificity, in terms of the skills required (making coffee

versus programming versus teaching versus caring). Service jobs are less homogeneous. For the same reason, the wage scale is more dispersed. Here is the difference between the experience of industrial workers, becoming a compact mass, and the experience of service workers, confronting an endless differentiation of tasks.

2 Real subsumption concentrates workers into massive combines, where they work with huge quantities of fixed capital. That is what gives industrial workers the power to stop society by refusing to work. There are many bottlenecks in the industrial production process: stopping work in one place can sometimes shut down an entire industry. The opposite is true in services: many service workers are littered across innumerable shops, and most of those are involved in final sales to consumers (a major exception is distributional services).

3 Real subsumption is the potentially limitless growth in labour productivity. Workers experience those productivity gains as a contradiction: we produce a world of freedom, but we know that freedom to mean, potentially, our own unemployment, and therefore unfreedom. By contrast, the service workers' experience is not linked to the triumph of free time. On the contrary, it is the failure to generate free time that creates employment. Endless busy-work, which is nevertheless essential for valorisation, is what creates jobs and generates incomes. Direct human labour remains central to the work process; it is not a supplement to the power of machines.

WORKERS AT THE LIMIT

The response of the workers to this change in fortune was—against the standard interpretation of May '68—in fact quite weak. The relatively low-amplitude of the wave of struggles in the advanced industrialised countries from 1968 to 77, the fact that they never directly challenged the mode of production, is largely explained by the depletion of rank-and-file-militancy in the earlier period. When confronted with the external limit, the unions proved to be hollow monoliths, unable to appeal either to the membership they had systematically dis-empowered, or to the state on which they had become increasingly dependent. It was the prior incorporation of aspects of the workers' movement into the state that dampened the response of the workers to capital's restructuring. But that defeat was inevitable, since the very industries on which the workers' movement had been based were the ones that were undermined by the restructuring.

All that remains of the workers' movement are unions that manage the slow bleed-out of stable employment; social democratic parties that implement austerity measures when conservative parties fail to do so; and communist and anarchist sects that wait (actively or passively) for their chance to rush the stage. These organisations have hardly been consigned to the dustbin of history. Yet none is likely to rejuvenate itself on the world scale. The workers' movement is no longer a force with the potential to remake the world. That it was such a force was what gave life to these currents within the workers' movement: they no longer make sense; their coordinates have been scrambled.

But of course the end of the workers' movement is not the same thing as the end of either capital or the working class. Even as more and more workers are rendered superfluous to the needs of capital, the relation between these two terms continues to define what counts as a life worth living. Thus, the class relation has outlived the real movement that was supposed to destroy it. Indeed the class relation has only become more dominant since the end of the workers' movement: for women everywhere, for peasants, etc.

What has changed in this period is that the diverse fractions of the working class no longer shape themselves into a workers' movement. Except in reactionary ways (when one part of the class defends its access to a diminishing pool of stable jobs), workers rarely affirm their shared identity as workers. There are a number of reasons for this transformation, all of which have followed from the "restructuring" of the class relation in the 1970s. As the profit rate declined after 1973, a surplus of workers and capital swelled into existence. It became possible to attack workers' material existence, and necessary to do so, since competition among capitals was intensifying. Because they were under attack, nationally situated workers' movements found themselves unable to score the material gains that had been their final reason for existence. Workers abandoned the organisations to which they had — even as those organisations proved to be counter-revolutionary — formerly clung.

Everywhere, the working class is less homogeneous — it is stratified across high- and low-income occupations; its work is more precarious; and it switches jobs more frequently. More and more workers feel like work has no purpose; for more and more are employed in dead-end service jobs, or are unemployed or unemployable. Like the housewives of an earlier era, they produce little more than the everyday reproduction of the class relation itself. For these reasons, we cannot follow the autonomists in supposing that an "objective" recomposition of the class will find its correlate in a new "subjective" affirmation of class identity.

It's not that it's impossible today to glorify work or workers; it's that those who can do so are necessarily a minority. They can no longer pose their activity, or the activity of any concrete fraction of the class, as having universal significance. The workers' movement rested on a vision of the future that turned out to be a dream. In the second half of the twentieth century workers awoke from this dream to discover that all that was supposed to bring them together had actually separated them.

CONCLUSION: THE METAPHYSICS OF CLASS STRUGGLE

The machinery of accumulation is breaking down. As yet, no revolutionary force appears ready to oppose its global reign. It makes sense then that we mourn the workers' movement, that we look back nostalgically on a time when that movement presented itself as a counter-force, even if a problematic one. How could one not feel a nostalgia for the past, living in a time when there is little to stop the ravages of capitalist social dynamics? But we must not let nostalgia cloud our understanding, making us believe that it would be possible to renew the struggles of an era that has come to an end. People do not make history under self-selected circumstances, but rather under existing ones. Humanity has survived the era of the birth of capitalism, although not without trauma. Now, we must get on with its destruction.

How is this task to be accomplished? The workers' movement embodied a certain idea about how it was to be done. At its heart was a metaphysical conception, that of the collective worker, which has since dissolved.[3] Society is still the product of all these working people: who grow and distribute food, who extract minerals from the earth, who make clothes, cars, and computers, who care for the old and the infirm, and so on. But the glue that holds them together is not an ever more conscious social solidarity. On the contrary, the glue that holds them together is the price mechanism. The market is the material human community. It unites us, but only in separation, only in and through the competition of one with all. If the world's workers stopped working—turning their attention instead to routing the capitalists and their goons—they would not find at their disposal a ready-made mode of social organisation, born of their

3 As is hopefully clear from the argument laid out, above, this metaphysic was not simply a 'wrong idea', which could have been otherwise. It emerged more or less organically out of workers' struggles within a particular social and political frame, which no longer pertains.

"actual" unity (that is, the collective worker). Instead, they would be thrown into a social void, within which it would be necessary to construct human relations anew.

The reason it is no longer possible to believe in the collective worker as the hidden truth of capitalist social relations is simply this: the extension of capitalist social relations to the ends of the earth was not associated with an ever more class-conscious workforce; quite the opposite. In the period immediately following World War I, a number of theories emerged to explain why this was the case.[4] After all, revolution had taken place in "backwards" Russia but failed to come off in "advanced" Germany, where the working class had been more industrialised. Why had industrial organisation failed to generate class consciousness?

One set of explanations focused on the role of bourgeois ideology: the emergence of a class consciousness had been blocked by a false consciousness, which was implanted in workers' minds by the apparatuses of bourgeois society: its presses, its schools, its churches. This institutional machinery was putting drugs in the workers' drinking water. Another set of explanations focused on the role of mediating institutions of the working class itself. Trade unions and parties were supposed to shape workers' wills into an immense hammer, with which the old world would be smashed. Instead, this hammer either sat idly by, or else was turned against the class itself (such betrayals were frequently explained as a matter of a certain embourgeoisement of party and union leaderships).

In reality, it was neither bourgeois ideology nor the mediation of workers' organisations that was to blame, most fundamentally, for the failure of a revolutionary consciousness to generalise. As it turned out, the extension of capitalist social relations gave birth not to the collective worker, but rather to the separated

4 See Anton Pannekoek's *World Revolution and Communist Tactics*, V.I. Lenin's *Left-Wing Communism: An Infantile Disorder*, Herman Gorter's *Letter to Comrade Lenin*, and Antonio Gramsci's prison writings.

society. The more workers' lives were imbricated in market relations, the more they were reduced to the atomised observers of their own exploitation. In the course of the twentieth century, socialist revolutions did not emerge where the full efflorescence of capitalist social forms had been achieved. Rather, they emerged where those relations had only recently extended themselves.[5] With time, revolutionary potentials appeared to diminish everywhere that capitalist society developed. At that point — except in rare circumstances, which we will come to momentarily — workers could embody their combative will only in mediated forms, such as trade unions and parties. These institutions were part of this society, and as such, reflected its basic character. It took almost half a century after 1917 for this reality to clarify itself. For all its inadequacies, Guy Debord's *Society of the Spectacle* intuited at least this sad reality: the extension of capitalist social relations was reflected in the increasing separation of workers from one another, even as they became increasingly dependent on one another for their survival.

5 Of course, none of these revolutions led to anything remotely like communism.

Constructing an "actual" unity, under these conditions, had to be a political project: it was that of the workers' movement itself. Acting within this society — against a current that became ever more intense — the movement pressed forward. It became lost, however, in a sea of differential interests: those of women and men, young and old, "white" and non-"white", and so on. Workers could bridge the gaps among their sectional interests only insofar as they believed, and convinced others to believe, in a shared identity: the collective worker. However, the unity thereby named was not a "real" unity, given immediately by the full flowering of capitalist social relations. It was a fiction presupposed and posited by the movement itself.

On this basis of shared identity, workers' day-to-day struggles — from which many workers benefited only indirectly, if at all — appeared to be universally utilitarian: "an injury to one" became "an injury to all". By some measures, this project was wildly successful. By means of solidarity and sacrifice, workers were able to win social protections for the unemployed, the elderly, and the destitute. Furthermore, by limiting the circumstances under which they were obliged to sell their labour, workers also compressed wage hierarchies. However, their efforts did not produce a revolutionary rupture. Eventually, the corrosive character of capitalist social relations dissolved the fictive unities of the workers' movement. And here we are, today.

Today there is everywhere a commonly felt absence of the institutional forms of solidarity that formed the backbone of the workers' movement. When we need to find a job, or when we have problems with a landlord, there are no chambers of labour, no mutual aid societies to which to turn. We are left with nothing but the state and its ancillary charities. Today's strategic thinkers thus urgently try to invent new organisations of this kind (places to dwell and share), or seek to revive those of the past (union, party, co-op). But these new or revived structures lack staying power, for they are built on the shifting sands of the fully separated society: no matter how much water one pours on them, they refuse to cake up.

It's true that in many ways the differences among workers that the labour movement had to overcome, in the first half of the twentieth century, have been significantly reduced. In the high-income countries, and in many low-income countries as well, the vast majority of workers live in urban areas. Their only country of residence is commodity-land. They obtain almost everything they need — paying mortgages or renting apartments, buying food, clothing, and assorted gadgets, and purchasing entertainment — by selling their capacity to labour. In this context, subcultures emerge and die off, but these are all overlaid on an abiding cultural flatness. For many people, national identity has become little more than a matter of national languages and cuisines. National monuments stand in for any more engaging historical awareness. Meanwhile, there are women CEOs, black CEOs, gay CEOs, and so on.

Yet even so, certain social differences have hardened. The wage scale continues to instantiate a hierarchy among workers, generating differential life chances for workers and their children. These life chances are also determined by differential accumulations of assets: the children of some workers inherit handsome sums, which may not allow them to stop working, but at least ensure that they will live no less well than their parents did in their later years. For most workers, however, there is no such personalised safety net. Nor are unemployment and underemployment randomly distributed across the class. They continue to correspond to differences of gender, race, nationality, immigration status, etc. Interests among workers tend to diverge most strongly when the economy is growing slowly, or stagnating. Of course, in most countries the economy has not grown quickly for a very, very long time.[6]

Today crises are more frequent. More and more people are shunted into an existence defined by low-pay, irregular work, and informality, in other words, everything we have called surplus populations. The division between the still regularly employed and the fractions of the surplus population is becoming the key division within struggles, today. Because we reiterate this point, our analysis is often taken to imply that we think things are looking up because everything is getting worse: *la politique du pire*. It is certainly unlikely that revolutions will take place in a time when things are simply getting better — nor when they are statically bad.

6 A deeper transformation has occurred, as well, which has further diminished the chances for a resurgence of a class-based politics of shared interest: being a worker is no longer one's essence, even if one is poor. Society tries to convince those at the top of the wage hierarchy that they can work at what they love, and that therefore they may identify the totality of their lives with their working lives. That is also true of certain jobs – nurses or teachers – where workers could imagine a different form of social organisation, in which they could be more useful, and even recognised as such. For most people, however, work is what they do to survive. The work they do is the sort of work they hope their children will never have to do.

However, there is no hope in things getting worse, by themselves. Revolutionary hopes are found only in revolts, which tend to emerge out of a frustrated optimism. That is, revolts follow a disruption of everyday life, or a series of such disruptions, that fractures the dream by which humanity is cowed into believing that the rigged game of social life will work out in their favour. The picture of calm and unanimity presented by the forces of order breaks down; conflicts among elites are suddenly on display before the people. Anger building up for years or even decades rises and spills out onto the surface. There is hope, then, only in the opening of a new cycle of struggle, in the flight of populations into ungovernability.

Indeed, the real unity of the class lies neither in some organic unity given by the development of the forces of production, nor the mediated unity achieved by means of the unions and parties. Rather, that unity has and always will be forged in self-organised struggle, when workers overcome their atomisation by creatively constructing a new basis for collective activity. In the previous issue of *Endnotes*, we tried to find a way to describe that unity without appeal to a pre-existing metaphysical entity, the collective worker. We showed how a historically specific form of struggle emerges out of the historical specificity of class relations in capitalist society (determined by the unity-in-separation of the exploited).[7]

This way of understanding struggle — grounded in but also taking leave of the perspectives of left communists — can be applied equally to the past as the present. But it is important to recognise, here, the chasm that separates us from the past. The creative generation of new forms of organisation, new tactics, new content — all immanent to the unfolding of struggle — is orientated toward a given horizon of communism. In the past, revolutionary rupture was orientated towards a particular project, which we

7 'Spontaneity, Mediation, Rupture', *Endnotes* 3, September 2013.

have described in detail in this article. We have also shown why this project is no longer given today.

Thinking through the new context in which struggles are taking place requires a pivot at the deepest level, in the very categories of communist theory. We can no longer appeal to the notion of class consciousness, with all it implies. We are forced to confront the fact that the working class is a class of this mode of production, unified only in separation. Of course there are still moments when, in their struggles, workers come together in a mode that interrupts their unity for capital, allowing them to organise both within and across lines of division. However, today when they come together they no longer do so as a class, for their class belonging is precisely what divides them. Instead, they come together under the name of some other unity — real democracy, the 99% — which appears to widen their capacity to struggle. In such moments a conflict can open up between this ideal unity of the class, as something other than a class, and the fact of the actual disunity of the class, as a class of this mode of production.

It is in such diverse and diversified conflicts that the communist horizon of the present may announce itself, not in a growing class consciousness, but rather, in a growing consciousness of capital.[8] At present, workers name the enemy they face in different ways: as bad banks and corrupt politicians, as the greedy 1%. These are, however, only foreshortened critiques of an immense and terrible reality. Ours is a society of strangers, engaged in a complex set of interactions. There is no one, no group or class, who controls these interactions. Instead, our blind dance is coordinated impersonally, through markets. The language we speak — by means of which we call out to one another, in this darkness — is the language of prices. It is not the only language we can hear, but it is the loudest. This is the community of capital.

8 This point has been made by Théorie Communiste. See, for example, 'Théorie Communiste Responds' in *Aufheben* 13, 2005.

When people make the leap out of that community, they will have to figure out how to relate to each other and to the things themselves, in new ways. There is no one way to do that. Capital is the unity of our world, and its replacement cannot be just one thing. It will have to be many.

AFTERWORD: THE IDEA OF THE WORKERS' MOVEMENT

The first issue of *SIC* lays out the main historical claim of the communisation current. "In the late 1960s and early 1970s, a whole historical period entered into crisis and came to an end — the period in which the revolution was conceived ... as the affirmation of the proletariat, its elevation to the position of ruling class, the liberation of labour, and the institution of a period of transition."[1] This claim leaves unanswered what would seem to be an essential question: what was it that this "period of transition", for which revolutionaries fought, was a transition *to*?

After all, the socialists and communists of the late nineteenth and twentieth centuries did not take as their final goal to hoist the proletariat into the position of a new ruling class. Their final goal was to abolish all classes, including the proletariat. This aim was stated in the Erfurt Programme of 1891, which became the model for many revolutionaries, across the world: "the German Social Democratic Party ... does not fight for new class privileges and class rights, but for the abolition of class rule and of classes themselves."[2] Towards that end, the SPD fought against "not only the exploitation and oppression of wage earners" but also against "every manner of exploitation and oppression, whether directed against a class, party, sex, or race".[3] To focus on the transition period only — the so-called dictatorship of the proletariat — is to miss its intimate connection with this final goal — the abolition of class society.

Some might respond that, when the SPD spoke of the abolition of classes, they meant something very different than we do. What did the SPD mean by the abolition of "classes themselves?" In his commentary on the Erfurt Programme, published as *The Class Struggle* in 1892, Karl Kautsky provides the following gloss: he says, "it

1 'Editorial', SIC 1.

2 The Erfurt Programme, 1891; available on marxists.org

3 The Erfurt Programme. That the SPD vowed to fight oppression directed against parties is presumably a reference to the passage of the 1878 Anti-Socialist Laws in Germany, which limited organising around social democratic principles.

4 Karl Kautsky, *The Class Struggle*, 1892; on marxists.org. We will quote from Kautsky a lot here. Much more than Marx, and precisely because he interpreted him for a broader audience, Kautsky laid out the basic theoretical perspective of the labour movement. Insofar as Lenin, Trotsky, or even Pannekoek reacted against Kautsky, it was

is not the freedom of labour" for which the socialists are fighting, but rather the "freedom from labour".[4] They are fighting to bring "to mankind freedom of life, freedom for artistic and intellectual activity".[5] Kautsky did not see socialist parties as fighting to preserve or extend an already grey world, a world of choking smog, a world of mental and physical exhaustion brought on by years of work.

On the contrary, the goal of socialism was to reduce the role of work in everyone's lives, to create time for other pursuits. This goal was already given in the major workers' struggle of Kautsky's time, the campaign for the eight-hour day: "the struggle of the proletariat for shorter hours is not aimed at economic advantages ... the struggle for shorter hours is a struggle for life."[6] In Kautsky's estimation, only socialism could realise this goal. The party programme claimed that only socialism could transform "the constantly growing productivity of social labour ... from a source of misery and oppression into a source of the greatest welfare and universal harmonious perfection."[7] Productivity growth was widely seen as the source of present-day misery, but also of a potential liberation, which could not but be the liberation of humanity.

Kautsky's own vision of productivity-based liberation was of a world of art and philosophy not unlike ancient Athens. Whereas Athenian culture was based on the slavery of men, socialism would be based on the work of machines: "What slaves were to the ancient Athenians, machinery will be to modern man."[8] Socialism would thus realise the dream of Aristotle, who imagined that "if every instrument could accomplish its own work, obeying or anticipating the will of others, like the statues of Daedalus, or the tripods of Hephaestus" there would no longer be any need for the debasement of the many to create free time for the few.[9]

usually on some basis that they shared with him. See Masimo Salvadori, *Karl Kautsky and the Socialist Revolution* (Verso 1990); Paul Mattick, 'Karl Kautsky: from Marx to Hitler', 1938 in Mattick, *Anti-Bolshevik Communism* (Merlin Press 1978); Gilles Dauvé, 'The "Renegade" Kautsky and his Disciple Lenin', 1977. In *Lenin Rediscovered: What Is to Be Done? in Context* (Brill 2006), Lars Lih has recently made similar arguments whilst drawing the opposite political conclusions.

5 Kautsky, *The Class Struggle*.

6 Ibid

7 Ibid.

8 Ibid.

9 Aristotle, Politics 1:4 in *Complete Works* (Princeton 1984).

THE PRIMARY CONTRADICTION OF THE WORKERS MOVEMENT

So, was Kautsky the original theorist of anti-work? How did this liberatory perspective turn into its opposite in the twentieth century? That is to say, how did the liberation *from* labour become a liberation *of* labour? What we need to recover here is the primary contradiction of the labour movement. The socialists and communists of the late nineteenth and twentieth centuries wanted to abolish the working class and with it class society. However, *they believed this abolition could be achieved only through the universalisation of the proletarian condition*. To end a world of hard labour, most of humanity had to be transformed into labourers: they had to be set to work according to the latest techniques and technologies of production.

Today, most of humanity has been proletarianised. Across the globe, huge masses of people must sell their labour in order to buy what they need to survive. That is true in spite of the fact that, for many, proletarianisation has taken place without an accompanying integration into modern capitalist enterprises: a large portion of the world's labour force consists of workers without (regular) access to work. It is obvious that this situation has not brought us any closer to being liberated from a world of work. Indeed, it is difficult to imagine how anyone might have thought otherwise, in the past: how could you seek to end domination by spreading one of its forms to the ends of the earth? Yet this idea animated an era of revolutionary energies: *to usher in a world of workers became the order of the day*.

That explains why, almost half a century after the publication of the Erfurt Programme, Leon Trotsky could look back on his interventions in Russian history as having pushed towards the realisation of the socialist project, in spite of the Stalinist nightmare that the USSR became. He thought he had contributed to this project, not because the Bolsheviks had reduced the amount of work the Russian people performed, but rather, because they had increased it: "socialism has demonstrated its right to victory, not on the pages of *Das Kapital*, but in an industrial arena comprising a sixth part of the Earth's surface — not in the language of dialectics, but in the language of steel, cement, and electricity."[10] It was a massive increase in production, not a reduction in labour hours, that was the measure of socialism's success.

Although he did not himself oversee it, it was in this vein that Trotsky praised the war against the Russian peasants — undertaken in the course of the collectivisation drives of the early 1930s — as a "supplementary revolution" to that of 1917.[11] This supplementary revolution had been demanded since "the kulak did not wish to 'grow' evolutionarily into socialism" (by this Trotsky meant that the peasants had refused voluntary proletarianisation, and thus subjection to the will of the central planner and local bureaucrat).[12] Trotsky saw a fuller proletarianisation as a necessary step before any reduction in labour time was possible.

Indeed, he believed that the threshold at which work could be reduced was still far in the future, even in advanced capitalist countries: "A socialist state, even in America ... could not immediately provide everyone with as much as he needs, and would therefore be compelled to spur everyone to produce as much as possible. The duty of the stimulator in these circumstances naturally falls to the state, which in its turn cannot but resort ... to the method of labour payment worked out by capitalism."[13] Not only a world of work but also a system of wage payments would have to be retained for the time being![14] We take Trotsky, here, as one key example (he is not necessarily representative of the range of socialist perspectives).

10 Leon Trotsky, *The Revolution Betrayed*, 1936 (Socialist Alternative 2013).

11 Ibid. p. 59.

12 Ibid. p. 59.

13 Ibid. p. 64.

14 As Lenin says, 'The whole of society will have become a single office and a single factory, with equality of labour and pay.' Vladimir Lenin, *State and Revolution*, chapter 5, 1917; available on marxists.org. Lenin imagines this office-factory as organised 'on the lines of the postal service', with all technicians, as well as workers, receiving a 'workman's wage'.

The point is that, in any case, the extension to the world of the English factory system (later, the American one displaced the English) — with its frightful pace, its high rate of industrial accidents, its periodic speed-ups, and its all-round subjugation of human beings to the needs of the machine — this was the dream of many revolutionaries.[15] On that basis, it is easy to see why socialism, in its seemingly interminable, intermediate stage of development, came to seem to many people to be not so different from capitalism. Indeed, many socialists saw themselves as doing the work that capital had not done or had refused to do. *The incompletion of capitalist development presented itself as a communist problem.*

THEIR FUNDAMENTAL VISION

In the vision of the future laid out in the *Communist Manifesto*, the development of the productive forces was supposed to bring about heaven on earth. As we have seen, the socialists looked forward to a time, not far in the future, when machines — moving by themselves and producing a cornucopia of goods according to designs of scientists — were going to bring about an end of suffering, and so also of the conflict born of that suffering, which made man into a wolf for other men. The fuller development of the productive forces was not going to end suffering immediately: all this productive power would as yet remain concentrated in the hands of capitalists, who used it for their own ends (hence the impoverishment of the masses in a world of plenty). Nevertheless, in stoking development, what these capitalists were producing "above all" was their "own grave-diggers".[16]

Here we come to the as yet unmentioned key to the labourist vision of the future. The fuller development of the productive forces was expected to propel the workers into the leading role. The development of the

15 Antonio Gramsci not only popularised the term 'Fordism', he also identified with it. Fordism was the 'ultimate stage' of the socialisation of the means of production, based on the primacy of industrial capital and the emergence of a new kind of morality. Such intimations of the 'new man' could emerge in America because the US lacked the unproductive classes that formed the social base of European fascism. The moral depravity of the latter conflicted with the new methods of production, which 'demand a rigorous discipline of the sexual instincts and with it a strengthening of the family'. *Prison Notebooks* (International Publishers 1971), p. 299.

16 Marx and Engels, *The Communist Manifesto*, 1848 (MECW 6), p. 496.

productive forces was simultaneously "the multiplication of the proletariat", its becoming the majority of bourgeois society.[17] Crucially, proletarians were not only becoming the majority; they were also made over into a compact mass: the *Gesamtarbeiter*, or collective worker. The factory system was pregnant with this collective worker, which was born of bourgeois society in such a way that it would destroy that society.

17 Karl Marx, *Capital*, vol. 1, (MECW 35) p. 609 (Fowkes trans.). See 'Misery and Debt', *Endnotes 2* for a more thorough discussion of this famous line from Marx.

Antonio Gramsci captured this vision best when, in his pre-prison years, he described the collective worker in terms of workers' growing "consciousness of being an organic whole, a homogeneous and compact system which, working usefully and disinterestedly producing social wealth, arms its sovereignty and actuates its power and freedom to create history."[18] Of course, in order to become conscious of themselves as an "organic whole", workers would have to give up various particularising identities related to skill, ethnicity, gender, etc. Coaxing them to do so turned out to be more difficult than socialists supposed.

18 Antonio Gramsci, 'Unions and Councils', 1919. Gramsci thought that the council was the proper form for this collective worker, and also the germ of a future society. See 'A Collapsed Perspective', below.

Yet in spite of such difficulties, workers were confident that history was moving in their favour. Theirs was no free-floating vision. It was grounded in an *experience* of history's unfolding. The working class could feel history unfolding, in stages: the old world begets capitalism, and capitalism begets socialism. The transition through these stages could be read off the landscape, as the countryside gave way to cities. The same disjunction was reflected in the surface of British steel: one could compare its straightness to one's own crooked instruments. The factories of England were supposedly the most advanced point in history. They had traveled the furthest along a linear trajectory. All of England was being made over by the factories; all of Europe was becoming England; and all of the world was becoming Europe.

This allegorical reading of the English factory system grounded a fervently held belief that the future belonged to the working class: "The proletariat was destined — one only had to look at industrial Britain and the record of national censuses over the years — to become the great majority of the people".[19] It was inevitable. By contrast, every other social stratum was doomed to disappear: peasants, artisans, small shopkeepers, etc. On that basis, many socialists felt no need, at least at first, to take a stand against colonialism, or against the genocide of faraway populations, in settler-colonial countries, to make space for Europeans. History was going to stamp these peoples under its boots and march on.

19 Eric Hobsbawm, *Age of Empire* (Weidenfeld & Nicolson 1987) p. 117.

SOME PROBLEMS

Yet history marched at a halting pace. The Marxist understanding of history turned out to be only partially correct. The entire world was not made over in the image of the English factory. Industrialisation took place in some regions; however, it largely failed to give birth to the collective worker as a compact mass. We have provided a historical account of these problems, above. Here, we focus on internal debates among socialists and communists. At issue was the question: would capital eventually give rise to a working class that was large and unified enough to take over and then to destroy bourgeois society — and how quickly?

Kautsky made the clinging-on of the moribund classes into a centerpiece of his commentary on the Erfurt Programme. He admitted that there was still a large remainder of peasants, artisans, small shopkeepers in Europe (to say nothing of the world as a whole, where these classes were preponderant). Kautsky explained this reality as follows: in capitalist society, "private property in the means of production fetters the small producers to their undeveloped occupations long after these have ceased to afford them a competence, and even when they might improve their condition by becoming wage workers outright."[20] In essence, smallholders refused to become wage-workers because to do so would require that they subject themselves to the insecurities of the market and the despotism of the factory director. In the face of these dire prospects, smallholders did whatever they could to retain their autonomy.

Of course, Kautsky still thought these smallholders were doomed. But he now supposed that capitalism would snuff them out much more slowly than Marx and Engels had expected. Socialism, once achieved, would have to complete the process of proletarianisation. In socialism, to be a proletarian would no longer mean a life of insecurity and subordination. For that reason, socialism would be able to coax the remaining smallholders into the factory: they would willingly give up their small pieces of property to join the proletariat, thereby reducing economic irrationality and bringing us ever closer to communism. Kautsky thus conceived the leveling down of the new world as a precondition for absorbing the remainder of the old world.

In his revisionist critique, Eduard Bernstein argued that smallholders would never get the chance to partake in these sorts of socialist schemes. Bernstein, too, began from the argument that, in fact, "the industrial workers are everywhere the minority of the population."[21] At the turn of the century—and even in Germany, one of the leading industrial powers—the remainder of peasants, artisans, and shopkeepers was very large. Industrial wage-earners, "including industrial home-workers", represented merely "7,000,000 out of 19,000,000 people earning incomes", or in other words, about 37 percent of the workforce.[22] Below the 50-percent hurdle, it was flatly impossible for the class to obtain a majority in parliament.

20 Kautsky, *The Class Struggle*.

21 Eduard Bernstein, *Evolutionary Socialism*, 1899; available on marxists.org.

22 Ibid.

Even more problematic, for Bernstein, was the fact that these "modern wage-earners are not a homogeneous mass, devoid in an equal degree of property, family, etc., as the *Communist Manifesto* foresees."[23] That is to say, the factory system was not giving birth to the collective worker as a compact mass. Between workers of different situations and skills, it might be possible to imagine a "lively, mutual sympathy;" however, "there is a great difference between ... social political sympathy and economic solidarity."[24] Moreover, the factory system was tending to accentuate divisions between workers, not reduce them.

Bernstein argued that socialists would have a hard time maintaining equality among workers, even if they managed the factories themselves. For as soon as a factory "has attained a certain size — which may be relatively very modest — equality breaks down because differentiation of functions is necessary and with it subordination. If equality is given up, the corner-stone of the building is removed, and the other stones follow in the course of time. Decay and conversion into ordinary business concerns step in."[25] Bernstein's solution to these embarrassments was to to give up on the goal of a revolutionary transition to socialism altogether and to try to find a more inclusive, liberal-democratic way forward.

For the mainstream of the socialist movement, it was not yet time to give up on the goal. One part of the movement drew the conclusion that it was now necessary to bide one's time: they should allow capitalism to mature, and await the further integration of the population into the modern industrial workforce; meanwhile, they should continue to organise that workforce into a conscious, coherent mass through the mediations of the trade unions and the social democratic parties. By contrast, for the romantic revolutionaries — including Trotsky — there was no time to wait. History had stalled, half-complete. The revolutionary communist international would thus

23 Bernstein, *Evolutionary Socialism.*

24 Ibid.

25 Ibid.

constitute itself in the decision to de-arrest the dialectic of history. What was supposed to be a historical inevitability would now become an act of will. *Everyone is being proletarianised, and so, to achieve communism, we must proletarianise everyone!*

Regardless of which faction they joined, socialists shared this overall perspective. As the catastrophes of history piled ever higher, they put their faith in the full development of the productive forces. Movement strategists saw that development, and the class power it would bring, as the only way to break out of the penultimate stage of history and into the final one.

A COLLAPSED PERSPECTIVE

Before we go any further, it is important to recognise that what we have called the primary contradiction of the labour movement—that the generalisation of one form of domination was seen as the key to overcoming all domination—eventually resolved itself in a "collapsed" perspective, which fused the two sides of the contradiction together. Thus, the universalisation of the proletarian condition was identified *directly* with the abolition of class rule, rather than as a precondition of the abolition of all classes. In fact, this collapsed perspective—we might call it "Lasallian"—was hegemonic before the Marxist vision displaced it, and it also became popular once again in the middle of the twentieth century. Lasallianism had its root in the defensive struggles of artisanal workers against capitalist industrialisation.

For artisans, capital appeared as an external parasite: artisans did the same amount of work as before, but instead of receiving all of the income from the sale of the products of their labour, they received back only a portion of those revenues as wages. Hence the nearly universal slogan among struggling craft workers was that labour was entitled to its "full product". Artisans' struggles were not only about resisting "the wages system". Craft workers also fought battles over shopfloor control. They resisted employers' efforts to rationalise the labour process, to increase the division of labour and to introduce labour saving technical change.[26]

Although the artisans were eventually defeated (in fact, the battle dragged on for a long time), their vision of skilled workers' self-management was adapted for an industrial era. What "semi-skilled" workers lost in terms of skill and control, they gained in terms of numbers: they formed — to a greater extent than any other set of workers — a compact mass in large-scale workplaces, which could be seized as strongholds. Workers dreamed that, once they were in control, they would be able to run the now-established factory system in the interest of the workforce, without the capitalists. In terms of both wages and shopfloor control, class conflict was perceived more or less as a zero-sum game: it was class against class, with the possibility that the exploited class might take the "full product", eliminating the capitalist.[27]

This Lasallian perspective was the one that Marxism defeated, in the last quarter of the nineteenth century: a Marxist story about dynamic productivity growth displaced the Lasallian one about a zero-sum contest between classes. However, such a static perspective was later revived in the early twentieth century, above all in the radical current of the labour movement called anarcho-syndicalism (which is not to suggest that syndicalists were pro-market, like Lasalle, just that they came to see communism as a sort of workers' paradise).

This sort of perspective also became the *de facto* position of the socialists and communists, if not their *de jure* position, throughout the first half of the twentieth century, and into the mid 1960s, when the goal of wholly or nearly automated production — having already

26 See David Montgomery, *The Fall of the House of Labour* (Cambridge 1989).

27 '[T]he craftsmen pushed together in the manufacture ... could dream of an industrialisation that would turn its back on the big factory and return to the small workshop, and to a private independent property freed of money fetters (for example, thanks to free credit à la Proudhon, or to Louis Blanc's People's Bank). In contrast, for the skilled electricity or metal worker, for the miner, railwayman or docker, there was no going back. His Golden Age was not to be found in the past, but in a future based on giant factories… without bosses. His experience in a relatively autonomous work team made it logical for him to think he could collectively manage the factory, and on

receded towards the horizon — fell below that horizon and disappeared completely from view.

The dynamic given by growing productivity, and the tendency towards automation (which was so central to Marx and the socialists of the late nineteenth century) thus fell out of the story, once again. Only the struggle to end capitalist exploitation remained. As Rudolf Rocker explained, "For the Anarcho-Syndicalists, the trade union is by no means a mere transitory phenomenon bound up with the duration of capitalist society; it is the germ of the Socialist economy of the future, the elementary school of Socialism in general."[28] Here, it really was explicit that the working class was to be the ruler of society. Taking over society was to inaugurate a transition, not to a world without work, but rather, to a workers' world.

A History of Separation has attempted to explain why the primary contradiction of the labour movement resolved itself into this collapsed perspective. The key was that, for a long time, the development of the productive forces really did tend to increase the size of the industrial workforce. Like Marx, Kautsky and the other socialists expected a second phase of industrial development to arrive and sooner rather than later: rising productivity was supposed to bring about a reduction in the demand for labour and hence the ejection of the workers from the space of the factory, leading to widespread unemployment. In fact, this second phase did not arrive until the 1970s.[29] When it finally did, it spelled doom for the labour movement.

A PARTIAL CRITIQUE

Rummaging around in our theoretical toolbox, we might be inclined to retrieve the following critical perspective. The socialists lacked a proper theory of value, as well as of the possibility and the inner tendency of its

the same model the whole society, which was conceived of as an inter-connection of firms that had to be democratically re-unified to do away with bourgeois anarchy.' Gilles Dauvé and Karl Nesic, 'Love of Labour, Love of Labour Lost', *Endnotes 1*, 2008.

28 Rudolf Rocker, *Anarcho-Syndicalism: Theory and Practice*, 1938. Rocker's summary of anarcho-syndicalism does not mention productivity-enhancing technical change.

29 It was probably difficult to see the collapse of 1929/30 as having its source in automation, but it would be worthwhile to examine that period's politics carefully.

self-abolition.[30] According to this critique, the labour movement failed to conceive of a real break with the value-form. It therefore ended up reinforcing the categories of the capitalist mode of production, not least the category of productive labour. Hence, finally, the labour movement "affirmed the proletariat", instead of abolishing it.

The mistake of the theorists of the labour movement was as follows. They often described capitalist social relations in terms of a foundational fracturing: the separation of peasants from the land generated a propertyless proletariat. However, the class relation is not only established through a foundational fracturing; it also confirms that fracturing in every moment. Capitalism realises the fracturing of social existence as the "unity-in-separation" of market society, an interdependence of everyone on everyone else, which nevertheless reduces individuals to isolated atoms, facing off against one another in market competition.[31] This is especially true for proletarians, whose very survival depends on competing with other proletarians, and who therefore face the most barriers to collective organisation (as we have argued elsewhere, it is not the eventual decline of working class identity, but rather its emergence despite these barriers, which needs to be explained).

The cleaving off of human beings from their capacities — the expropriation of "workers" set against the "means of production" — is simultaneously the social separation of individuals from one another, of the sphere of production from that of reproduction. It is also the separation of the economy from politics. All that is given in the phenomenon of market dependence and market exchange: we are cut off from nature and from other people, in such a way that we relate to both almost exclusively through the mediation of markets, overseen by states. We remain dependent on one another, but in a way that keeps us separate from one another. This practical

30 For a reading of *Endnotes* along these lines see Matthijs Krul, 'Endnotes: A Romantic Critique?', *The North Star*, 28 January 2014. For a critical response see Atë, 'Romantic Fiction: Notes on Krul's critique of Endnotes', Endnotes blog, February 2014.

31 'Separation is itself an integral part of the unity of this world', Guy Debord, *The Society of the Spectacle*, 1967, ¶ 7.

unity-in-separation instantiates itself in a set of ideas, which come to seem self-evident: "a fair day's work for a fair day's pay"; "he who does not work shall not eat".

All of these separations, together, would have to be overcome in order to achieve communism, that is, a world in which the connection between how much one "works" and how much one "eats" has been definitively broken. For the labour movement, only the initial separation of workers from means of production came clearly into view as something to be overcome: this they hoped to achieve by abolishing private property in the means of production, and replacing private exchange with centralised planning of production and distribution.[32] By contrast, the commodity — as "use-value" but not as "exchange-value"— appeared to be neutral and transhistorical; it was the same in every era. And so, they thought, the more the better: if more wheat will feed everyone, then why not more of everything else? That can only be a good thing.[33] Commodities, heaped together in great piles (an "immense collection of commodities"), were seen as the overcoming of alienation, not its realisation. More importantly, the factory system — as "labour process", but not as "valorisation process" — was to survive the end of the capitalist mode of production. It was understood as the foundation of socialism, not as the material embodiment of abstract domination.

To call these notions "productivist" or "progressivist" is to mark out the obviousness of our disconnection from a former era. But neither of these epithets should be taken to mean that, today, we think the dream of freeing human beings from existential insecurity is not a beautiful dream. Nor would we question the human needs, however apparently frivolous, which such production was imagined to satisfy (the critique of consumerism is itself an outgrowth of productivism). It is simply to point out that the identification between the realisation of this dream — that "no-one shall go hungry any more"[34] — and

32 Socialists often spoke about a future moment when the separation between mental and manual labour would be overcome, but they saw this overcoming as a technical matter.

33 'When Spanish anarchists speculated about their utopia, it was in terms of electricity and automatic waste-disposal machines.' Hobsbawm, *Age of Empire*, p. 138.

34 Theodor Adorno, *Minima Moralia* (Verso 2005), p. 156.

the extension of capitalist social relations, or the massive expansion of the factory system, is not only false; due to global warming, it now has the potential to bring extreme harm to humanity as a whole.

As few were able to see in advance, the machinery and products of the capitalist production process were not neutral; they reproduced all the separations of capitalist society.[35] It is perhaps surprising that contributions towards a critique of the neutrality of the factory system did not emerge within the workers' movement until the 1950s (in the writings of Phil Singer and Grace Lee Boggs, as well as Raniero Panzieri and Cornelius Castoriadis).[36]

Among the few who did see this side of things, in an earlier moment, was Marx himself. Quoting Fourier, he equated the factories to "mitigated jails".[37] For the factory is the very embodiment of capitalist domination, of the separation of human beings from their capacities and from one another. It is the perfect realisation of the topsy-turvy world of capital in which man is dominated by the products of his own labour. Marx failed to finish *Capital*, his masterwork on these phenomena of alienation and embodied domination (or real subsumption). However, based on the volume he did finish, it is hard to see how the factory could be thought to have a liberatory content. In her critique of Bernstein, Rosa Luxemburg conceded this point: "It is one of the peculiarities of the capitalist order that within it all the elements of the future society first assume, in their development, a form not approaching socialism, but, on the contrary, a form moving more and more away from socialism."[38]

A SELF-UNDERMINING TRAJECTORY

That the factory was part and parcel of the unity-in-separation of capitalist society made it difficult for the collective worker to struggle its way into existence.

35 Orthodox Marxism tends to see technology as neutral between alternative socialist and capitalist uses, c.f. Lenin's interest in scientific management and his definition of communism as 'soviets plus electrification'. In fact, the capitalist transformation of the labour process does not take place simply as a means of increasing productivity, but also as a means of increasing the control of the capitalist over the workers.

36 Paul Romano and Ria Stone, *The American Worker* (Facing Reality 1969)and Raniero Panzieri, 'The Capitalist Use of Machinery' in Phil Slater ed., *Outlines of a critique of technology* (Ink Links 1980).

37 Marx, *Capital*, vol. 1 (MECW 36), p. 553.

38 Rosa Luxemburg, 'Reform or Revolution' (1900) in *The*

In spite of rhetorical statements to the contrary, it turned out that the "actual unity" of factory workers — as opposed to their unity-in-separation — could be achieved only through the mediations of the trade unions and the parties, as well as through their myriad cultural organisations (we will come to the problems associated with unifying through those mediations, as opposed to directly on the factory floor, a little later). We can go beyond this critique.

The theorists of the labour movement expected that the unity of workers within the four walls of the factory would cut against the tendency of capitalist society to atomise workers and to oppose them to one another outside the factory (in labour-market competition and in the isolation of household reproduction). Yet this strategy seems likely to have been effective only in the early phases of industrialisation, that is, during the phases of what Marx, in *Capital*, called "cooperation" and "manufacture".[39]

During these phases, capitalists took workers from many small shops and collected them together in gigantic combines, where they were able to see and experience themselves all working in concert, producing all the materials of a new world. Thus, it was in these early phases that workers appeared to be the ultimate source of material wealth (as we showed, above, remnants of these phases tended to last a very long time, much longer than Marx expected). Bernstein dismissively pointed out that it was precisely "cooperative" work that people usually thought of when they imagined the collective worker's self-actualisation: "What one usually understands by associated labour is only a mistaken rendering of the very simple forms of cooperative work as they are practiced by groups, gangs, etc., of undifferentiated workers."[40]

With the advent and extension of "large-scale industry", this sort of imagining lives on only as nostalgia.[41]

Essential Rosa Luxemburg (Haymarket 2008), p. 92.

39 Marx, *Capital*, vol. 1 (MECW 36), chapters 13 and 14.

40 Bernstein, *Evolutionary Socialism*, chapter 3.

41 Marx, *Capital*, vol. 1 (MECW 36), chapter 15.

Machines, designed according to the latest scientific knowledge, become ever more central to the production process. The very centre of society shifts: science and, perhaps more than that engineering, replaces labour at the heart of the production process, as the key source of material wealth. Indeed, here is the fundamental, self-undermining tendency of the capitalist mode of production: social life continues to be founded on the exchange of labours; yet with the extension and development of the fixed capital base, labour is no longer the key to production. Direct human labour plays an increasingly subsidiary role in production, even though the exchange of equivalents continues to be measured in terms of labour time.

The development of large-scale industry expresses itself, finally, in the extrusion of workers from the factory—deindustrialisation. Beyond the factory gates, workers find themselves wandering in an immense infrastructure, that of modern life, which reflects back to them not their growing power, but rather, their impotence. They see not a world of their making, but rather a runaway world, a world beyond their control, perhaps beyond anyone's control.

Insofar as they put their faith in the development of the productive forces (insofar as they themselves contributed to that development), industrial workers actually undermined the basis of their power. The fuller development of the productive forces did eventually lead to everything Marx imagined: worsening crises, the expansion of surplus populations, and the immiseration of vast numbers of people in a world of plenty. But at the same time, that development made it impossible for workers to experience themselves as an aliquot part of the collective industrial worker, and hence as the savior-destroyer of society. In short, atomisation won out over collectivisation (and did so in the USSR as much as in the US).[42]

42 'Because the production relations are transparent, most individuals in inferior social positions are dissatisfied with the system ... The only way the system can be maintained is through the effective atomisation of the population.' Hillel Ticktin, 'Towards a Political Economy of the USSR', *Critique*, vol. 1, no. 1, 1973, p. 36.

WAS THERE AN ALTERNATIVE?

In the above sections, we have noted a gap between Marx's late critique of political economy and the theories of the labour movement, towards which Marx otherwise expressed an infinite fidelity. Some have described this gap in terms of an "exoteric" and an "esoteric" teaching. Evidence for their perspective can be found in Marx's critique of the Gotha Programme, an 1875 pre-cursor to the Erfurt Programme of the 1890s, quoted above. The first line of the Gotha Programme affirmed that "labour is the source of all wealth and all culture", to which Marx replies, no! "Labour is not the source of all wealth. Nature is just as much the source of use values (and it is surely of such that material wealth consists!) as labour."[43] It is only within a value-producing society that labour becomes the centre of social activity, and nature is pushed into the background as something to be used, but not really valued in itself. Marx is confident that the further development of capitalist economies will render this Lasallian perspective moot.

But do Marx's later writings really present us with an alternative to the path taken by the labour movement? In the *Critique of the Gotha Programme*, Marx goes on to lay out his vision of the stages by which capitalism will actually be overcome. In the "first phase of communist society", he explains, the same principle will apply as in bourgeois society, except that "content and form are changed, because under the altered circumstances no one can give anything except his labour, and because, on the other hand, nothing can pass to the ownership of individuals, except individual means of consumption."[44] Marx here expresses the same sort of contradictory position that Kautsky and Trotsky expressed in their writings: to achieve the abolition of the proletariat, it is first necessary that each individual be reduced to a proletarian. The universalisation of this form of domination is the precursor to the end of domination.

43 Karl Marx, *Critique of the Gotha Programme*, 1875 (MECW 24), p. 81. Marx is here explicitly expressing his frustration with the Lasallian perspective, which lacks the dynamic given by the tendency towards automation.

44 Ibid. p. 87.

For Marx, it is only in the higher stage that domination is actually overcome. This overcoming is, once again, apparently possible only on the basis of a fuller development of the forces of production: "after labour has become not only a means of life but life's prime want; after the productive forces have also increased with the all-around development of the individual, and all the springs of co-operative wealth flow more abundantly — only then can the narrow horizon of bourgeois right be crossed in its entirety and society inscribe on its banners: From each according to his ability, to each according to his needs!"[45] Marx's statement is, to be sure, a beautiful one, laden with mysteries worthy of further consideration. For our purposes, it is pertinent simply to note that, even according to Marx, it is not until we achieve a state of abundance that we can hope to break the link, inaugurated by capitalism, between the amount of work one does for society and what one receives back from it.[46]

45 Marx, *Critique of the Gotha Programme*, p. 87.

46 Even more than Kautsky, George Plekhanov was the one who developed these ideas into a fully fledged stage-theory. See, for example, his 'The Development of the Monist Theory of History' (1895).

THE FINAL MARX

Yet very late in his life, Marx called this whole stagist perspective into question. Indeed, he came to believe that the theory of the succession of modes of production, which he had laid out in the *Communist Manifesto*, as well as his vision of the stepwise transition to communism, was incorrect. Instead of finishing *Capital*, Marx became increasingly obsessed with non-capitalist communities, among them the Russian peasant commune, the Mir.[47] Marx's insight was that, while there were classes in the Russian countryside, the domination of one class over another was not achieved on the basis of "private property"; on the contrary, domination was imposed externally on a community that retained "common property" in the land.[48] Within the Mir, relations were not mediated by markets, but by communal decisions made in accord and in conflict with local customs. That was of course true outside of Russia, as well, in the vast global countryside beyond the European continent.

47 See Kevin B. Anderson, *Marx at the Margins* (Chicago 2010).

48 Karl Marx, draft letters to Vera Zasulich, in Theodor Shanin, *Late Marx and the Russian Road* (Monthly Review 1983), p. 100.

On the basis of these investigations, Marx upended the stage-theory of history. Maybe universal proletarianisation was unnecessary. In areas where proletarianisation was not yet achieved, it might be possible to move directly from the rural commune to full communism, without an intermediate stage. In a draft letter to Vera Zasulich, Marx suggested as much: the rural commune "may become a direct starting-point of the economic system towards which modern society is tending; it may open up a new chapter that does not begin with its own suicide; it may reap the fruits with which capitalist production has enriched humanity, without passing through the capitalist regime".[49] It is important to note that Marx is not looking backwards here, or imagining some alternate reality in which capitalism had never arisen; the point is that communes could take on capitalist innovations, without proletarianising.

The same idea was expressed publicly in the corrective preface to the Russian edition of the *Communist Manifesto*, published in 1882, that is, just one year before Marx died. With Engels, he wrote: "If the Russian Revolution becomes the signal for a proletarian revolution in the West, so that both complement each other, the present Russian common ownership of land may serve as the starting point for a communist development."[50] The hopeful note Marx sounded, here, on the role that the peasant communes might play in the coming Russian revolution was echoed — at least initially — in the spontaneous activity of the peasants themselves, in the course of the revolutionary era that opened in 1917.

According to Jacques Camatte, in his 1972 text, "Community and Communism in Russia", the communes, which had undergone a process of dissolution in the late nineteenth and early twentieth centuries, were actually revived in the course of the Russian Revolution.[51] Camatte suggests — woefully considering what was about to happen — that "this could have been the

49 Shanin, *Late Marx and the Russian Road*, p. 112.

50 Marx and Engels, The Communist Manifesto, 1882 Russian Edition (MECW 24), p. 426.

51 Jacques Camatte, 'Community and Communism in Russia', Part II. See also Loren Goldner, 'The Agrarian Question in the Russian Revolution', *Insurgent Notes* 10, July 2014.

beginning of the reformation of the communities on a higher level, on the condition that the peasants were supported by the new state, which had to remove the elements harmful to the development of the communes, as Marx had stated in the drafts of his letters to Zasulich."[52] Perhaps there would have been a way forward, here, for the world as a whole, a new sort of revolution, which would have made possible the "reconciliation of men at various moments of their development, without necessarily putting these on an axiological scale."[53]

It is not clear how this new revolution would have been achieved, when Russia was decimated by the Civil War, and when revolutions in Europe failed to come off. Ignoring these impediments, Camatte simply notes: "the victory of Marxism hindered the realisation of this solution."[54] Camatte is surely right that, instead of being repudiated by events on the ground, Marx's earlier, stagist perspective was hereby "codified in the name of Marxism", as a programme of economic development and then put into practice by the Bolsheviks.[55] The latter determined that "everything archaic and Asiatic had to be eliminated over the whole huge empire (and given that the revolutionary flood affected the peripheral countries, this took on a global importance)."[56] Realising that the peasants could not really be coaxed into this modern world in formation, the Bolsheviks eventually set out to destroy the commune, to proletarianise the peasants, and to develop the forces of production as Russian capital had not. *This* programme became that of communist revolution in the twentieth century.

A MOMENT FOR REFLECTION

For Camatte, humanity had "the possibility of leaping over the CMP [capitalist mode of production]," but has now "lost" that possibility.[57] We have paused to consider this "lost" possibility for a few reasons. First, among all the vaunted red threads of history—which trace their

52 Camatte, 'Community and Communism in Russia', Part II.

53 Ibid.

54 Ibid.

55 Ibid.

56 Ibid.

57 Camatte continues: 'We have been most incapable of conceiving of [the leap over the CMP], infested as we were by the idea that progress is for all people the development of the productive forces. i.e. in the end, capital, which was the affirmation inside the proletariat of the interiorisation of capital's victory. Thus it is natural that, before the peoples whom we have forced to submit by our agreement with the deadly enemy, the infamous path of the passage to the CMP, we should stand accused (violent criticisms of Marx's ethnocentrism have

way back to an initial moment of betrayal, and hence to an unrealised potential for salvation — this one seems to go back furthest: to the conflicts within Marx's own conception of the pathway to communism. But more than that, this alternative vision seems to us to get closer than any other to the heart of the matter, that is, the primary contradiction of the labour movement: to end all domination supposedly required the extension of one form of domination, namely proletarianisation, to the ends of the earth, with all the violence this process necessitated.[58] The proletarian class — unified in and through the extension of the factory system — was thought to be the only class powerful enough to make the revolution.

In fact, instead of being a century of proletarian revolution, the twentieth century turned out, like the centuries that had passed before it, to be largely a century of peasant revolts. These revolts were aimed, initially, at securing a renewed access to non-market means of existence, which had been eroded both by the capillary action of capitalism and by the violent impositions of colonial administrations. Peasants were often backed by communists, who adopted peasant slogans while simultaneously turning them towards the new goal: industrial development, with the aim of creating the preconditions for full communism. Communists aimed at the maximal programme: freedom from want, freedom from labour, "freedom of life", to be achieved, first of all, through the incorporation of humanity into the industrial proletariat, and only later by the abolition of that class and by the withering away of the state.[59]

As mentioned above, the premise behind this project proved false. Universal proletarianisation has now been achieved: through the combined action of capitalist and socialist development, as well as by means of other, unforeseen forces (the spread of the demographic transition). Consequently, there is no longer an outside to capitalist social relations. Almost everyone has been

been made by various ethnologists originating among these people).' Camatte, 'Community and Communism in Russia'.

58 'Alas, we who wished to lay the foundation for kindness, could not ourselves be kind.' Bertolt Brecht, 'To Posterity'.

59 It's easy enough to denigrate this project retrospectively, but it was only terrible insofar as it failed to achieve its goal. If it had succeeded, it would have been worth it. The sufferings of humanity, already an omnipresent reality, but augmented by the communists, would have been redeemed by the victory of communism. That redemption never came.

incorporated into the modern world, at least tendentially, although frequently without finding employment within capitalist enterprises. Yet the train wreck of world history has not arrived at communism, nor even come nearer to it. Universal proletarianisation did not give rise to the collective worker, as a "real unity" to stand against the unity-in-separation of capitalist society. And of course the peasants — on to whose revolts this project was grafted — were defeated even when their revolts were victorious.

REFLECTIONS CONCLUDED

In his texts — which to our mind pose the greatest challenge to Marxist history — Camatte seems almost exasperated that false ideas, or in other words, the Marxist-developmentalist project, somehow won out over the true ideas, based in Marx's repudiation of stagism. This exasperation signals his failure to supercede an *idealist* perspective, which is the primary perspective that revolutionaries have taken with respect to their own history. In fact, history is not made by ideas, whether true or false, but rather, only in a clash of forces. There is one force that Camatte did not include in his discussion..

The peasantry, the peasant commune, persisted well into the twentieth century, that much is true. But almost everywhere *the persistence of peasant communities also meant the persistence of old regime elites*, whose massive power was also based in the countryside. These elites did not really form one class, but a set of overlapping power-structures. Their power was based, not in successful competition, but rather, on privileged access to resources, such as land and credit, and rights, such as the right to streams of income deriving from their ownership of, e.g., mines or positions in government.

As it turned out, these same elites were not displaced by bourgeois factory owners, with their purportedly enlightened, liberal ideals. Instead, the bourgeoisie was largely absorbed into the sabre-rattling old regime. This amalgamated ruling class typically set out to exclude workers from the polity. In some regions, they wanted more: they tried to turn back the clock, to "re-introduce caste society, that is, human groups with radically different entitlements and duties", and so to re-establish regimes of personal domination in place of abstract ones.[60] Such was true not only of the fascist parties of the mid-twentieth centuries. It was the notion of a whole range of political groupings, basing themselves on Social Darwinist ideas.

As long as these amalgamated elites retained power — in fact, their power was often augmented by what modernisation took place — the overall development of the productive forces was blocked outside of the core capitalist states. Trotsky makes precisely this point, at the start of *The Revolution Betrayed*, which we quoted above: "the history of recent decades very clearly shows that, in the conditions of capitalist decline [they were actually just a middling phase of capitalism's rise], backward countries are unable to attain that level which the old centres of capitalism have attained."[61] He attributes this to the persistence of the old regime: "the overthrow of the old ruling classes did not achieve, but only completely revealed the task," namely to undertake proletarianisation, as the precondition of communism.[62] This task was not otherwise going to be undertaken, according to Trotsky, due to "the insignificance of the Russian bourgeoisie", and the consequent weakness of the proletariat.[63]

Indeed, wherever the old regime remained at the helm, the peasantry persisted, while the proletariat remained small and weak, unable to play a decisive role in history. This peasantry, while sometimes willing to rise up against its oppressors, was at other times obedient to its overlords, particularly in the context of (often rigged)

60 G.M. Tamás, 'Telling the Truth about Class', *Socialist Register* 2006, p. 24.

61 Trotsky, *The Revolution Betrayed.*

62 Ibid.

63 Ibid.

parliamentary elections. The same could be said of small but formally employed industrial workforces, which were often conciliatory towards the forces of order. All of this is clearly on view in the histories of low-income countries — particularly in Latin America, the Middle East, and South and Southeast Asia, but not in East Asia — where old regime elites retained much of their power.

It was in this context that, as we mentioned before, the strategists of the labour movement came to see history itself as blocked, and the unblockage of history as an urgent task. That task would require a further development of the productive forces, whether within capitalist society or in a planned, socialist developmentalist one. In either case, further development seemed to be the only way to strengthen and unify the proletariat against its enemies, which were legion (and this in spite of the fact that, in reality, that development spelled the doom of the labour movement itself). Meanwhile, old regime elites, backed by imperial powers — later including the United States — were actively engaged in turning back any movement in a liberatory direction.

Without condoning or condemning, we claim that these facts grounded the workers' movement. Marx's idea had been that the industrial working class would come to exist, and that circumstances beyond its control would force that class to call itself into question. But really, in the nineteenth and twentieth centuries, the question was whether the class would exist at all, as a class of free commodity sellers, outside of a few centers in Northern Europe and among whites in the white-settler colonies. The world was changing rapidly, and it did so in ways that tended to enhance the power of the oppressors, both in the factories of Europe and in the colonies. In this context, *fighting to exist became a revolutionary position.*

GATHER US FROM AMONG THE NATIONS

The February 2014 protests in Bosnia-Herzegovina

When, on 10 February 2014, we crossed the frontier between Serbia and Bosnia aboard a tiny Eurolines bus, one of our fellow passengers, a young man in his late teens, was asked to step down from the bus and disappeared into the police station. The officers had suspicions he was part of the crowd that had gathered in front of the Mostar Canton government building on 7 February as it went up in flames and wanted to know more about it. After a 30-minute interrogation, they finally let him go. As he stepped back into the bus and it was clear he had definitely made it across the border, his joy erupted. Of course he was there! Like in Tuzla, like in Sarajevo, people attacked and burned down the government building, and it was a wonderful sight! Even better, in the divided city of Mostar, he saw people from both sides, Bosniaks and Croats, hugging each other in front of the burning building! He was hoping to be back in time for the plenum; he was constantly receiving text messages from his friends who were now in the streets in Mostar, and he could not wait to be there.

1 These interviews were conducted by the video collective Year01, of which one of us is a member. The collective went to Bosnia-Herzegovina twice, in February and October 2014, to conduct interviews with participants of the struggle and to report on the causes and consequences of the revolt. See the Facebook page and YouTube channel: Year-01-Videocollective.

▪ ▪ ▪

> A lot of people in February had unrealistic expectations. A majority of them thought that deep and far-reaching changes were possible and were going to happen in this short period. It was unrealistic to hope that a bunch of angry people in the streets could undo the developments of the past 30 years. I always recall this old lady with a red scarf telling us, very angrily: "If this fails, I will never forgive you". At the time I thought, "What are your criteria for failure?". You could sense that people really wanted a revolutionary change; a lot of people expected something very radical to change. But for a number of us who have more political experience, we knew that nothing so radical could really happen. (Interview with a plenum organiser, Sarajevo, October 2014)[1]

> There will be nothing here without revolution! What burned is zero, believe me. I repeat: the second period will be bloody, bloody in Tuzla! It started in Tuzla, it must finish in Tuzla. There is no other way. Look at the politics: all the same nationalists stayed in power and kept their positions. (Interview with a worker of the Dita factory in Tuzla, member of Solidarnost — a new independent union — October 2014)

As they had long been doing every week, on Wednesday 5 February 2014 the workers of several privatised factories of Tuzla took to the streets to demand payment of months of overdue wages and social contributions. Most of them had been fighting for years, occupying their factories; several hunger strikes had even been undertaken, to no avail, and the weekly Wednesday demonstration seemed unlikely to make a difference. But on that day they were joined by several hundred young people. Together they tried to storm the building of the Tuzla canton government. The demonstrators managed to rush inside before eventually being forced back by the police. As clashes occurred, some workers were beaten up, and these images, captured on camera, went viral.

By the next day, demonstrations of solidarity were occurring in Tuzla, and also in Sarajevo and Mostar. On Facebook, groups like UDAR in Tuzla, and the page "50,000 For a Better Tomorrow", called for massive protests in the coming days. On 7 February, thousands of people turned up to demonstrations in all the major cities of Bosnia-Herzegovina. In Sarajevo and Tuzla, after violent clashes with the police, people stormed the canton government buildings and set them on fire. In the divided city of Mostar they also burned the headquarters of the main political parties.[2] In panic, the canton government ministers of Sarajevo, Tuzla and Zenica resigned.

2 On the division of the city of Mostar into a Bosniak and a Croat part, see Vanni D'Alessio, 'Divided and Contested Cities in Modern European History: The Example of Mostar, Bosnia-Herzegovina', in Sabine Rutar, ed., *Beyond the Balkans* (LIT Verlag 2013).

3 While the term 'ethnic nationalism' helps capture the specificity of nationalism in the region, it has often been used in the literature on nationalism since the 1940s (especially since Hans Kohn's 1944 book *The Idea of Nationalism*) to denote a 'bad' Eastern nationalism in contrast to a 'good', Western 'civic' variant. This idea was popularised again in the 1990s in the context of the Balkans by Michael Ignatieff in *Blood and Belonging: Journeys into the New Nationalism.* For a critique of the ethnic/

In the following days, people started to organise "plenums" (assemblies) to discuss what to do next, and to formulate demands. Many more turned up than expected — several hundred in Tuzla and Mostar, often more than one thousand in Sarajevo. The plenums quickly became the main locus of the movement as the protests dwindled. Unlike in the Occupy and Indignados movements, the assemblies did not take place in the streets but in separate buildings. At each session, in each city — more than 20 cities in Bosnia-Herzegovina had their own plenums — long lists of demands were formulated, among them the end of privatisations and of golden parachutes for politicians, and the setting up of a "government of experts".

A recurring theme in slogans, in graffiti and within plenums, was the rejection of nationalism. In the context of Bosnia-Herzegovina, however, "nationalism" — and therefore anti-nationalism — refers to a very specific reality, which must be taken into consideration if we are not to be led astray. Rather than the sign of an internationalist movement unexpectedly emerging before our eyes, what was actually being rejected here was *one form* of nationalism which had dominated the country since the 1992–95 war, dividing it between Serbs, Croats and Bosniaks. This is often referred to as a kind of "ethnic nationalism"[3], whose aim is to push the economic and political interests of one or another of the three "ethnic groups"[4] within Bosnia-Herzegovina.

But in no way does this mean that this rejection was a trifling matter. Indeed, ethnic tensions have been at the centre of everyday life in Bosnia-Herzegovina since the creation of the country amid the ruins of Yugoslavia. They had already started to rise in the 1980s as the latter began restructuring its economy to counter the after-effects of the global economic crisis of the 1970s. With the growing political and economic autonomy of its several republics, imbalances arose between

civic nationalism dichotomy, see Pavlos Hatzopoulos, *The Balkans Beyond Nationalism and Identity* (IB Tauris 2008).

4 While it is obviously problematic to refer to ethnicity and ethnic groups as if they were givens rather than socially constructed, these are – as with race and gender – *really existing* constructs and must be analysed as such. Etienne Balibar and Immanuel Wallerstein helpfully analyse races, nations and ethnic groups as three 'peoplehood constructs' that are 'all inventions of pastness, all contemporary political phenomena', yet all have different structural relations to the capitalist mode of production (see esp. 'The construction of peoplehood' in Balibar and Wallerstein *Race, Nation, Class* (Verso 1991) pp. 79-85). Their analysis of

them, since the previous spatial division of labour within Yugoslavia had concentrated most industry in the north — particularly in the Slovenian and Croatian part — and agriculture and raw material extraction in the south, including in Bosnia. The managerial and political elites of the different republics soon started fighting for their particular economic interests, and cultivating nationalist discourses, each holding the other republics — and the other "ethnic groups" — responsible for their local economic difficulties. These claims increasingly resonated with the proletariat of each republic as its standard of living declined and its interests divided from those of the others. Tensions mounted until the Yugoslav wars erupted in the early 1990s, first in Slovenia and Croatia, then in Bosnia.

The war was particularly bloody in Bosnia, the most ethnically mixed of all the republics. More than 100,000 people were killed (some estimates place the number closer to 250,000); mass rape and genocide were used as weapons of war; nearly half the country's prewar population was displaced. This was part of the ethnic cleansing that was used to create the relatively ethnically homogeneous zones of today's Bosnia-Herzegovina. Since the Dayton peace agreement of 1995, the country has consisted of two entities and one district, formed along ethnic lines: located at the centre of the country, the *Federation* of Bosnia-Herzegovina (not to be confused with the country itself) is administratively divided into 10 cantons and mostly populated by Bosniaks and Croats. Wrapped around this, on the northern and eastern sides of the country, the entity of Republika Srpska — which has its own president, parliament, government and police force — is mainly populated by Serbs. Between the two geographical regions of Republika Srpska is located a further self-governing administrative unit, the Brčko District, which also has a separate status. All institutions at the level of the country as a whole themselves reflect these

the 'ethnic group' only makes sense, however, in the context of an 'ethnic minority' within a country, and is therefore of limited use in understanding the construction of ethnicity in Bosnia-Herzegovina, where there is no ethnic majority per se (it is estimated that Bosniaks represent 48% of the population). The difference between concepts of ethnic group and nation is further complicated in Bosnia-Herzegovina by the relation of two of the groups within Bosnia-Herzegovina – the Croats and the Serbs – to the Croatian and Serbian neighbouring states.

divisions, with the three major ethnic groups guaranteed, according to the constitution, an equal share of power. The Presidency of Bosnia and Herzegovina, for example, consists of three members: one Bosniak and one Croat elected from the Federation, and one Serb from Republika Srpska.[5]

Ever since the peace agreement, ethnic tensions had dominated all aspects of society, which made any revolt or movement almost impossible, since it would immediately run up against accusations of playing one ethnic group off against another. But this situation started to change in June 2013, with several protests that were termed the "Baby-lution". Earlier that year, due to ethnic divisions, the government of Bosnia-Herzegovina had failed to enact a law for the registration of newborn babies, leaving them without identity numbers, and thereby preventing them from getting access to healthcare, and from leaving the country. After the scandal of one three-month-old baby who died because she couldn't leave the country to get medical treatment, Bosniak, Croat and Serb protesters — mothers with strollers on the front line — formed a human circle around the parliament and kept the MPs and government employees locked inside. It was the first movement to unite people across ethnic boundaries since the war. Though this movement was relatively small, it was important as a forerunner of the February 2014 revolts; many activists who were central in organising plenums had met each other during the protests of the previous year.

During the Baby-lution, women's assigned roles as primary caretakers placed them at the centre of the demonstrations. The connections they formed, and the experiences they had in that movement, probably contributed substantially to their importance in the protests that followed. As in the global squares movements of 2011, many women were involved in the demonstrations and plenums in February 2014 and

5 To complicate the matter even more, since 1997, a non-elected body, the Office of the High Representative in Bosnia and Herzegovina, has the power to 'adopt binding decisions when local parties seem unable or unwilling to act' and 'remove from office public officials who violate legal commitments' (these are referred to as the Bonn powers). This body, which has already dismissed more than 100 officials, including judges, ministers, civil servants and members of parliament, has often been criticised for the unaccountability of its decision-making and for its repeated interference in the politics of the country.

played an especially important role on social media.[6] They were equally present in the riots of 6–7 February and particularly active among the workers of privatised factories. However, while they sometimes had to fight to be equally represented in plenums, especially among delegates, the question of gender did not come to the forefront of the protests, as we will try to explain later.

6 On the significant role of women in the February movement, see Nedim Hadrovic, 'Women are at the forefront of grass-roots movements in Bosnia', available on muftah.org

SOCIAL COMPOSITION

At the centre of the protests, at least at the beginning, were factory workers from the privatised plants of Tuzla: mainly Polihem, Dita, Guming, Aida and Konjuh. However, the status of these "workers" must be treated with caution, for production in their respective factories has long been at a standstill, and they should therefore be considered more or less unemployed — though they can't formally claim that status, since this would cancel their rights to the back-pay they are owed. In many cases, the owners — who mainly use the factories for money laundering — prefer to simply stop paying workers, rather than laying them off. On the one hand, these workers have a very strong identity derived from the importance of these factories within Yugoslavia, and the preeminent role played by the figure of the worker in the imaginary of those times. On the other, they are unable to use their position within the production process to push their demands, and are often totally ignored, not only by the owners but also by unions and government officials. Typically, these workers without work haven't received wages or social contributions for years, and months of occupations, protests — even hunger strikes — have not made any difference. It is in this context that they took to the streets every Wednesday until things took an unexpected turn in February 2014.

Indeed, it is only when these workers were joined by thousands of young, mainly unemployed, people on the streets of Tuzla on 6 February, and in all major cities the next day, that the movement achieved a tipping point, forcing several canton governments to step down. The parents of this younger generation typically became impoverished during the war, or during the wave of privatisations and economic collapse that followed. In Tuzla, they often have family ties with the workers of privatised factories, which surely played a role in the crystallisation of solidarities. In Sarajevo, this cohort is sometimes referred to by better-off activists as "foster home children", since many children lost their parents during the siege of Sarajevo and fell into deep poverty at that point. Amongst this category, some are organised in football fan clubs such as the "Red Army" in Mostar, or "Fukare" (have-nots) — the supporters of the football club FC Sloboda in Tuzla.[7]

Finally, in Tuzla and Sarajevo in particular, graduate students and academics played a big role in the movement, especially in organising and spreading the idea of plenums. In Bosnia-Herzegovina, the level of education is still very high — a remnant of socialist Yugoslavia — but many struggle to find jobs after university. Within this category, there are wide divergences of income and expectations, with many living on the brink of poverty, while others can still afford to travel abroad or study in foreign universities. But the frustration of the latter group remains high, as their only chances of getting a good job depend upon aligning themselves with a political party and playing the corruption game.

Of course, some participants do not fall into any one of these three categories — which are themselves somewhat fluctuant and imprecise. Still, these groupings capture in broad outline the diverse distribution of social backgrounds and stakes among the protesters. Though close attention must be paid to the specificities of each local case, there are clearly some broad parallels between the key terms of this composition and those of the 2011 squares movements.[8] While systemic

7 As in Egypt and Turkey, football fans/ultras played an important role in the riots, as well as on social media. They were also active in helping people who suffered from the floods that hit Bosnia-Herzegovina in May 2014.

8 For an analysis of those movements see 'The Holding Pattern', *Endnotes* 3, September 2013.

conflicts among these sections would emerge increasingly during the ebb of the movement, this diversity is itself a measure of the momentum of a struggle that managed to bring together people who normally have little to do with each other.

REASONS FOR REVOLT

The most immediate reason for people taking to the streets in such numbers on 7 February was clearly outrage at the way police treated workers who were demonstrating. In this sense, like most riot-waves of recent times, the proximate cause of this movement was police brutality; but that the latter could have such an effect is the result of a more general context of social injustice and — in this case — economic collapse. In explaining the movement, it is thus to this context that we should look.

Most industry in Bosnia-Herzegovina has been devastated since the war, due not only to the destruction of fixed capital in the war itself, but also the series of clientelist privatisations, bankruptcies and asset-stripping that followed it. The country is dependent on imports, and the trade deficit grows every year. Bosnia produces raw materials (metal, wood, coal) as well as electricity from hydroelectric sources, which it exports abroad, to Germany, Croatia, Serbia and Slovenia. But most consumer goods have to be imported. Employment is low and concentrated in the service sector: 65%, compared to 26% in the — largely "legacy" — industrial sector and 8% in agriculture. The state and its various apparatuses are the biggest employers in the country. Unemployment is among the highest in Europe, estimated at 44% overall and 60% for young people. Almost one-third of Bosnia-Herzegovina's population is considered to be in poverty or on the verge of it. The gray economy plays an important role, representing more than 20% of overall economic activity according

9 See Rajko Tomaš, *Crisis and Gray Economy in Bosnia and Herzegovina*, (Friedrich Ebert 2010).

10 See Nermin Oruc, 'Remittances and Development, the Case of Bosnia', 2011.

11 And more recently to assist the US military in regions affected by Ebola. See Adam Moore, 'Bosnians recruited to support US military's fight against Ebola in West Africa', *Balkanist*, 27 October 2014

to estimates. 290,000 people are thought to be working in that sector, while the number of people officially employed is circa 700,000.[9]

Transfers by Bosnian workers living abroad help many families to get by. It is estimated that about 1.35 million Bosnians live abroad, and their remittances represent around 23% of GDP.[10] Many of these people are highly educated — the "brain drain" that started during the war is ongoing — but unskilled youths also often leave in search of employment elsewhere. For example, since 2007, American companies such as Fluor Corporation and DynCorp have been recruiting thousands of contractual workers from Tuzla and the region to work in US military bases in Afghanistan and Iraq.[11] In 2013, deals were also made between the Bosnian government and Qatar to authorise young Bosnian women to work there as domestic workers.[12] In some cases, with these contracts, workers can get four times the average salary in Bosnia-Herzegovina, allowing them to send home a considerable remittance. Financial aid and loans from other countries also remain major sources of money, even if they have been decreasing since 2000.[13]

THE END OF WORKERS' IDENTITY

With its important mines, Tuzla was once among the industrial centres of Yugoslavia, so it is highly symbolic that the movement started there. Since the Husino rebellion in 1920 — an armed rebellion by striking miners that was violently repressed — the figure of the miner in struggle has been central to the history of the city. In Yugoslavia more broadly, the specific form of workers' identity was one centred on the idea of workers' self-management of the means of production.[14] While it is clear that the decision-making power that was given to workers within the production unit was limited — especially during Yugoslavia's final

12 See Lily Lynch, 'Qatar seeks Balkan housemaids', *Balkanist*, 2 September 2013.

13 See Timothy Donais, *The Political Economy of Peacebuilding in Post-Dayton Bosnia* (Routledge 2005) and Lana Pasic, 'Bosnia's vast foreign financial assistance re-examined: statistics and results', Balkanalysis.com, 21 June 2011.

14 On the specificities of workers' management in Yugoslavia, see Goran Musić, 'Workers' Self-Management as State Paradigm' in Immanuel Ness and Dario Azzellini, eds, *Ours to Master and to Own: Workers' Control from the Commune to the Present* (Haymarket 2011).

decades[15]— self-management has had an important influence on the self-image of workers, who often express a strong bond with their workplace as *belonging to them*— something reinforced by the fact that many received shares in these factories after the collapse of Yugoslavia. However, if this identity is still very much present in workers' understanding of their role in society— as could be witnessed in their statements and interventions at plenums— it is, as already mentioned, a contradictory one: a workers' identity held by people who have been *de facto* unemployed for years.

15 On how the realities of self-management evolved between 1948 and 1991, see Vladimir Unkovski-Korica, 'Self-management, Development and Debt: The rise and Fall of the 'Yugoslav Experiment' in Srećko Horvat and Igor Štiks, eds, *Welcome to the Desert of Post-Socialism: Radical Politics After Yugoslavia* (Verso 2015).

And every statement from the authorities shows how indifferent they are to values such as workers' pride. In this context, the non-working workers whose protests were blatantly ignored by employers and politicians alike became the symbol of a workers' identity fighting desperately against its obsolescence, whose fate strongly resonated in a younger generation for whom formal labour had long-since become an inaccessible dream. In this sense, these workers became the symbol of the surplus character of labour in Bosnia-Herzegovina. Indeed, if an important factor in the socio-economic composition and stakes of many recent movements, including the square occupations of 2011–12, has been the general low-level of demand for labour on a global level, in individual cases local factors can drastically exacerbate this general predicament. With its historical particularities, Bosnia-Herzegovina represents a quite acute case. Unemployment levels here are extreme, production is devastated, and there is hardly any international economic interest in the region— which also explains why the international media carried so little coverage of the protests.

While in other European countries where squares movements occurred it was the 2008 crisis that accelerated the rise in unemployment and poverty, in Bosnia the economy has been in a deep crisis since the war, when the country's GDP fell to only 10% of its pre-war level, so the effects of the financial crisis were less clear-cut against this backdrop. Still, there had been modest improvements in the economic situation since 1996—improvements halted by the effects of the European crisis in 2008. Indeed, while the Bosnian economy is only indirectly integrated into the EU's, as countries like Croatia and Slovenia—the main importers of Bosnian products—were affected by the EU crisis, the growth trend went into reverse. Exports to these countries slowed down while internal consumption remained low, diminishing employment possibilities even further.[16] In this context, aggravated by a reduction of financial aid from international funds during the last decade, and a decrease in transfers from Bosnian citizens abroad (by about KM300–€600 million in 2008[17]) the economic situation became even more unbearable for the poorest segments of the population.

16 See the Statistics of foreign trade, no. 3, BH Agency for Statistics, 2009, p. 3

17 See Rajko Tomaš, *Crisis and Gray Economy in Bosnia and Herzegovina*, (Friedrich Ebert Stiftung 2010), p.101.

CORRUPTION

As in other squares movements, corruption was seen by protesters as the main cause of the economic problems affecting Bosnia-Herzegovina. The latter is often listed as one of the most corrupt countries in Europe, along with Ukraine, Belarus and Kosovo. The channels of corruption run through all layers of society, from the allocation of money injected by foreign institutions and NGOs, to the state sector (including universities, schools, cultural projects and healthcare), to the private economy and various local mafias. Its central structures, however, seem to be the ethnically-divided political parties, sometimes referred as the "ethnocrats", who run this "foreign-sanctioned national-clientelistic machine".[18] Indeed, since the war, these parties have been allocating the available jobs and resources along ethnic lines in a clientelistic manner, blatantly increasing their own wealth in the process. They are therefore the primary target of the protesters where corruption

18 See Stef Jansen, 'Rebooting politics? Or, towards a <Ctrl-Alt-Del> for the Dayton Meantime' in Damir Arsenijević, ed., *Unbribable Bosnia and Herzegovina: The Fight for the Commons* (Nomos 2015), p. 91.

is concerned, and several political party headquarters were attacked during the demonstrations.

The functions of the state are divided between members of these parties, since, as mentioned above, every position must be held by three representatives: one Bosniak, one Serb and one Croat. This multiplication of positions makes of the state an enormous machine, and indeed, according to Aleksandar Hemon, the "largest and only reliable employer in the country".[19] However, corruption is not limited to political parties and state employees; for most proletarians in Bosnia it is a very concrete everyday experience. Indeed, in order to get a job, it is typically necessary to bribe a member of a political party—which can cost several thousand euros, requiring a loan that will take years to repay. Membership of the party linked to the job in question, and a demonstration of loyalty to it, are also typical requirements: in particular, participation in protests, or anything else that might endanger in any way the party's prospects, is ruled out. That is, of course, not to say that the majority of people in Bosnia-Herzegovina benefit from corruption, but rather that they are forced to play by the rules and be part of the big corruption machine. Agreeing to play the game is also a prerequisite of access to healthcare, since the health system is highly dysfunctional and doctors must be bribed for assistance and medication. The same applies in universities, where students have reported having to pay bribes to get their diplomas.

In this sense, though it may sound quaint, the designation of the February protesters as "Unbribable Bosnia"[20] may well be useful, if we set aside the moralistic connotations. Along with university professors and academics who refused to be corrupted and belong to a political party, a substantial part of the protesters may well be "unbribable" because they are simply too poor to participate in the corruption machine,

19 See 'Beyond the Hopelessness of Survival' in *Unbribable Bosnia and Herzegovina,* p.62.

20 See Damir Arsenijević's introduction to a collection of texts by participants in the protests: *Unbribable Bosnia and Herzegovina: The Fight for the Commons.*

unable to pay the bribes that would buy them a place in those networks. This may actually help to explain why *so few* people took part in the protests, considering the terrible economic and social conditions most have to endure: while, according to surveys made shortly before the October 2014 elections, the majority of the population saw them as positive events, no more than a few tens of thousands of people (in a country of only 3.8 million inhabitants, it must be said) took part in the protests and plenums around the country. Among the fears preventing them from doing so was that of losing a position, or access to a service, by not showing one's loyalty to the regime in general, and a political party in particular.

But, according to Jasmin Mujanović, "This process cannot merely be understood as one of banal 'corruption', as there is no functioning state that is being corrupted, per se".[21] Indeed, a central demand of the movement was to get "a functioning state". Moreover, corruption as organised through these clientelist networks may be effectively *the form the state takes* in *Bosnia*, the way it (dys)functions. Or, as L.S. says in the context of Tunisia: "Corruption is then not simply an exception to the normal functioning of the relationship of the state to civil society, nor merely the concern and cause of the established middle class citizen, but a moment in the state's habitual, harassing reproduction of the mass of marginals."[22]

Discussions around corruption and its causes often revolve around the alternatives of either blaming foreign institutions such as the IMF or viewing it as a matter of the clientelism and patronage to which some "cultures" are especially prone. In the context of recent revolts, corruption has been discussed primarily in cases where what Jack Goldstone has termed a "sultan" is able — in the context of a rentier state — to redistribute revenue via patronage networks. In Bosnia-Herzegovina, though,

21 Jasmin Mujanović, 'The Baja Class and the Politics of Participation' in *Unbribable Bosnia and Herzegovina*, p. 141

22 L.S., 'Hanging by a thread: class, corruption and precarity in Tunisia', *Mute*, 17 January 2012. He continues: 'For the unemployed poor of the interior most notably, but for Tunisians suffering declining incomes and rising prices generally, corruption and the attendant experience of violence and injustice at the hands of state officials is an everyday fact of social reproduction. From the point of view of the state, it is a way of managing the growing surplus population: a specific way in which authoritarianism is modulated to control and integrate the proletariat of the restructured and globally integrated neoliberal economy.'

there is no sultan, no dictator — not even a particularly strong figure.[23] This peculiar state-form is the direct result of the Dayton agreement, designed by "the international community". While there is a form of top-down clientelist redistribution — particularly of foreign aid, one of the main resources the state and NGOs can redistribute — corruption has also emerged at the base of the social structure, through the development of an informal economy that is necessary for the most basic reproduction. This economy is organised through various small mafias that ruthlessly exploit the desperation of the bottom layer of the population.

23 See Jack A. Goldstone, 'Understanding the Revolutions of 2011', *Foreign Affairs*, May/June 2011. An exception here is the case of Republika Srpska and its nationalist president, Milorad Dodik, who is famous for his 'bombastic public performance of personal strength and authority'. See Jasmin Mujanović, 'The Baja Class and the Politics of Participation' in *Unbribable Bosnia and Herzegovina*, p.135.

For neoliberals such as Hernando de Soto, the informal economy is a result of corruption, and corruption in turn a result of the rigidity of the labour-market. But causation may flow in the opposite direction — corruption resulting from the informality of the economy, itself the effect of a low demand for labour, which makes the reproduction of a significant part of the proletariat contingent to capital. The gray economy is an inefficient terrain for capital accumulation: in Bosnia it is estimated that profits are 20% lower here than in the formal economy. But it nonetheless helps shore up a crumbling social structure that might otherwise collapse entirely. Rather than being straightforwardly unemployed, people still find meagre, residual sources of income here and there, and allegiance to corrupt officials prevents them from revolting. While the economy tends towards informality — i.e. avoiding formal taxation — when profits are weak, in such a context the corruption which both riddles the state and props up such political structures as do exist may be interpreted functionally as a last-instance mode of taxation:

> Corruption is the most successful business of quasi-democratic authorities; gray economy is their most powerful social program, and "racketeering" is the favorite method of "taxation". Corruption is also

one form of gray economy. Ultimately, it is an illegal method of taxation. The gray economy actors need corrupted civil servants, and the corrupted civil servants need gray economy.[24] The construction of this clientelism along ethnic lines involves alliances between business partners, mafia networks and political parties — all united by an allegiance to the interests of one ethnic group against the others. Business opportunities and cash resources can be gained through networks of influence within the state, and there are benefits to be had from the turning of a blind eye to illegal activities. These ethno-nationalist networks distribute ethnic privilege — that is, the ability to exclude other people from jobs and resources. In this sense, it is no wonder that these networks, as well as corruption more generally, have been one of the main targets of those who are largely deprived of such resources.

24 Rajko Tomaš, *Crisis and Gray Economy in Bosnia and Herzegovina*, p.131

AN ENORMOUS DEMANDS-PRODUCING MACHINE

The most widely-discussed aspect of the Bosnian movement was its systematic creation of plenums — "citizens' assemblies" — in all the affected cities. This form of organisation has been popular in the region among left students and academics since the Croatian student occupation of 2009, and it was discussed, but never put into practice, in Bosnia-Herzegovina during student protests in Tuzla in 2009 as well as during the 2013 Baby-lution. This time it turned out to be extremely popular, and, from 8 February onwards, more people went to plenums than to demonstrations or gatherings. While the number of protesters fell to a few hundred, some 500–1000 people of diverse ages and backgrounds gathered in the plenums of Tuzla, Mostar and Sarajevo, at least until the end of February. Through plenums, the movement expressed an enormous need for communication, exchange of experience and transparency.[25] It is often reported that the first plenums were a sort of

25 This transparency led to a formalism even more acute than that of Occupy Wall Street: people were given only two minutes to talk; all decisions were written down and projected on a wall at all times; most plenums were filmed and the videos put online. These arrangements were clearly meant to avert corruption, at least symbolically.

collective psychotherapy, with people mentioning for the first time in public their war traumas and post-war experiences. Given that this is a country where each "ethnicity" has had to go through a parallel — and often biased — remembrance and mourning process, this function of the plenums should not be downplayed. It has often been said that it profoundly changed people's perception of the collectivity and of the capacity of different "ethnic groups" to communicate together.

However, the plenums quickly crystallised around another central aim and purpose: that of formulating demands. Each session produced dozens of them, from "revisions of the privatisations of public firms", to the "right to work" and "linear pension increases".[26] Talks and interventions seemed to become mere preambles to their formulation: "Come to the point, what is your demand?" A frenzy of demand-making could be witnessed, with each city sending one list after another to their respective governments. Does this contradict the common claim that an absence of demands has been a central aspect of recent movements around the world? Consideration of the proliferation of demands in the Bosnian movement may help us to clarify some points about the issue of demands, and to question some more simplistic readings of their alleged absence.

Let's start by probing the idea of demands per se, and of the purely demandless struggle. All struggles short of revolutionary insurrection must necessarily have something determinate at stake within a continuing relation to another social subject — a specific employer, the state, the police. And it would seem reasonable to consider such stakes as amounting to "demands" that are at least implicit in the very fact that the struggle is taking place at all. An everyday struggle entirely lacking demands in this sense is inconceivable. We might consider all-out insurrection as lacking these kinds of demands, but this is because when this occurs, the

26 For a list of the main demands formulated at the different plenums, see 'The Demands of the People of Bosnia-Herzegovina' on jasminmujanovic.com. According to Valentina Pellizzer, an activist involved in plenums in Sarajevo, 2200 demands were received by the plenum organisers in that city alone. See 'The politics of division and sabotage', on 'Bosnia-Herzegovina Protest Files'.

27 It would seem reasonable to doubt that struggles are ever so purely nihilistic. Even the struggles which have been described as 'suicidal' in 'communisation theory' (See Jeanne Neton & Peter Åström, 'How one can still put forward demands when no demands can be satisfied', *SIC 1*, November 2011, and *inter alia* Théorie Communiste, 'Self-organisation is the

time for negotiations is already over, and the subjects to whom one might put demands are no longer recognised as interlocutors. Yet, even then, they will become so again if the uprising falters or hits some deadlock short of all-out victory, and it becomes necessary to "sue for peace". That is, as long as another social subject is recognised as a persistent pole in a relation of struggle, there are always demands implicit in the situation. The struggle that truly "demands nothing" can thus only be one that either has full revolutionary ambition, as well as some concrete, practical sense that this ambition can be achieved — or, perhaps, is absolutely nihilistic or suicidal.[27] Everything short of that is in the last analysis a "demand struggle", whether or not demands are formally written up and handed over to the opponent, scrawled on a banner, chanted in a slogan, or merely implicit in what the struggle *is*.[28]

The simplest valorisations of demandlessness in recent movements may be read as a token of radicality in the here and now; an expression of maximal revolutionary ambition. Such inclinations to demandlessness will inevitably prove "premature" in every context short of the all-out revolution in which it becomes genuinely possible to step beyond demands-making and to start creating a new situation directly. On the one hand we thus have here an instance of the anarchist broken clock that manages to tell the right time twice a day. On the other we should not be eager to habitually announce such prematurity, for while counsellors of moderation in struggle always know what time it is — too early — when the moment finally comes it will stop all the clocks. And such valorisations are not always uniformly inappropriate, even this side of revolution: in certain conditions they can gain a certain resonance. For example, where all routes for conventional, ritualised demand-making appear blocked, the refusal of empty negotiations, and the decision to struggle anyway, outside of normal formalised paths, may be a way to bring about a new

first act of the revolution; it then becomes an obstacle which the revolution has to overcome', 2015) cannot be understood as purely demandless. They are better described as last-ditch forms of 'demand struggle', where the odds are so hopeless that desperate measures are taken in an attempt to secure the most minimal of victories. One can view even the most negative examples of such struggles as not merely 'irrational', and as related overall to negotiating strategies. In all such struggles it is clear that there are determinate stakes, and thus always demands – however latent or implicit.

28 See Zaschia Bouzarri, 'Arson with Demands – on the Swedish Riots', in *Sic 3* (available on sic.journal.org) for an analysis of the 2013 Swedish riots in

situation in which different possibilities can emerge. These possibilities will generally involve new capacities for demand-making, though very rarely they might involve a capacity to push beyond demand-making to all-out insurrection. In such conditions, then, while there will be underlying, latent stakes, refusal to make these explicit as formalised demands for the negotiating table can be considered a rational tactic to open up space for further struggle. We might thus say that the assumption of the most abstractly radical subject position here can be a reasonable speculative orientation to bring about a new situation, even if this falls short of the all-out revolution in terms of which this subject position is constructed.

What happens if we now regather some mediations and return to a more emphatically socio-historical level? It is clear that many recent movements have experienced *problems* of demand-making. Either they've been unable to conjure any conviction about their ostensible demands in the face of an awareness of the sheer meaninglessness of even pretending that such things are still up for negotiation; or they've spent weeks and months in endless discussion, trying to discover what their demands actually are; or they've embraced a condition of demandlessness as a *de facto* admission of despair; or they've produced such a disordered mass of demands that the "meaning" of the movement itself loses legibility. These real experiences of a problem of demand-making may explain the resonance of abstract valorisations of demandlessness in such movements. The slogans that named the conversationalist encampments of Occupy were forged in the much more insurrectionary postures of the student movement that preceded them. But the very abstractness in those postures functioned differently in Occupy, transformed into a positive space in which to infinitely thrash out the problem of demands.

this light. A striking example during some of these riots – which were partly fueled by a drastic increase of rent in the neighborhood – was 'graffiti with demands' such as: 'lower the rent by 50%'. See also 'A Rising Tide Lifts All Boats', *Endnotes 3*, on the 2011 English riots: 'Anyone who, for political reasons, wants to hold that "The Riots" were entirely "demand"-free, a mere matter of the "negative language of vandalism" etc, will at minimum need to offer some explanation as to how they would separate these events, at which clear demands – on banners, in chants, in attempts to negotiate with cops – were present, can be separated from the riot-wave in which they issued, and which would not have occurred in their absence.'

Let's venture a hypothesis: that the problem of demands is identical to the problem of composition. For any singular, consistent social agent in struggle, the essential demands of the struggle will be evident in the simple facts of who the agent of the struggle is, and what has caused this agent to form in struggle. But where a struggle manifests an unsynthesised multiplicity of social agents — where it expresses a problem of composing a unified agent of struggle — by the same token it will express a problem of demand-making.[29] In such a situation it is not that demands are absent, for in fact there's a multiplicity of them, but rather, that they're not synthesised at the general level, as unifying demands of the whole movement. Thus their absence in one sense is directly related to their multiplicity in another. What should then probably be done in pursuing the question of demands in a particular movement is, rather than simply posing the question of their presence or absence, to ask what the *consistency* of demands, as well as their content, tells us about composition. Demands, we could say, are a direct index of the composition and texture of a movement.

29 See 'A History of Separation', in this volume, for a consideration of related points in the context of the workers' movement.

Both the absence of demands and their multiplicity represent attempts to temporarily overcome the fragmentation of the class, to come to a common mode of struggle despite divergent stakes for different class fractions. In Bosnia, there was a risk that the workers, the students, the retired would have irreconcilably different aims in the struggle, and instead of attempting to gather everybody around one central demand — which would have been impossible — plenums let everybody add their demands to a never-ending list. This frenetic proliferation was an attempt to avoid leaving anybody out, to make sure this was the protest of all Bosnian citizens; an attempt to achieve unity through multiplication.

But it remained a weak unity, and as the movement ebbed, conflicts between the various fractions emerged in the plenums. They also appeared within these groups themselves, depending on the concrete situation of each. Among workers from privatised factories, for example, there were conflicting interests between older workers — focused on getting their pensions and due wages — and younger ones who wanted to prioritise the restarting of production.

DECLINE

The gradual fading-out of the movement in March and April 2014 sadly makes a particularly interesting case-study of how a movement comes to an end. In this case, no external factor, such as direct repression by police, can really be blamed, and it is clear that the end had to come from the limitations of the movement itself.[30] Many participants are currently in a phase of intense reflection about this: for a lot of them, those days in February were the best days in their lives, and they are still trying to understand how and why the movement could just die out like that.[31]

In particular, people gradually stopped coming to plenums. Most would agree that as soon as the protests disappeared the plenums had no leverage, no way to pressure the institutions, which quickly stopped taking their demands seriously. Some politicians came to the plenums to push their own interests, and some allegiances were revealed, breaking the trust that had been so important in bringing people together. As people went on with their lives, they continually experienced pressure — threats that they would not be able to find a job because of their participation, street harassment by police etc. As the movement ran out of steam, the weak unity that had arisen from the struggle started crumbling. Conflicts broke out between different groups: workers were accused of being corporatists, only caring about their own struggle, while rifts developed between those with jobs and the

30 A disastrous external factor must be mentioned though: the flood that hit the country in May 2014 and caused incredible damage. This was indeed the last blow to the movement. However, this doesn't explain why the latter had been declining since March. Still, it has been reported that two of the main organised groups of participants, the plenum-ers and the football fans, were important in organising help during the flood, while the government once again showed its total uselessness. See Aleksandar Hemon, 'Beyond the Hopelessness of Survival' in *Unbribable Bosnia and Herzegovina.*

31 Some participants in Tuzla have referred to this as a process of mourning.

32 For example, on 15 March, a candidate for chief executive of

unemployed; between young and old; between people with various levels of education.

But what did participants expect of the plenums? After the first cathartic phase it seems that people understood the plenum as a new form of institution. And indeed, it did try to mimick the state: different working groups were created whose names would parallel those of the different ministries: a working group for the economy, one for culture and sport, one for internal affairs. Quickly, the plenums agreed to form connections with former politicians and candidates in the next elections.[32] The plenums started a dialogue with the very politicians they at first rejected. At one point, it looked like they might even aim to become a permanent institution that would play an intermediary role between the population and the government, gathering demands on the one hand, putting pressure on the other—and one might say—preserving some level of social peace in the meantime. But it is important not to fall into the trap of blaming plenums for putting an end to the movement. In Sarajevo for example, the first one was organised as people were already deserting street protests.[33] If some plenum-ers were pleased to discover that their organisational form seemed capable of diverting people from the more violent forms of protest[34], many were also conscious that, without such protests, the plenums would lose both their legitimacy and their main leverage.[35]

While some activists in Bosnia accused plenum organisers of being responsible for the institutionalisation of the movement, the latter would typically blame a certain passivity on the part of participants, who would come expecting to be told what to do. In the first theorisations of this organisational form in the Croatian student movement and its *Occupation Cookbook*, plenums were supposed to extend themselves, multiplying on different levels of society: in universities, workplaces,

the Tuzla Canton government came to the plenum to present his program for the local elections of October 2014.

33 In contrast to the relatively large numbers of protesters on the streets in the first days of the movement, only 300/400 people participated in the protests in Sarajevo on 10th and 11th February before the first Sarajevo plenum – which around 1000 people attended – took place on the 12th.

34 See the interview with a Sarajevo plenum organisor, Šejla Šehabović, on Face TV, a Bosnian television channel, on 14th February (available with English subtitles on bhprotestfiles.wordpress.com).

35 This doesn't mean organisers share no responsibility in their insistence that plenums should

etc... Though this was mentioned at points, it never really caught on. Similarly, and quite paradoxically, if the idea of plenums was greatly influenced by the *Occupation Cookbook*, one thing that was never on the cards during the Bosnian movement was the occupation itself. And this is where the similarities with Occupy movements stop.

As a result of this absence, there was no attempt to reorganise social life on another basis, beyond the level of representation. In most local instances of the squares movements, people not only met at assemblies and protests, but shared significant periods of their everyday life together. In some cases, they organised alternative forms of reproduction that did not involve money. The clearest example of this is the Gezi Park movement, where people organised free food, free access to health care, free barbers, a library, even a redistribution of cigarettes. Not that these explicitly alternativist moments didn't have serious limitations: the money-free zone could only exist because monetary-exchange continued a few meters away from the square, and those with jobs simply continued going to work, coming back to the square at the end of their work-day. Still, there was an idea that the protesters could not simply appeal to some institution to solve their problems, and that some attempts at changing social relations should take place within the struggle itself.

This also has specific implications when it comes to the challenging of gender relations. When protesters occupy a square for more than a few days, living together in tents, organising cooking, childcare and so on, they cannot avoid being confronted with the question of the separation between spheres of social life, and with it the question of gender.[36] This can itself take place in a conflictual and violent way, as demonstrated

take place in official buildings rather than on the streets. As we witnessed during the first plenum in Sarajevo – which could not take place because the room chosen for it was too small – many explicitly questioned the strategy of the organisers in waiting for the authorities to provide a bigger room, and demanded that the plenums be held in the open. Organisers continually insisted that plenums were a serious matter, requiring proper sound equipment, and thus couldn't be organised spontaneously.

36 On the link between gender and the reproduction of social spheres within the capitalist mode of production, see 'The Logic of Gender' in *Endnotes 3*.

by the many attacks on women in Tahrir square, for example. Unwaged reproductive activities take place among assemblies and street battles, and the question of their repartition cannot remain hidden: the occupiers have to take the question of their own reproduction as an object; it itself becomes a political question.[37] In the absence of occupations, during the protests in Bosnia-Herzegovina the challenge for women was to participate equally — which they certainly did, possibly even more actively than men — in plenums, riots and protests, while having to take care of these reproductive activities on the side. They struggled to be heard in plenums, to be equally represented among delegates, but, since there were no occupations, the question of their managing of reproductive activities during the protests remained a private concern.

Indeed, if the Bosnian movement was looking for an alternative, it was only at the level of decision-making: the movement demanded more democratic institutions, less corruption, to replace a government of crooks with a government of experts. This aspect, which was present in other squares movements, was especially central here. Indeed, more than direct democracy, people seemed to be mainly longing for a properly functioning state.[38] Most participants said they just wanted the infrastructures and the institutions to function; that they were fed up with administrative procedures being blocked, public transport being unreliable, even the most basic help not being provided while the country was being ravaged by floods. Most people did not mind the state, but they wanted a non-corrupt, efficient one capable of distributing a basic level of welfare. In this sense, as in other countries where revolts have taken place in recent years, protesters expressed a certain pining for a previous order of things, some form of welfare state — a certain *Yugo-nostalgia* could even be felt, especially among older people.[39]

37 On this question, see Rust Bunnies & Co., 'Under the riot gear' in *SIC* 2, Jan 2014.

38 The two first demands of the Tuzla plenum are telling in this regard: while the first one called for a 'maintaining [of] public order and peace in cooperation with citizens, the police and civil protection, in order to avoid any criminalisation, politicisation, and any manipulation of the protests', the second one demanded 'the establishment of a technical government, composed of expert, non-political, uncompromised members.'

39 On this phenomenon, which has 'less to do with the embellishment of the past than with its invention', see Mitja Velikonja, 'Mapping Nostalgia for Tito' in *Welcome to the Desert of Post-Socialism.*

ANTI-NATIONALISM AS DEMAND FOR A FUNCTIONING STATE

This has gone hand in hand with a rejection of the ethnic divisions that have been responsible for the fragmentation of institutions. If nationalist conflict appears here as the main barrier to the formation of a proper state, the anti-nationalism that was one of the main positive aspects of this movement cannot be separated from its longing for a functioning state, for a "united Bosnia-Herzegovina" that would bring all ethnic groups together.[40] It is perhaps striking, in an era in which some longstanding state structures in Europe — Great Britain, Spain — have been newly threatening to unravel under national pressures partly driven by social movements, that in the fractious region which two centuries ago gave us the word "balkanisation", nationalism could be confronted like this as a political problem for movements to solve in the name of a functioning state. If a common political problematic for many recent movements has been that produced by the enfeeblement of local and national mediations on the vast field of capital's worldly movements (and the entwinement of these mediations with capital's regional and global managements) the Bosnian case seems notably distinct. In this region in which global capital is barely interested, there is no properly functioning state to be defended in the first place. To have one appears to be a privilege to aspire to; to be properly exploited by capital is another.

In another context, these tendencies might have taken the form of an explicit movement towards the creation or defence of a nation-state, giving rise to a new nationalism. Indeed some Bosnia-Herzegovina flags could be seen here and there in demonstrations, but in numbers that are in no way comparable with the movements in Greece or Egypt. This is because the specific situation of Bosnia-Herzegovina makes such a prospect inherently problematic. The longing for a united Bosnia is itself associated with Bosniak nationalist discourse, and

40 Elements of this rhetoric could be heard for example in the 9th plenum in Tuzla, the 20 first minutes of which can be seen on the 'Bosnia-Herzegovina Protest Files' website with English subtitles.

thus also with a prospective diminution of the autonomy of the Brčko district and Republika Srpska, directly contrary to the aspirations of Bosnian Croat and Serb nationalists respectively — the latter of whom actually hope for an incorporation into "Greater Serbia". This projection of the Bosniak nationalist imaginary is itself a response to the fear of a division of Bosnia-Herzegovina that would leave only a tiny Bosniak-populated region.

By defending the creation of a united Bosnia-Herzegovina, pushing, for example, for the abolition of Republika Srpska and the Brčko district as obstacles to the creation of a functioning state, the movement would have destroyed any possibility of support from other regions. Indeed, some Serb and Croat nationalists already insisted on describing the protests as a Bosniak phenomenon — even spreading rumours that the protesters wanted to attack Republika Srpska residents. This partly explains why the demonstrations were almost non-existent in those regions.[41] Pushing for the formation of a single nation-state would thus have put in danger the very unity that such a state would require. This explains in large part why nationalist/patriotic tendencies were largely absent within the movement, in contrast to recent movements in Egypt or Spain.

But beyond this level, protesters in Bosnia also understood themselves as part of a larger wave of movements in the region, using forms and ideas first developed in neighbouring states such as Serbia and Croatia.[42] Such sentiments of solidarity were reciprocated: during the protests, there were demonstrations of solidarity with the Bosnian movement in almost all ex-Yugoslavian countries, including Macedonia, Serbia, Croatia and Montenegro. Revolts in ex-Yugoslavia seem to have been watching each other closely and influencing each other's modes of action in recent years. Indeed, before the Bosnian movement itself, many observed a wave of protests in the region, comparing it to the 2011–13

41 There have been reports that small gatherings took place in Republika Srpska in support of the protests but were quickly repressed by police and nationalist thugs.

42 Many protesters had only the vaguest knowledge of Occupy or even of the Arab Spring. But they knew a lot more about other revolts in ex-Yugoslavia and about the movements in Greece, Turkey, and – further away but at the centre of many debates – in Ukraine.

global wave of struggles, and even raising the prospect of a Balkan Spring.[43] In Croatia, Slovenia, Bulgaria, Serbia, commentators noted the rise of new modes of protest with — albeit on a smaller scale — similar aspects to recent squares movements.

Probably the most obvious example is the Slovenian protest wave of 2012–13, and the small Occupy movement that preceded this in October 2011. After a big demonstration against austerity on 15 October, around 30 tents were erected in a square in front of the Ljubljana Stock Exchange, where they remained until early 2012. Assemblies that sometimes gathered 150–200 people took place regularly, sharing similarities with those of Zuccotti Park in New York, even if activists at the core of the movement put forward a principle of "democracy of direct action vis-à-vis the consensus-based decision making of OWS".[44] Protests reappeared again in November 2012, first in Maribor, the second largest city, before spreading to many others and gathering tens of thousands of people. They were mainly directed against corrupt politicians — the mayor of Maribor being a blatant example — and contributed to the fall of a number of officials.

Beyond Slovenia, the whole region has witnessed a surge of social protest: in Bulgaria in 2012–13[45] people took to the streets because of a huge increase in the price of electricity, and against corruption in general. In Romania protests have erupted sporadically since 2010, in response to austerity measures and health-care reforms. Demonstrations have also taken place in Croatia, Serbia, Montenegro, Kosovo, Albania, and most recently in Macedonia. Despite their differences, these movements have displayed similarly "alternativist" tendencies, particularly in their experimentation with collective forms of decision-making, outside traditional, hierarchical structures, privileging plenary assemblies as organisational forms, and the use of social media.[46]

43 See Michael G. Kraft, 'Insurrections in the Balkans: From Workers and Students to New Political Subjectivities' in *Welcome to the Desert of Post-Socialism*. This collection of essays was published in 2015 but most texts contained were written before the Bosnian movement. In a postscript, Srećko Horvat and Igor Štiks recall how, after the submission of the manuscript, the 'most important social upheaval in the post-socialist Balkans' took place in Bosnia-Herzegovina, as a clear proof of the return of protest movements in the Balkans they had been documenting through the book.

44 See Maple Razsa and Andrej Kurnik, 'The Occupy Movement in Žižek's hometown: Direct democracy and a politics of becoming', *American Ethnologist* 39(2): pp. 238–58, May 2012.

The forms the February movement took in Bosnia-Herzegovina should therefore ultimately be understood in the context of this more general wave.

Workers' struggles have also been recurrent in the region, especially in Serbia and Croatia, and many are strikingly similar to those that have been taking place in Tuzla. Goran Music speaks of a new workers' movement in Serbia, and analyses three specific types of workers in the private sector, who each use different modes of protest.[47] The first are employed by large profitable companies — often multinationals — and while they suffer intense exploitation, they usually get their wages on time and have less trouble making ends meet. The second type are employed in small privately owned businesses — shops, bars, sweatshops — and are extremely exploited, regularly doing unpaid overtime. They are very atomised, with few possibilities for fighting collectively. Lastly there are "those workers left behind in large and midsized companies bypassed by new investments". As Music points out: "These workers are faced with challenges of a specific type, as their exploitation is not primarily the result of intensive labour processes at the place of formal employment." According to him, it is this category of workers that has been pushed to the forefront of resistance since the 2008 crisis, using forms of protest such as hunger strikes and even self-mutilation to press their demands.[48] Concerning this layer of the working population and their modes of struggle, Music asks the most pressing question: "After years of social decomposition of the industrial working class, would it make more sense to view these protesters as workers or a declassed layer of impoverished citizens?" He summarises the situation of these workers particularly well. Here the resemblance with the Tuzla workers is striking:

> On the one hand, the collective memory of socialism made sure the protagonists still saw themselves

45 See Mariya Ivancheva, 'The Bulgarian Wave of Protests, 2012-2013', *CritCom*, 7 October 2013, available online.

46 See Michael G. Kraft, 'Insurrections in the Balkans: From Workers and Students to New Political Subjectivities' in *Welcome to the Desert of Post-Socialism.*

47 Goran Music, *Serbia's Working Class in Transition 1988–2013* (Rosa Luxemburg Stiftung 2013)

48 Zoran Bulatović, a worker from the Raška textile factory who cut off a finger from his left hand in protest against his forced unemployment, has become a symbol of the desperation of this part of the working class in Serbia.

primarily as workers. The image of the past as a better time serves as the source of self-respect for this group of workers. Regardless of it standing idle for years, the local factory remained a place of identification and pride. Even after multiple privatisations, the workers still saw the enterprise as something belonging to them. The preferred final outcome of the strike for most strikers was the renewal of industrial activity.

On the other hand, the methods of struggle showcased during these protests had little to do with traditions of the labour movement. In many cases the workers occupied factories only to turn themselves into hostages. Hunger strikes, self-mutilations and suicide threats carried more resemblance to the tactics of struggle inside a prison than an industrial facility. With assembly lines remaining motionless for years, workers lost the most powerful weapon they once had in their hands — control over the production process. Even in cases when they recaptured the factory halls, it seemed that nobody cared. Neither the state, nor the new owners had any intention of using that space for manufacturing anyway. The "Gradac" factory incident, where the boss cut off the water supply while the hunger strike was taking place inside the building, is a good example. The workers were superfluous people — a burden inherited from the time of socialism which should be discarded together with the timeworn machinery.[49]

The increasingly desperate situation of the workers in Tuzla is clearly far from unique in the region. In this context, it is unsurprising that they would try to gather support from other parts of the population, bringing their struggle out into the open, demonstrating and blockading roads. Their situation has hardly improved since the February movement.[50] Shortly after the protests, the new cantonal government — the so-called "government of experts" — promised to renationalise the Dita factory,

49 Musić, *Serbia's Working Class in Transition*, pp. 44–45. Musić also gives the example of the former workers of 'Zastava Elektro' who organised nine roadblocks of the train tracks connecting Serbia and Macedonia between June and December 2009, 'placing their bodies across the tracks as a symbolic act of workers' collective suicide'.

50 Nonetheless, many would say that they at least gained a sense of pride in protesting, resisting pressures, and being the spark for many important experiments such as the plenums, giving them hope that such a movement might reappear quickly in the future.

51 In Tuzla and Sarajevo, more than one year after the protests, the Cantonal governments had still not repaired the burnt buildings or removed

which had been at the forefront of the movement. But it soon became clear that this would not actually happen, since the renationalisation of a company with such vast debts (approximately 15 million euros) was ruled illegal. For a while, some workers from Dita nurtured hopes that things could change before the October 2014 general elections, but these expectations quickly dissipated.[51] The new independent union, Solidarnost, has been struggling to gain legal recognition, and while it has helped organise bigger demonstrations, has so far been unable to achieve more concrete results.

the graffiti. Instead they just moved to other locations. The damaged buildings at the centre of these cities remain monuments to the protests, and reminders of how little change they actually brought. The latter signification was perhaps intentional.

An action organised by the workers of Tuzla on 24 December 2014 was highly symbolic: to demonstrate that they no longer had anything to hope for in Bosnia-Herzegovina, several hundred left the city on foot, in harsh winter weather, to walk to Croatia, enter the EU and ask for asylum. When they reached the border on 28 December, lacking passports, some were refused entrance to Croatia. Those who did have papers crossed the border symbolically, but returned in solidarity with the others. Exhausted from the long walk in the snow, several people needed medical attention. On their way back to Tuzla, angry as ever, the workers marched past the government building chanting "thieves!, thieves!" and "you'll be beaten up!"

To many — particularly the younger — emigration seems one of the only ways of improving their situation, continuing, one might say, class struggle by other means. This betrays the lack of options left to the workers — and, to a degree, to the rest of the population — in Bosnia-Herzegovina.[52] If it is true that, as Serbian economist Branko Milanović claims, inequalities between countries have now grown bigger than those within countries,[53] emigrating to a richer country may be by far the most effective way of increasing the price of one's labour power. Commentators in the autonomist marxist tendency, including Antonio Negri and Michael Hardt,

52 According to a survey conducted in 2012 by the Youth Information Agency of Bosnia-Herzegovina, 81% of young people declared they would 'leave the country tomorrow if they had a chance'. The same agency reports that from 2006 to 2012 at least 150,000 young people from Bosnia moved to the Western Balkans, North America and Australia.

53 Branko Milanović, *Global Income Inequality by the Numbers* (World Bank 2012)

have tended to analyse such emigration in a roseate light, seeing "desertion and exodus" as a "powerful form of class struggle within and against imperial postmodernity".[54] But as long as workers in those richer countries themselves experience immigration as bringing the prospect of *reductions* in the price of their labour power, the question of the nation — despite the positive developments we have witnessed in Bosnia-Herzegovina — is unlikely to recede easily in the future global unfolding of class struggle.

54 See Hardt and Negri, *Empire* (Harvard 2000), p. 213.

EPILOGUE

All prospects of the Dita workers getting their due wages vanished when the owner declared himself bankrupt in April 2015. In June, however, the workers decided, with the agreement of the creditors, to restart production in a self-managed fashion. Using materials left in the factory, and repairing some of the machines, they started turning out some of the main detergents previously produced there, under the names of '3de', 'Blic grill', 'Alls' and 'Broncho'. On 30 June, they agreed with the creditors that they would only have to repay the factory debts when they started making a profit. For the creditors, showing that the factory is viable may be a major help in the search for a new investor, and would thus increase their chances of getting their money back. For the workers at Dita, the restarting of production, even on a small scale, brings them not only an income but also a clear source of pride and hope. In this context, it is important not to get blinded by the ideological debates around self-management, either from those who praise it as a step towards a society of free producers or those who reject it per se as conservative and counter-revolutionary. However implausible it may seem as a long-term solution, in the context in which these workers find themselves, self-management appears as one of the few survival strategies remaining to them, and — from their point of view — at least worth a try.

ITS OWN PECULIAR DECOR

Capital, urbanism, and the crisis of class politics in the US

Chris Wright

In *Society of the Spectacle*, Guy Debord noted in rapid succession several elements of the relation of capital to space, which he brought under the concept of urbanism. Capital unifies and homogenises space so that it becomes the free space of commodities, of the valorisation of values. This eliminates geographical distance only to create a kind of inner distance — separation — in which transportation serves to make each place as much like every other as possible, so that, finally:

> A society that molds its entire surroundings has necessarily evolved its own techniques for working on the material basis of this set of tasks. That material basis is the society's actual territory. Urbanism is the mode of appropriation of the natural and human environment by capitalism, which, true to its logical development toward absolute domination, can (and now must) refashion the totality of space into its own peculiar decor.[1]

This concept of urbanism identified the separation under conditions in which it appeared that 1) "industry" as discussed in *Capital* vol. 1 was the highest and last form of the organisation of labour,[2] 2) capitalism would never be able to overcome the material impoverishment of more than a small minority of wage-labourers in any country, including the wealthiest ones, and 3) the working class would remain always and forever — or at least until the revolution — outside the legal and political forms of capitalist society; that is, it would retain the status of an estate with its own semi-autonomous political and cultural institutions marking it off from the bourgeois and petit-bourgeois classes. In crucial respects, these three conditions no longer apply.

These changes are expressed not merely in production, distribution, and consumption, but in the working up of the spaces in which these take place. For example, the elimination of geographical distance today relies more on

1 Debord, *Society of the Spectacle*, trans. Donald Nicholson-Smith (Zone 1994), p.165–9.

2 This is often conceived of today as the real subsumption of labour under capital, but I believe this is mistaken. As I will argue, industry in this case should be understood as 'mechanical industry', and is itself a surpassable organisation of the labour process.

capital as such and the abstract nature of its forms of domination, and the conflation of a class relation with the condition of being an estate. To put it another way, both have acted as if capitalist society was a direct form of domination of one group by another, as in slavery or feudalism, when in fact it involves an indirect form of domination through abstract social forms. Of course, in its initial development capitalism arose amidst such direct, concrete forms of domination and they do not simply disappear of themselves, but only under a protracted development, which is itself determined by continual crises and the potential overthrow of capitalism.

CAPITAL AND SPACE

Labour in capitalist society requires the constant separation of people from their powers, from the means of production, from the products of their labour, and from each other. Separation is the premise of all accumulation, or paraphrasing Guy Debord, it is the alpha and omega of capital.[3] Separation is internalised within the experience of everyday life, where it becomes naturalised and consensual, and does not appear as domination. Separation is essential to capital as a total social circuit — that is, the separation of production, circulation, and consumption. This separation of the total circuit can be expressed spatially. For example, production occurs in "places of work", from factories, mills and mines to offices and engineering campuses, while circulation takes place in commercial warehouses and retail stores, and consumption loops back into production in the workplace or the home.[4] From the opening of the capitalist era the latter has been constructed as private by the separation of non-waged labour — into the feminised space of the home — from the masculinised, public, waged labour of the workplace. This separation of the private is in fact doubled: as the separation into spheres of waged and unwaged labour, but also of public and private, of the political and the economic.

3 *Society of the Spectacle*, p. 20.

4 As Marx noted in the *Grundrisse*: all production is consumption, all consumption production.

LABOUR PROCESS AND CAPITAL CIRCUIT

Marxian urbanism was concerned largely with conceptualising the contradictory unity of spatial and formal concentration: bringing together geographically to separate socially—producers from means of production; home from workplace; reproduction of labour power from reproduction of capital; producer from product; producers from each other, and so on. Capital seemed to *categorically require* an increasing density of population and a geographical concentration of the means of accumulation. However, this concentration has ultimately proved contingent; something which capital sought to overcome, and it achieved this through a transformation in its capacity to negate physical distance: the crisis of urbanism was thus temporarily resolved through the spatial deconcentration of capital and labour.

Capital is not only separation, however: its entire circuit—M → C...P...C′ → M′—has to be taken into account.[5] The question is how the logical forms are simultaneously both maintained in their separation and brought together in a unity. Many of the central problems of urbanism flow from the contradiction that capital is not only its activity of separation but this entire circuit of buying, selling and productive consumption—and that in order to complete the circuit, producers, means of production, and products all have to be brought together in great concentrations. Consumption also takes place, in Marx's classic formulation, between capital's two "departments"—capitals engaged in the production of means of production and in the production of means of consumption—which is another way of considering productive consumption by capital and labour. Here we will focus in on changes that have occurred within only part of the circuit: C...P...C′. That is, we will look at changes to production, communication, energy, and transportation, due to the importance of these for understanding spatial de-concentration.

5 Money → commodities ... production ... commodities + surplus value → money + surplus value. This formula places an emphasis on money, since it falls at the circuit's extremes, and is thus specifically the circuit of money capital, but it can also be viewed in rotation, with either the commodity or production at its extremes, thus giving us the circuits of commodity and productive capital. All of these circuits should nonetheless be grasped as facets of a single, socially general process. For Marx the circuit of commodity capital was actually the more concrete, since it articulated the circuits of individual capitals with the broader social context, via the market.

Urbanism arose and took its classical forms as manufacture and mechanical industry gave rise to ever denser populations under conditions which helped produce a collective self-identification as workers, as a class, as a political power, as proletariat. The modern industrial city, as well as the great cosmopolitan centres, grew out of this process, under conditions determined both by technical restrictions on capital's diffusion in space and by the economic and political exclusion of labour. The crisis of the phenomenal forms of capital in the first half of the 20th century was then also a crisis of the modern industrial city and of the relationship between the urban and the rural. Out of many discontinuous and contested changes a process of rationalisation took place, both within the labour process and in urbanism.

The process of rationalisation under capitalism is not about technological solutions to technological problems, but re-organisation of the class relation. This process is typically described in terms of the transformation of the labour process through technological innovation, but it also entails the transformation of the environment, which is much less discussed. The replacement of living with dead labour is not just quantitative, replacing *x* human labour with *y* machinery, but involves qualitative combinations of labour displacement and deskilling. The widespread employment of a particular technology to achieve systematic rationalisation is always also a question of the problem of reproducing labour as a social mediation. The old machinery and methods become reduced to mere technology subsumed to the new labour process.[6] This progressive rationalisation cannot be adequately grasped by the notion of a movement from formal to real subsumption. Capitalist "progress" is exactly this process of successive transformations in the labour process, undertaken to overcome problems of valorisation. "Technological solutions" mediate these broad-ranging transformations that alter the organisation of space, time, and

6 This is why craft labour, for example, does not go away; nor did the implementation of large-scale electrification and the combustion engine after WWII simply do away with mechanical industrial processes. But neither do they any longer have the possibility of being the form in which a new period of valorisation might take place. Either the new class relation fundamentally alters the means, opening up different possibilities, or the older technology simply subsists in those areas where its replacement by other labour processes is not practical in a profitable manner.

rationality, which is also why these progressive rationalisations appear as technological revolutions, giving rise to technological determinist theories.[7] This process of rationalisation is the way in which capital's domination is reasserted, through the transformational reproduction of the capital-labour relation.

These transformations radiate and generalise because capital is a dynamic totality that can accommodate an almost infinite variety of political and cultural forms, and absorb forms of resistance. The totalising nature of the dynamic is evident in the global scope and simultaneity of these transformations, which have been given an abundance of names: Fordism, the mass worker or state capitalism to refer to the period from 1917 to the early 1970s, where power and production seemed increasingly to collapse into each other; globalisation, neo-liberalism or Empire to refer to the changes which have taken place since the 1970s, in which the separation of state and economy seemed to be the dominant trend.[8] At the same time, these rationalising transformations can manifest themselves in a seemingly infinite variety of concrete shapes, and the global shift is therefore only evident after the fact. Often, the fact that we can talk about a change indicates that it is already passing, or has already passed.

We will now take a closer look at these successive and progressive rationalisations through which the capital–labour relation has re-asserted itself, transforming the way in which it is experienced and produces space.

7 Moishe Postone recognises this in terms of the productivity of capital outstripping labour with the current application of science, but he cannot adequately relate it to the mode of producing and labour process, because it reflects something more specific than the 'real subsumption' of labour or even than the 'micro-electronics revolution' specified by Robert Kurz and Norbert Trenkle, which misses the transformation of the labour process in its concreteness.

8 Or perhaps one should say: the reduction of the state to a more indirect intervention in favour of so-called 'market mechanisms'.

THE CHANGING RELATION OF WORKERS TO WORK

The transformation of machinery and the labour process alters the relation of labour and capital, and the relations of workers to each other. Machinery and the labour process mediate the actual relations between workers, because workers come into contact with each other through the production process. They also mediate the relation between capital and labour, because capital is experienced first and foremost as machinery, raw materials, and the command of the production process, while capital experiences labour as variable capital. Machinery and the labour process materialise the class relation and thus form the basis for its perpetuation and particularisation.[9] Social relations are thus embedded in the labour process and machinery, and this formation in turn shapes sociality.

9 Just as we can refer to the class relation as a kind of symbolic order, so with machinery and the labour process we have a kind of material semiotic.

The introduction of a labour process based on machinery gives work an indirect relationship to nature, as work is performed on nature to either turn it into a raw material or to turn a raw material into a product, but in neither case is the whole labour oriented towards the whole process from beginning to end. This abandonment of handicraft production opens up the way for the pre-planning of coordination, transport and assembly, and the rationalisation of the work activity via practical analysis and deskilling. Planning in turn becomes the price-form in process, with the value already being calculated prior to being brought to the market. Out of this comes the divorce of operational and technical planning from realisation via physical labour, which introduces the difference between the worker and the planner, engineer, and overseer.

Following Hans-Dieter Bahr:

> Machinery sets free an intellect formerly bound to the feudal-handicraft labour process, an intellect which carries the possibility of forming a political collective worker out of the divided partial workers. In contrast to the work ethic of the guild, the political cooperation of wage-workers comes into external opposition to production as such, since the social ends of production confront the proletariat as an external force, i.e. as the ruling class. The leveling

down of the specialised workers by means of production technology creates the condition for turning the wage-struggle into the potential political socialisation of a working class in the process of organising itself. On the other hand, the contradiction between the specialised worker and the technological intellect responsible for the direction, construction and transmission of the isolated detail operations, prevents the working class from recognising its own social character in this intellect, which in fact represents its own intellect, even if in the form of an unconsciously collective product alienated from the working class and acquiring independent shape in the form of planners, technicians and engineers. The proletariat therefore stands in outward opposition to its own intellect, which the capitalist process of production has created in formal independence. In part, it was this hostility which weakened and nullified the resistance of the working class to fascism. In addition, the absence of a practical-theoretical critique of the productive intellect blinkers the working class, binding it as a variable moment to the aggregate social capital; in this respect, the working class is merely an antagonistic, but nonetheless fixed component of bourgeois society. Its blindness towards its own, but alienated, intellect means that it contributes to the maintenance of the false totality of this society. And a "liberation" which takes place behind the backs of the producers posits freedom as mere ideal.[10]

10 Hans-Dieter Bahr, 'The Class Structure of Machinery', in Phil Slater ed., *Outlines of a Critique of Technology* (Ink Links 1979), p.6.

The formal independence of the intellect has become its real independence. This shift means that the worker more thoroughly divorces himself from a labour process which is incomprehensible to him in the absence of highly specialised, scientific knowledge. This independent intellect fosters a culture of giving orders and obeying which is prevalent in today's permissive society. Both authority and obedience flourish where they are least expected.

With the internalisation and objectification of the whole labour process into machinery, the circulation of commodity capital is itself industrialised, while "industrial and commercial capital fuse via the functional role played by financial capital."[11] Despite this fusion, however, the limitations of the means of transportation and communication prior to WWII still necessitated relatively dense and connected facilities, with large concentrations of workers able to see the entire production process. This concentration brought about industrial union-type organisations and labour-type political parties. Forms of mass communication such as the newspaper, film, and radio, developed to artificially resolve what Bahr refers to as the "'ideality' of the collective worker" into that of an individual consumer and citizen.[12] The various strands came together in the form of organisations of the workers which took on an autonomous existence, developing bureaucratically, and in the end becoming a brake on the very revolutionary intellect from which they grew.

11 Ibid.

12 Ibid. The notion of the ideality of the worker as a subject is important. As Bahr notes, Lukács mistakes this ideality for a reality, and thus imagines a supra-historical Subject.

Critical changes took place in energy, communications, and transportation that provided the infrastructural foundations for the dissolution of the spatial and communicative conditions of collective working class life. National energy grids were developed to provide power across large areas without the need for facilities to have dedicated power plants. This broad network of energy provision was combined with the mass proliferation of the automobile and truck, and the development of massive road and highway infrastructures to support them, which made it possible to expand laterally in space at a much lower population and capital density than had previously been imaginable. In terms of intercontinental transportation there were also huge strides in transoceanic shipping and air transport. This expansion of power and mobility for the commercial, the retail and the residential went hand-in-hand with improved communication networks, starting with the phone, but expanding into radio, television, and eventually computers.

These developments also involved the massive, more or less direct, engagement of the state in the economy. In poorer countries only the state could gather and coordinate enough capital to engage in development. In wealthier countries it regulated the commonly required systems of power, communication, transportation, education, healthcare and sometimes housing, whether directly in the form of nationalisations, or indirectly via regulatory bodies and investment in infrastructure, which was then made up as a gift to private capital. This development of capital's means of transport and means of communicating its orders and instructions deepened the spatial isolation and separation between workers, and disrupted collective and public forms of communication and of movement in space.

THE RELATIVE END OF MATERIAL IMPOVERISHMENT AND THE IMPOVERISHMENT OF SPACE

One major change after WWII was the massive increase in spending power of workers, especially in the US, which amounted to 50% of the world's wealth and 25% of world productive capacity, but only 5% of its population. The unionisation of the 1930s resulted in a desire by the institutional representatives of capital *and* labour to ensure social peace and profitability in the post-war period. The wage–productivity deal worked out between the unions and major industries meant that, in return for productivity that increased faster than the rate of wage growth, wages were nonetheless able to grow far higher than ever before. This played a critical role in the development of the worker as mass consumer, as the material impoverishment of the pre-WWII period was left behind. This took the form of a large part of the working class having the means to buy cars, houses, and to move away from the dense urban networks of working class life to the relative isolation of the suburbs.

The new means allowed individuals and groups to find "solutions" to the problems associated with the industrial city, such as overcrowding, lack of access to nature, crime, landlords, and so on. They also made it possible to flee into places purged of, and walled off from, the racial and immigrant Other, simultaneously escaping and reinforcing racial formation and its conflicts. Suburban development and sprawl, through which the existing order produced such solutions for some at the expense of others, combined with the transformation of those workers into mass consumers, to result in a process of de-concentration. This would become the basis of "white flight", "urban decay", and eventually "urban renewal". The more pronounced and extensive the development of the suburb proper, the more the dismantling of the industrial city implied its falling into a state of ruin, and not necessarily its transformation into a "rejuvenated" sprawl city.[13] Where the formation of the suburb was less pronounced or even largely absent, the older cities were often nonetheless re-shaped according to the forces of this ex-urbanism. There was also an emergence of wholly new cities, which from their inception were suburban in design.

It was never for the working class alone that housing and the geography of social relations were a problem. Large concentrations of people from all social classes meant large concentrations of poverty, of garbage and shit, and of discontent. Water and air pollution from factories and homes, garbage, and poor housing put up simply in order to provide the minimum of shelter, meant illness and disease. Current conditions in Mexico City, Lagos, Shanghai, Hyderabad, and Sao Paolo differ in scale from the 19th century conditions of the English working class in Manchester or Leeds, or the 20th century worker living in Chicago, but except for a highly developed consumer society which has increased the power and pressure of money over the working class

13 While 'industrial city' or 'financial metropolis' differentiate between the kinds of cities that predominated under urbanism – say, between Detroit and New York – it is difficult to conceptualise the new kind of city along production lines. Post-industrial seems a cop-out, much like 'post-modernism' or post-anything. Other options like the 'cybernetic' or 'bio-informatic' city seem odd. It is an environment so wholly given to the totality of capital, so much a smooth surface encapsulating the entire cycle of M–C–M', I think it necessary to alternate between 'suburban city', as an indicator of its sub-urban status, and 'sprawl city' to identify its material and organisational feel. Such terminological difficulties are indicators of a genuine conceptual knot that

globally, many of these conditions would be familiar to those workers.

needs to be revisited and wrestled with.

CASE STUDY: THE UNITED STATES AND SUBURBIA PROPER

The problems of environmental planning created a new field of activity for the management of class power. As early as the 1830s in England, middle class social reformers and utopians attempted to find a way to deal with "the housing problem", with both sides generally proposing a combination of individual ownership and state intervention into workers' housing. This problem reflected fundamental dilemmas of capitalism: capitalists in the building industry needed demand to exceed supply; capital would flow towards the more profitable building projects; ground rent — which plays a key role in determining housing costs alongside of the actual costs of construction, maintenance and interest on mortgages — was too high in cities, because of industrial and commercial development.

Engels mocked those who proposed such solutions in his 1872 articles on "The Housing Question". He also warned that, were such panaceas to succeed, they would result in the de-proletarianisation of the working class, and that widespread homeownership was incompatible with — and would be a reactionary development in relation to — the working class as a revolutionary class. Anticipating the current state of affairs by more than a century, he suggested that it would render workers immobile and put them deeply into debt, and therefore at the mercy of capitalists. Against the claims of Proudhon and some of his German followers, Engels argued that far from providing security and a civilising effect, individual home ownership would turn workers back into peasants, clutching their little piece of land and — whatever their misery — ultimately narrow, provincial, and fixated on the security of their property.

Far from representing a solution, at the time wide-scale home ownership by workers seemed utterly impossible. None but the highest paid workers had access to the money or credit necessary to secure a mortgage, although even in the 1887 edition of Engels's articles there was already a note on the purchase of homes by workers in Kansas, on the outskirts or in the suburbs. Built by themselves, of extremely poor quality, with little in the way of modern conveniences like sewage and public garbage removal, some workers still purchased these little dwellings at $600 each.

The real breakthrough in housing construction was the "balloon frame" house. This could be built from precut wood, with relatively little effort, time and therefore cost — especially compared to the older brick and stone buildings. It thus made possible the mass-production of houses at prices that many workers could afford, if they could manage the land or the ground rent, and if they could get a mortgage that they could pay off.

Land prices make up a large part of the cost of a house, so houses for workers had to be built on cheap land, on the edges of, or outside, cities, but the limitations of existing means of transport posed a critical barrier to use of that land. Train travel over short distances, and even horse-drawn omnibuses, were still too expensive for most workers and the lower middle classes, and no other means of transport made it feasible to work 10–14 hours a day and still get to and from work without living within walking distance, even if walking distance was often several miles. Even reformers complained that long walks to and from work contributed to workers' exhaustion and reduced productivity. However, the widespread introduction of mass transit in the form of the trolley or tram would come just a few short years after Engels's death, undermining the force of this argument.[14]

14 It is important to note that in the 19th and most of the 20th century, suburbanisation in continental Europe had a different character from the Anglo-American trend. In Europe, the city centre was claimed by the bourgeoisie and upper middle classes, while the working class and industry were pushed to the edges of the cities and suburbs. Even today, American-type suburbs remain the exception on the continent. Therefore it is unsurprising that the 2005 French riots took place in the banlieus – that is, the suburbs – and mostly involved North African youth. In the US, the riot is almost always an 'inner city' phenomenon, though as events in Ferguson, MO have shown, this is not exclusively the case. [See 'Mike Brown's Body', in this issue, for an analysis of the latter.]

Before the automobile, the electric trolley made possible a spreading-out over a much larger area of land. Through state subsidies in Europe — where ownership of a trolley or cable car line involved legal prohibitions on real estate speculation — and privately in the United States, where the owners of such systems were almost all land speculators, mass transit came into existence, greatly extending the distance workers could live from their homes. The much cheaper land on the edges of, or outside, cities thus suddenly became accessible to a larger part of the working class. Los Angeles — today known for its vast car-driven sprawl and expressways — was originally developed as a low-density, de-centreed city based on the trolley system, and was unlike anything imagined in Europe or east of the Mississippi. By the early 1900s, Los Angeles had the largest mass transit system in the world, put into place as a way to turn a profit on land bought cheaply by large real estate speculators. Los Angeles was the product of land speculation mixed with the new system of mass transit and balloon frame housing, and became the first urban suburb, even before the automobile could have a significant impact on public transportation.

In the United States, the trolley systems usually ran at a loss, and owners hoped to profit heavily from the land speculation and housing development that they facilitated. By the 1920s, however, the trolley was in competition with the noisier, less efficient, polluting bus — and, to an increasing extent, the car. A coalition of companies, including automobile, trucking, steel, rubber, and others, lead by the president of General Motors, systematically bought up and destroyed the trolley mass transit systems in dozens of cities, including New York. This process of systematic acquisition and destruction continued into the 1940s. The destruction of Los Angeles' mass transit system by General Motors is only the most well-known incident at the end of a long process that had begun almost 20 years earlier.[15]

15 Bradford Snell, 'The Streetcar Conspiracy: How General Motors Deliberately Destroyed Public Transit', *The New Electric Railway Journal*, Autumn 1995. For an international view of the struggle between mass transit and the automobile, see Colin Divall and Winstan Bond, *Suburbanising the Masses: Public Transport and Urban Development in Historical Perspective* (Ashgate 2003).

As the trolley systems were being destroyed bit by bit, however, mass transit in the form of buses continued to predominate in the 1930s. The vast majority of American workers used either their feet or mass transit to get to work, to shop, to visit their friends, and to otherwise conduct their lives. Even so, home ownership was an increasingly common feature of working class life in the United States, especially among the children of immigrant workers — now considering themselves white American — who were more likely to buy homes than were those who had preceded them by several generations. They were also more able to get credit and buy homes than were black workers, who were either trapped in the sharecropper/tenant farmer contracts of the Southern rural areas, or relegated to the lower strata of the working class in the Northern cities after the first Great Migration from WWI onwards.[16]

Expansion further outside of the cities required two key elements. The first prerequisite was even more individualised transportation, allowing travel to anywhere that roads went, instead of being circumscribed by bus and trolley lines. This meant the building of a large motor vehicle road system outside of the cities, in areas where the money for such vast projects was scarce. This process began in the 1930s, but really expanded in the 1950s with the federal Interstate Highway Program under Eisenhower, directed by a former General Motors executive.[17] Supported also in the name of "national defence", this was in fact a thinly disguised way to increase the dominance of the car as the primary means of transport. This programme received 90% of its funding from the federal budget and 10% from the states; approximately 50% came from federal, state and local fuel taxes, vehicle taxes, and tolls, the rest from other federal taxes. It was an investment, over 35 years (the formal completion of the programme came as late as 1992, with the completion of Interstate Highway I-70), to the tune of $425 billion.[18] This makes it one of the

16 David H. Onkst, '"First a Negro ... Incidentally a Veteran": Black World War Two Veterans and the G.I. Bill in the Deep South, 1944–1948', *Journal of Social History*, vol. 31, no. 3, spring 1998, pp. 517–44.

17 Francis Dupont, whose family money created GM, became the head of the Federal Highway Commission. See Mary Zepernick, 'The Impact of Corporations on the Commons, address at the Harvard Divinity School's Theological Opportunities Program, 21 October 2004.

18 Figure adjusted for 2006 dollars. These sums include maintenance costs for bridges and other items on highways, as well as the highways themselves. Al Neuharth, 'Traveling Interstates is our Sixth Freedom.' *USA Today*, 22 June 2006. For total

largest public works programmes in human history. On top of this original plan, interstate highways have of course continued to be constructed. In 2007, funding appropriated for the total Interstate Highway System budget totalled $147 billion.

budget see 'Spending and Funding for Highways, Congressional Budget Office Economic and Budget Issue Brief', January 2011.

The other key element was a transformation of the home loan and building industries. Mortgages were a problem because they tended to be short term — at most 15 years — with a large down payment, a large lump sum due at the end, and fairly high interest rates. In response to the depression, the Roosevelt administration created agencies and passed bills that completely restructured the mortgage industry. Focusing on low interest, long-term loans and federal guaranteeing of many mortgages, the mortgage industry was radically restructured. Even though federal housing loans did not force private lenders to adopt their rules, federal loan guidelines and guarantees against losses due to foreclosure promoted a restructuring of practices, and facilitated a vast extension of private lending.

The Federal Home Loan agency — and following it, the so-called GI Housing Bill implemented during and after WWII — defined the guidelines for underwriting mortgages in the official Underwriters Manual. This identified areas where lending was most likely to succeed or fail by defining four different zones, marked by colour; thus was created the practice of "redlining". Red-line districts were those where mortgages, and the federal insuring of mortgages, were more or less automatically denied. The main criterion was race. Areas that were non-white or "mixed" were automatically redlined, so that neither the federal government, nor ultimately private lenders, would lend to "black" people trying to secure a mortgage. Despite the GI Bill and Federal Home Loan agency accounting for over 50% of suburban housing construction mortgages from 1945 to 1960, less than 1% of those loans went to prospective black homeowners.[19] This also reinforced the devaluation of housing in predominantly black or mixed areas, so that many whites, able to secure a home loan, fled to the suburbs in a steady flow after 1945. The Underwriters Manual also gave preference to — and in many cases actually required — racially-restrictive housing covenants that would prevent black people from purchasing homes within a federally insured housing development.

The Underwriters Manual also made it difficult to get an insured loan for already-built housing, and certain construction guidelines — such as requiring a certain amount of distance between the house and the street — forced people to move to newly constructed housing in the suburbs instead of purchasing in the cities. This provided a huge boost to home builders by forcing prospective homeowners to purchase new buildings instead of existing housing stock.

The federal home loan and GI Bill housing programmes, combined with the eventual highway construction programme of the 1950s, involved billions of dollars of federal subsidisation of housing for whites of all classes, including a bevy of homeowner tax credits, so that it was often cheaper to buy in the suburbs, including purchasing one or two cars, than to rent equivalent housing in the city.

The construction industry — originally dominated by small to medium sized builders, who could only come up with enough capital to take on projects of a few houses at a time — was also transformed by federal underwriting of residential and commercial developments, and rationalisation of the mortgage system. While there were a few large residential construction companies, they were exactly that: few. Builders generally needed to have assurances that they could build with as little risk as possible from foreclosures and economic downturns. With each depression between 1877 and 1929, thousands

19 Tim Wise, 'Bill of Whites: Historical Memory Through the Racial Looking Glass', *ZNet,* 24 July 2000: 'the VA and FHA loan programmes [...] utilised racially-restrictive underwriting criteria, thereby assuring that hardly any of the $120 billion in housing equity loaned from the late forties to the early sixties through the programmes would go to families of colour. These loans helped finance over half of all suburban housing construction in the country during this period, less than 2% of which ended up being lived in by non-white persons.' Suzanne Mettler argues that, while the G.I. Bill got black workers into vocational and college programmes, it failed to provide housing: *Soldiers to Citizens: The GI Bill and the Making of the Greatest Generation* (Oxford University Press, 2005).

of contract builders went under, unable to survive the bankruptcy of more than a handful of mortgage holders. The federal loan programmes and agencies, and their *de facto* restructuring of the mortgage lending industry, provided the stability and insurance against losses that made it possible for larger construction firms and developers to build housing for workers on a scale that was unimaginable only 20 years earlier.

The relative power of white labour to secure higher wages and to move freely allowed many workers to purchase homes under the new terms of 30 year, insured, low interest mortgages. And, given the chronic weakness of the US labour movement, laws could be written to: 1) openly exclude black people, via redlining, which meant that 99% of federally guaranteed and subsidised mortgages between 1935 and the early 1960s went to whites only; 2) minimise investment in renovating existing housing, because loans were almost entirely reserved for new homes; 3) re-direct investment away from cities, because most space for new single-family residence housing was in the suburbs; 4) stop cities from growing by annexing immediately adjoining suburbs, since suburban residents and authorities wanted to keep taxes low, avoiding the cost of common municipal social services, which suburbanites could in any case still access simply by traveling into the city.

Even though a 1948 Supreme Court ruling formally outlawed racially restrictive covenants in housing, the practice has continued *de facto* to the present.[20] The structure of the economically homogeneous subdivision — where developers build a whole set of houses aimed at a single income bracket — continues to dominate suburban housing development, and typically remains racially uniform. Few projects have been on the scale of the original Levittowns, but the basic standard for subdivision — rather than individual lot — development, guarantees that uniformity.[21]

20 Supreme Court ruling in *Shelley vs. Kraemer*, 1948.

21 Levittowns: large post-war suburban developments pioneering the new model, created by the real estate developer William Levitt's company. In 1948 Levitt declared: 'No man who owns his own house and lot can be a Communist. He has too much to do.'

This kind of development has not remained purely in the suburbs or in newly developing areas. The opening up of areas outside cities for housing would have been insufficient in itself to shift the tide of development from urban to suburban. For this to happen, the rest of the city also had to move to the suburban and semi-rural areas. The city had so far been the location of both work and consumption. Factory and office, department store and multitude of small retailers, would all reside within the city, within neighbourhoods or city centres. But the same changes in transportation that allowed residential movement to the suburbs also opened the possibility of moving industry and offices out of the cities.

The personal car came hand in hand with the development of the trucking industry. Trucking gave the same flexibility in space to industry that the automobile gave to individuals and families. By the 1930s, the railroads were in steep decline, as trucking became the main means of transport for materials and commodities over land. Railroads remain the predominant long-distance, point-to-point method of land transport because under those conditions it is cheaper than trucking. However, the further one needs to move away from central cities and train lines, the more cost effective trucking becomes. This dynamic led to the eventual dominance of trucking for transport in the United States.

Soon after WWII, companies began to migrate industry and offices out of the cities and into the suburbs, and eventually into the "greenfields" — semi-rural areas that are often in a state of development between rural and suburban. From almost every angle, moving industry out of the cities benefited businesses. Suburbs, having less infrastructure to maintain and being on less developed land, offered low ground rents, and generally lower taxes. Prior to the "tax revolt" that began in the late 1970s, this movement allowed many suburbs to maintain lower residential and homeowner taxes through taxation levied on businesses, who still managed to pay less than in cities. At the same time, businesses thereby avoided conflicts with urban political machines, which had to maintain relative class peace in a much less homogenous environment than the suburbs. This mutually beneficial tax arrangement would eventually crumble in the 1960s and 70s as companies either moved further away from the cities, seeking better deals in newer suburbs and greenfields, or left the country.

Companies responded as much as the state to the huge class conflicts between 1919 and the end of WWII. Workplaces moved into the suburbs and greenfields in order to escape the concentrated mass of workers that proved so intractable in the first half of the 20th century. Dense concentrations of workers, their families and friends in generally rented housing, meant that thick networks of relationships could exist, and often near workplaces. Cities did not generally have land use regulations creating sharp divisions between residential, commercial, and retail areas. Many small businesses dependent on the workers within walking distance had close relationships with them. This tended to generate sympathy, and in times of strikes and lockouts workers could often depend on a certain degree of support from such businesses, where they bought their groceries and everyday goods. Such networks could prove a serious problem for capital.

Suburban design introduced rigid distinctions of residential, commercial and retail space. Zoning laws separated these in a way that they never had been in cities. Workers came to live apart from not only their workplaces, but also the businesses they bought consumer goods from. In post-WWII suburbs, urban planners and developers produced designs involving new arrangements such as the purely residential cul de sac opening onto a four to eight lane feeder road. Not only was there really no way to walk to the workplace or shops, but walking itself was actually discouraged by a design that made it hugely inefficient and even physically dangerous. Here physical design was also in part social engineering. Police harassment of those walking in suburbs would further reinforce the separations — focusing in on those lacking apparent purpose, or possessing an appearance atypical for a particular subdivision.

Suburbia changed the possibilities for the entry of chain stores into the space previously dominated by "mom and pop" neighbourhood stores. In the suburban setting, small retailers could not be situated within walking distance of consumers, because they could not be set in residential areas. At the same time, many people also wanted access to the downtown shopping experience stripped of the unpleasantness of beggars, homeless people, and other "undesirable elements". Enter the two most commonly recognised symbols of suburbanisation: strip malls and shopping malls, to which have been added "big box" stores like Walmart, which follow the same basic "one-stop-shopping" design as the traditional mall. While this took some time to develop — really only beginning in the mid to late 1950s — both the shopping mall and the strip mall took off in the 1960s and 70s, recreating the downtown shopping options, but within a far more controlled environment.

Communities began to fragment as large concentrations of workers in proximity with each other across multiple workplaces were broken up. As both waged workers and industry left, what remained in cities were populations pushed further and further to the social and spatial margins, with collapsing incomes and thus collapsing infrastructures and social services. Here we have the successor to the pre-WWII ghetto. The latter was, to be sure, a place of collective isolation, but it was also one rarely outside of capitalist reproduction in one form or another, due to the expanding need for labour in the period from the 19th to the early 20th century. But what came now was a new kind of ghetto, increasingly cut off from more than marginal access to waged labour, and also the object of increasing homogenisation and atomisation. In the United States this dislocation, de-population, and ghettoisation finds its highest expression in the former centres of industrial production and working class militancy: Detroit, Baltimore, Cleveland, Akron, Buffalo, Newark, St. Louis, Pittsburgh, and so on. In terms of division within the working class, it is most clearly expressed in the disparity in median wealth per household between black and white families, which has tripled in the last 25 years. Median white household wealth is $265,000 compared to $28,500 for black households, most of which is tied to home ownership.[22]

Even focusing purely on the support given to different types of housing, the divergences are stark. Public programmes, originally put into place during World War II to meet housing demand for war workers, were essentially the only subsidised housing non-white workers could get, while they were completely excluded from federal—and therefore largely from private—mortgage loans. Cities and states worked with the federal government to "clear slums"—often referred to as "negro removal"—putting workers into public housing located in relatively isolated areas of the city, often far from downtown and from the best paid industrial work. Based on the standardisation of neighbourhoods, real estate agencies and developers could profit vastly by engaging in "block busting": supporting the move of one or two black families into a neighbourhood, to then scare white families with the associated prospect of decline in their property values—underwritten as certainly as a federal loan by the federal government's mortgage lending policies—and eventually allowing

22 See Thomas Shapiro, Tatjana Meschede and Sam Osoro, 'The Roots of the Widening Racial Wealth Gap: Explaining the Black–White Economic Divide', Brandeis University Institute on Assets and Social Policy, February 2013. This study looked at 1,700 families over 25 years from 1984 to 2009. The Bureau of Labor Statistics reports an even greater relative gap (though smaller in absolute terms) of $110,729 vs $4,995 respectively. According to the BLS, the gap between black and white families nearly doubled from 2008 to 2010 because black, latino, and asian family wealth dropped collectively by 60%, while white wealth 'only' dropped by 23%.

them to cash in, as white families sold cheap and black families bought dear. In the longer term, this allowed them to also devalorise the land and buildings in a neighbourhood for eventual redevelopment, complete with government subsidies for slum clearance. Since the 1980s the formation of development zones, and the ensuing tax breaks to developers, have allowed the suburbanised gentrification of large sections of central cities.[23]

23 See, among others, Setha Low, 'How Private Interests Take Over Public Space', and Cindi Katz, 'Power, Space, and Terror', in *The Politics of Public Space* (Routledge, 2006); also Kenneth T. Jackson, *Crabgrass Frontier* (Oxford University Press, 1985).

New housing increasingly tends towards the single family residence, as public housing projects, long suffering from systematic neglect, are torn down. Where multi-unit dwellings go up, they are frequently for the well-off. The poorest populations are driven out of the city centres in a less overt but no less systematic work of "negro removal", though this is increasingly also extended to the poorest whites and latinos. Recent examples include the gentrification of lower Harlem in New York City, and the tearing down of Cabrini Green and other projects near Chicago's downtown, to be systematically replaced with single family residences, duplex condominiums, and luxury residential skyscrapers.

Spatial deconcentration goes hand-in-hand with the post-WWII expansion of consumption for a large part of the working class; the introduction of the machinery of one-way communication from capital and the state to the population; the mechanisation of household labour; the individualisation of means of transport over large distances via the automobile. Marginal cities, lacking the developed infrastructures and social services required both for industry and to accommodate a self-sustaining and often oppositional working class culture, with its own institutions and self-identity, are the fallow fields upon which the suburb city is constructed. Here we have the creation, in what appears as a kind of "all at once" rush, of the radio and TV audience, the model housewife, the commuter, and the suburban homeowner. The suburb proper, having no autonomy of its own, derives its model from the city. Just as the pre-WWII suburb was a mini-city, so the post-WWII suburb is a miniature Los Angeles.

There is also the loss — or failure to keep up the repair — of public amenities, from sidewalks to public parks, including both programmes and facilities. In the case of global metropoles like New York, or in cities such as Chicago which have similar status, the care of public facilities is partially or even wholly privatised, meaning that the majority of resources go to the facilities that most immediately serve local elites. In other cases, such facilities are annexed by gated or otherwise restricted communities, and thus effectively privatised insofar as they become inaccessible to non-residents of those subdivisions. In places such as Detroit and Baltimore, the dismemberment of the city takes place on such a scale that it is often cheaper to abandon housing than to attempt to sell it. Thus whole areas are in a sense reclaimed by nature, as weeds, grass and trees grow up and over the rusting cars, the crumbling buildings and empty lots strewn with garbage.

In the former industrial cities we of course also find industrial ruins: abandoned factories and steel mills; areas where the land has been rendered unusable by years of industrial waste; large production facilities and warehouses which may or may not become the "artists' lofts" of some lucky developer. Facilities which employed hundreds, thousands or even tens of thousands lie dormant, with little prospect of being put back into profitable use, even if from a technical point of view they remain completely functional.[24] As much as the transformation of housing, retail, and public space, the change in the space of production marks a significant departure from the past.

24 Sparrows Point steel mill in Baltimore is a case in point. The plant itself was until recently considered to have one of the best steel producing continuous caster units left in the US, but for lack of ability to produce steel as cheaply as in Brazil or Russia, the mill has been scrapped, its parts having been auctioned. See Jamie Smith Hopkins, 'With blast furnace down, Sparrows Point layoffs begin', *Baltimore Sun*, 8 June 2012 and 'Sparrows Point auction brings hundreds to buy mill's pieces', *Baltimore Sun*, 23 January 2013.

Through these developments, the city ceases to have many of the distinctive features which once demarcated it from the suburban and rural worlds. Relentless privatisation and policies of separation and demarcation undermine what remaining public space might be contested. Parks are replaced with fee-charging places like "Discovery Zone" or "Chuck E. Cheese's". What is allowed in public spaces is curtailed, "zoned" for certain activities while others are ruled out. Sidewalk space in "commercial areas" is restricted, as for example in Chicago where no more than three people at a time are allowed to gather in certain districts, in the name of stopping loitering by gangs — a law which of course is only systematically applied to youth, and especially of colour, as opposed to groups of drunken, but spending, yuppies.[25]

25 Rick Hepp, 'Police Enforcing New Anti-Loitering Law', *Chicago Tribune*, 22 Aug 2000.

While, in the US, the state played a central role in implementing housing policies that favoured a racially segregated suburbanisation, globally it was increasingly the provider of services that were not profitable for private enterprises, but which were necessary to mollify populations that had been in near-constant upheaval before WWII. The state was often forced into partially rationalising unequal social relations in the face of movements making demands for the extension of citizenship and the use of law to remedy *de jure* and *de facto* inequality. State programmes for nationalising healthcare, education, and public housing were the result.

The struggles of the labour movement which had engendered the partial incorporation of labour into citizenship were followed by the increasing demand for equalisation in other areas of life, which themselves took the forms of struggles within the labour movement and its organisations. This often lead to a fragmentation of working class culture along lines of race, gender, sexuality, registering fault lines which had been suppressed by a politics of working class identity.

However, as these struggles receded, their demands were partially incorporated. It became increasingly necessary for women to join the workforce full time in order to sustain household income levels. Meanwhile, non-wage benefits were increasingly privatised—which is to say, commodified—in the shift from social security and pensions to 401(k) retirement plans[26]; the replacement of direct wages with employee stock options; in increasing wage deductions for medical benefits; growing dependence on home ownership-based equity for loans and to maintain a certain credit rating. This last aspect has advanced to the point where many employers now check a potential employee's credit rating before hiring them—something which systematically, if unintentionally, discriminates against minorities, given their widespread exclusion from homeownership.

26 401(k) plans: an employer-contribution form of pension saving in the US that was introduced in the late 1970s to give tax breaks on deferred income.

As the crisis of urbanism has progressed, so too has the privatisation of spaces and services, as the socialisation of the fulfilment of needs once codified and executed through the extension of the powers of the state—or as Gaspar Tamás has described it, "the Enlightenment tendency to assimilate citizenship to the human condition"—is systematically rolled back. Homogenisation and privatisation—always part and parcel of capital's logic—have taken on a hitherto unprecedented scope in the face of the transformations looked at above. This cannot be separated from the simultaneously increasing material inequality and absolute material impoverishment both in the developed countries and in those places pushed outside the global circuits of legal accumulation. These tendencies represent a consistent undermining of any kind of progressive universality of the kind that was central to the notion of socialism in the workers' movement of the 19th and early 20th century.

If the ruined city is the first, negative product of the crisis of urbanism, this ruin has its photo negative in the suburban or sprawl city. The transformation of the urban world into sprawl cities had two distinct moments: on the one hand the creation of new cities along lines laid out by Los Angeles and the post-WWII suburb, and the transformation of *some* former industrial cities into sprawl or suburban cities; on the other the mere hollowing out of cities that could not be profitably transformed.

The typical sprawl city escaped the fate of the industrial city precisely because it was marginal, in a less industrially developed region, and so did not present the same institutionalised, structural resistance to the rationalisation of capitalist accumulation and urbanism. A lack of collective working class identity entailed a lack of opposition to the new technologies and labour processes. Provincialism and isolation thus proved assets. They were also something promoted by the new methods of de-concentration — indeed, their very rationality. For capital's part it was often simply easier to start again somewhere else than to try reforming the industrial city.

This goes a significant way to explaining why urban population decline in the United States — but also in many other countries; China comes to mind — has occurred largely in former industrial cities, while growth is almost entirely confined to suburb cities. Industry in these places is often very high tech, utilising small amounts of unskilled labour generally at very low wages, while what labour is employed intensively — such as in the many forms of engineering — is highly skilled and amounts to few jobs. Much of the workforce provides services to the core of highly paid, highly skilled workers and managers. What sprawl cities have in common with the moribund industrial city and the suburb is a lack of collectivity. Like them, these are places of atomised individuals, moving from work to home to the shops.

How then should we interpret the shift of some of the population back to the inner areas of New York City,

London or Tokyo? What about the apparent prospering of some older cities like San Francisco and Chicago, which have in some ways resembled industrial cities? Here we need to make some distinctions about the development of cities globally, even if we risk making overgeneralisations. New York, Tokyo and London have always been great financial-cosmopolitan centres of capital. Through them flow the vast rivers of money-capital, and it is thus no accident that these places are strongly identified with their exchanges or financial districts, whether Wall Street, the Nikkei or the City. As such, they have also tended to be centres of high bourgeois culture. This is utterly unlike the industrial cities, which were if anything animated culturally by the working class, since the upper classes in these places, and the political class in particular, were not only often at odds, but quite ignorant and immersed in *realpolitik* rather than any kind of deep cultural life. The cosmopolitan centres too may ultimately be transformed further by their central role in the circulation of capital—hollowed out as bourgeois society becomes ever more senile—but they also generally do not cease to be global poles of attraction, and as places seemingly made entirely of money they provide ground for all manner of adventures and ideas.

Cities like Chicago and San Francisco really throw into relief the combined and uneven character of capitalist development. Chicago was certainly part industrial city, but it has also long been a financial centre. As such, its course and its condition reflect this duality. San Francisco is not atypical of coastal cities that were major places for shipping and trade. Insofar as shipping remains a vastly important part of the global economy, port cities can sometimes retain some degree of centrality, or preserve stature while shifting to other focuses. But with containerisation, of course, many such places have died a death, as business is transferred to a deep-water dock elsewhere. Although San Francisco's own role as a port city declined dramatically — 134 other US ports now handle more traffic — the Bay Area as a whole remains massively important, and this has continuing implications for the San Francisco economy. The key to the city's fortunes is, however, its proximity to the suburban areas that became central to the microelectronics industry, namely Silicon Valley. What is most distressing about San Francisco is the degree to which it has become a bedroom community for the Silicon Valley set. A larger discussion of this is not possible here, but the city has increasingly become not where so many people spend their days, but only where they return, after 12-14 hour days, to consume and sleep. San Francisco, for all of its historic association with radical politics in the United States — as capital of the "Left Coast" — is now one of the most expensive places to live in the whole of North America; a place that, like New York, has precious little space left for the kind of milieus on which it built its reputation.

What has to be recognised here is that the apparent opposition of city and suburb, which existed in the post-WWII period, has been fundamentally undermined. The crisis of mechanical industrial urbanism, out of which the suburb and the suburban city arose while simultaneously dismantling the industrial-era city, has passed. Debord again registered this period clearly:

> The country demonstrates just the opposite fact — "isolation and separation" (*The German Ideology*). As it destroys the cities, urbanism institutes a pseudo-countryside devoid not only of the natural relationships of the country of former times but also of the direct (and directly contested) relationships of the historical cities. The forms of habitation and the spectacular control of today's "planned environment" have created a new, artificial peasantry. The geographic dispersal and narrow-mindedness that always prevented the peasantry from undertaking

independent action and becoming a creative historical force are equally characteristic of these modern producers, for whom the movement of a world of their own making is every bit as inaccessible as were the natural rhythms of work for an earlier agrarian society. The traditional peasantry was the unshakeable basis of "Oriental despotism", and its very scatteredness called forth bureaucratic centralisation; the new peasantry that has emerged as the product of the growth of modern state bureaucracy differs from the old in that its apathy has had to be historically manufactured and maintained: natural ignorance has given way to the organised spectacle of error. The "new towns" of the technological pseudo-peasantry are the clearest of indications, inscribed on the land, of the break with historical time on which they are founded; their motto might well be: "On this spot nothing will ever happen—and nothing ever has." Quite obviously, it is precisely because the liberation of history, which must take place in the cities, has not yet occurred, that the forces of historical absence have set about designing their own exclusive landscape there.[27]

27 Debord, *Society of the Spectacle*, p. 126.

Whereas Debord ends in the affirmation of the overcoming of the city and urbanism by the subordination of the environment to the needs of the workers' councils, what has in fact happened is the end of the conditions upon which councilism could exist. What can be decried in the structure of the sprawl suburb comes to redefine the city in nearly equal measure.

GATED COMMUNITIES AND THE END OF THE WORKING CLASS AS AN ESTATE

The individualistic, privatised resolution of the housing question in ex-urban deconcentration not only has objective effects, such as the re-segregation of America, it is part of the restructuring of the experience of the class relation. To understand this shift, it is necessary to grasp the role private home ownership plays in the US as a replacement for the types of benefits that are in many other places provided through social programmes and the state. There is a reason why neoliberal endeavours to annihilate the social democratic elements of the state, in favour of private solutions, often get their impetus from America. A private homeowner benefits in at least six ways that mask their reliance on the state:

1 The state provides a huge tax write-off, giving back significant income. With the end of the heavily graduated income tax in the late 1970s, more people were taxed at lower income levels than in the 1930s, 40s or 50s, and so the tax refund on the mortgage became even more important.

2 Given the low rates of interest and tax subsidies, mortgage outgoings can be far less than rent for an equivalently-sized home. This depends on relatively low property taxes, however, which in the suburbs are the single most important source of revenue for services provided by the town/city, such as police, fire, roads, and schools. The other major source of income comes from taxation on industrial and commercial properties, which are key to keeping property taxes low for homeowners.

3 A house acts as equity, improving the owner's credit rating, and thus allowing them to borrow considerably more for considerably lower rates of interest. For most families in the bottom 80% of the population, the house is by far the single most valuable item they own, and generally the only one they can use as a significant source of collateral.

4 A house acts as a form of inter-generational wealth transfer and income security.

5 The value of the house can be expected to increase in value over time. Thus the asset becomes a means of increasing one's wealth.

6 The combination of increasing value and equity also becomes a means of making it possible for one's children to go to university and escape the orbit of working class labour.

These six aspects of home ownership were, as we've seen, racialised by the housing policies of the FHA and HUD.[28] Since these policies meant that black families purchasing a home in a community would automatically devalue property, in the rare cases where they could qualify for housing assistance and loan support, home ownership went hand-in-hand with the desire for racial isolation and against integration. This racialisation of housing, equity, and property values, especially after the end of *de jure* segregation in the South in 1964 and 1965, meant that the threat of integrated housing became one of the most important factors in the right-wing shift of white workers to the Republican Party in the 1968, 1972, and 1976 elections.[29] White *renters*, on the other hand, were statistically much less opposed to integration/desegregation, in housing and in education, both before 1964 and after 1968.

Home ownership along these lines thus has a close relationship to political conservatism, but it is not necessary to stretch one's imagination very far to understand the further transformation of experience that home ownership entails. Here I will briefly list some key points:

- Hostility to any policies which might lower housing values. This includes not only the aforementioned racism, but also hostility to public housing and subsidised apartment programmes which do not lead to home ownership, as these tend to lower values by introducing lower-income families with worse credit ratings.

28 FHA: Federal Housing Administration; HUD: Department of Housing and Urban development.

29 See Richard Aviles, 'Racial Threat Revisited: Race, Home Ownership, and White Working Class Politics in the US, 1964–1976', 2009, draft paper available online.

- Hostility to anything which might increase the tax burden, including property taxes. This includes providing for services which would be available to everyone in a community, and not merely homeowners. The current push among the Tea Party-type populists to privatise education and fire departments provides a particularly nasty example.

- Hostility to anything threatening the privilege of huge tax breaks for home ownership. Renting is in effect penalised several times over, and homeowners have a vested interest in not being reduced to renters again.

What is at issue is not merely the title to the property itself, but the ability of the home to act according to the six characteristics outlined above. Of central importance here is also the degree to which home ownership has effectively functioned in the US as a partial form of compensation for the lack of a social safety net. While it may not have the absolute highest homeownership rates, the United States does have the highest inequality of any industrialised nation. More than any other developed country, it depends on a high level of private debt, based on equity derived from the home and better access to additional credit sources like credit cards. Such debt has of course grown massively since the early 1970s, effectively plugging a gap left not just by stagnating real wages, but also by the meagre "social wage". In the 2000s the securitisation of household debt both enabled its further expansion and articulated it with global financial flows as foreign banks bought up dollar-backed securities. The capacity for the American economy to support enormous levels of private debt itself depends upon the preservation of the dollar's value, which is effectively underwritten by the catastrophic effects that any devaluation of the dollar — as world money — would have on the global economy.

The increased home ownership extends the private into the public, and in turn transforms the public into a private affair, reducing public engagement into NIMBY (Not In My Backyard) politics. It is no accident that suburbanisation should give rise to a politics of re-privatisation. The overcoming of communal and collective existence was materialised in the post-WWII technologies of urbanism, especially the creation of the experience in one's private space of what previously had to be experienced publicly. The home was no longer simply a place to eat and sleep, but a self-sustaining microcosm in which the outside world only entered via electronic media such as radio, television and eventually the computer. The home became a refuge. At the same time, the yard provided a fenced-off replacement for parks and playgrounds and other public facilities in which nature might be experienced collectively.

Post-war mass consumer urbanism also held out the promise of homogeneity. As we've seen, the very structure of the post-war suburb depended on developers creating large areas with relatively similar incomes, and for a long time it was legally required that the community be racially homogeneous. Single women were also blocked from access by social conventions and credit ratings based on gender. Suburbanisation involved a flight from people "not like us", which was to say away from different races, creeds, ethnic groups, and so on. The tendency towards homogeneity and conformity means that suburbanisation has a logic of experience unlike that of the city. Therein lies a fundamental problem for the suburban city. The very extension of this homogenisation — privatisation of space and services; private management and even funding of parks and schools which are nominally public — butts up against the very structure of the city.

Homogeneity is also viewed as a source of safety. The absence of obvious class differences in a community where one leaves one's work somewhere else, where work and non-work life are cordoned off; the absence of "the lower classes" or "the poor"—or what is in fact the absence of those without sufficient access to *credit*—tends to result in reduced crime. The city is increasingly policed to keep people in their neighbourhoods, while suburbs are policed to keep people out. Profiling is exceptionally effective in suburbs due to their propensity for homogeneity. Being of a different race, driving a rusted old car, and walking on foot are all equally tell-tale signs of exclusion, of being Other. The gated community is merely the most obvious, overt expression of this tendency.

Thus the world outside the suburb is already prefigured and experienced as threatening, dangerous and especially as criminal: people from the cities want what those in the suburbs have, but living in the cities they cannot, by definition, have it, so they can only steal or achieve it by a degree of undeserved privilege. When George Bush Jr. announced that terrorists hate us for our freedom, he did no more than rearticulate the common sense of the suburban experience towards the dangerous masses of the cities as the national experience of the US in relation to the "dark masses" of the non-Euro-American.

The hostility to intellectual and cultural maturation as bourgeois, as elitist, is the reaction of the hillbilly and the slave master to modernisation. Anyone who has the temerity to suggest that their provincial utopia is not *as good as it gets* is a snob. While provincialisation cannot be reduced to suburbanisation and sprawl, it reinforces it. At the same time, intellectual language is transformed into that of the administrative side of society. Those who feel outside of, or unfairly constrained by, the managerial logic of liberalism thus find their inclination towards tribalism, insularity and corporatism reinforced. Suburbanisation magnifies and intensifies the experience of this alienation from the liberal administrative consciousness, even as it exists completely in dependence on state subsidy, and especially on the militaristic and overtly oppressive sections of the state.

Suburbanisation also promotes infantilisation and feminisation. By "feminisation", what is meant here is not a domination of some essential female values, but the extension of the root of gender relations in capitalist society, the separation of home and work. Suburbanisation extends this division by putting work in one place — maybe even a completely different suburb or in the city — so that one no longer lives where one works, and the social orientation of both men and women in suburbia becomes the home. Where work traditionally also meant that the worker who brought home the income also participated in public activities — whether carousing in bars or union activities or social clubs — non-work life is increasingly oriented towards housework: mowing the lawn, gardening, fixing up the house, working on the car in the garage.

The fetish of sports as both a communal voyeurism and a social imperative goes hand-in-hand with the loss of other collective referents and the process of identification with a brand and a tribe. American football is the most watched sport, asserting violent masculinity against cheerleader and "beer babe" femininity, and tribal collectivity. On the other hand there is the overwhelming popularity of golf, which is the actually-played sport of choice because it requires little physicality, is very individualistic and is associated with social status — both because it is expensive to play and takes place in another manufactured, pseudo-natural but utterly tame space. The dynamics that infantilise adults also promote an exaggerated focus on children. Public life ends up in many cases being about taking the kids to their "activities". The original excuse to move to the suburbs is often "for the schools" and to have a "healthy environment" in which to raise children. The latter become another kind of Big Other, a super-egoic compulsion to suburbanise. It is no accident that both parents and children resent each other in such situations.

POLITICAL AND LEGAL INTEGRATION AS THE CRISIS OF THE POLITICAL

Revanchist politics has expressed itself in many different forms over the last sixty or so years, from McCarthyism and the rise of Goldwater Republican populism, through the Taxpayers Revolt of the 1970s to Reaganism and the rise of the Christian Right. The Tea Party of today is only the latest incarnation of this political trend, encouraged by the threat to the financial conditions which made suburban and sprawl development possible. Post-WWII urbanism depended on a number of features, not least of which was a capitalist expansion linked to productivity rates outstripping income growth so that such growth could be accommodated by capital. De-industrialisation, the movement of production facilities to other countries, and other kinds of capital flight from the suburbs have contributed to increased dependence on state and federal funding, but states too have found themselves in dire straits. The political milieu of suburban revanchism seeks to relieve its problems by poaching the wealth of the cities and the tax base of the most urbanised areas.

The crisis of this urbanism is the spatial form of a crisis which in political terms Gáspár Tamás refers to as post-fascism.[30] The key features of the communalist expression of post-fascism include:[31]

- an extreme feeling of *ressentiment* towards the poor or non-creditworthy, the Other as bogeyman

30 Gáspár M. Tamás, 'On Post-Fascism', *Boston Review*, Summer 2000.

31 'Communalist' here refers to political movements such as the Tea Party, LePenism in France and the Jobbik Party in Hungary.

- *ressentiment* towards any kind of cultured or intellectually sophisticated, worldly sorts of people; feeling at home in the world—instead of simply at home—is a sign of corruption and treason

- denial of one's own dependence on state subsidies

- an orientation towards the privatisation of all social services that do not directly support private wealth

- overt identification with capital

- perpetual concern that people aren't "carrying their own weight"

- a lack of interest in non-work except for ritualistically masculine activities, a.k.a. sports

- pronounced nativism

- fear and thus hatred of anything one doesn't understand (linked to nativism, religiosity, militant heterosexuality, conformism)

At root, this amounts to the creation of a dual state where "true citizenship" goes hand-in-hand with one's credit score, race, religion, and so on. In other words, under the pressure of capital's inability to simultaneously sustain profitability and the expansion of citizenship, the spatial deconcentration and isolation of post-war urbanism lends itself to a post-fascist politics that drives towards the death of universal citizenship. Both of these phenomena are coterminous with what many refer to as neo-liberalism.

The same impoverishing influence of the goal—escaping and keeping out the Other; creating a community without conflict, sharing a common hatred and fear—does not easily translate into the city. The city simply *is* the space of Others residing alongside and amongst each other. That is not to say that some miraculously free and open public space existed before, but that what was free and open could at least be contested and fought over, while the space for such possibilities has now become systematically privatised and policed. Space in the city was always hotly contested — often violently so.

To survey some cases in Chicago, for example, 1919 alone saw white riots and the massacre of around 1,000 African Americans in events that occurred alongside and entangled with the meat packing and steel strikes. Many white workers who went on strike with black workers also participated in riots against the growing black population on the south side of the city. In 1937, in the "Little Steel Strike", Chicago workers were shot down by strike-breaking police. In 1966 racist mobs attacked a civil rights march attended by Martin Luther King Jr. in Chicago's Marquette Park with a degree of ferocity and hatred that King claimed was unmatched even in the South. In 1968, the parks were the site of massive protests against the Democratic Party at the Democratic National Convention, which was met with brutal violence by the Chicago Police Department and the National Guard. In 1990–91 more than 10,000 people marched in the streets of Chicago against the Gulf War. Police violence is of course a relative constant in this story, but what becomes more and more impossible to imagine is the open nature of the conflict and of the space itself. Where in a suburb would such mobilisations even take place?

The decline and marginalisation of the industrial city — its transformation into a site of ruins where what blossoms does so only where the green of finance and pockets of the microelectronic, software, and bio-chemical industries sow the land — is the decline of a kind of self-sustaining working class culture. These cities typically collapse into ghettos stripped of social life. What predominate are larger or smaller interpersonal networks, familial and private relations into which one can only enter by invitation. This is the complete opposite of the union, the working class political party, the self-help organisation, the community cooperative, and so on. In place of overtly political newspapers—whether from the Socialist or Communist Party or the Chicago Defender or Pittsburgh Courier—we have the overwhelming weight of the corporate media, and now even the dissolution of the journalistic, print-oriented segment of that into infotainment and the isolated blogger. Public institutions are replaced with commodified services. The state, which Marx once called "the illusory community", is seemingly no longer even contested as the community. If one wants to start a programme, say, to help "the youth of the city", it is necessary either to address oneself to the state—that is, to the schools or to state-run park districts—or to start one's own organisation and find funding. In the latter case one must either create a business oneself, become indebted to private business support, or rely on funding from the state. The rich and relatively independent institutional life that the working class had to maintain at the stage when it lacked social and economic integration first becomes unnecessary and then becomes unrecoverable.

The loss of universalising alternatives to capitalism as negations of class—and in a different manner, of race, gender, sexuality, and so on—does not mean an end to attempts at forms of collective organisation. Communitarian modes of accommodation take the place of universalising alternatives. Capitalism does not merely replace overt social relations with production relations as the determinate social relations; it subordinates them without necessarily doing away with them. Thus race, gender, sexuality, religion, nation, region, and so on, which seem to group people in various ways, in ways that allow them to associate for perceived mutual advantage — remain not only potent, but actually become more powerful. In a society of antagonistic, competitive relations between individuals with unequal power relations, such groupings are common.

Progressive social movements tended to associate citizenship with the right to a certain quality of life, and typically they worked to extend its domain to broader layers of the population. Communitarian modes operate in the exact opposite way, attempting to restrict the full extension of citizenship — and since the 1920s, they have sought to actively destroy the links established between citizenship and the right to a certain standard of living. Communitarian modes seek to create a homogeneous community and to pursue its interests; indeed the community is actually constituted in the pursuit of these interests, in the same way that the suburb is created by the flight to a space of homogeneity, away from what one imagines oneself not to be. While these tendencies supply the blueprints of fascism in the first half of the 20th century, and of post-fascist revanchist politics since the 1950s, religion is of course especially suited to such developments, predicated as it is on a community of believers contrasted to the unbelievers who are condemned to some manner of damnation in this world or the next. It should not surprise us then that in the enforced homogeneity of the suburbanist world, in the absence of a liberatory universalistic alternative, reactionary populism should so often find itself in religious garb, not only distinguishing between the deserving and the undeserving, but allowing the saved to locate the damned. We could say further — though this point cannot be developed here — that insofar as capitalism entails an indirect, abstract social relation which does not directly appear as a social relation, and thus seems also to lack meaning, the pressure for direct, concrete, and meaningful social relations takes on a new force. Finally, the religious institutions — which have no particular opposition to capital's domination of a world of sin or karma — take the place of other non-state institutions, able to provide services and even jobs and livelihoods, but supposedly in the name of the affirmation of the community of believers, without the indifference of the pure market relation of employee and employer.

The current constellation thus gives rise to a political crisis, but in the form of a crisis of the political as such. Jacques Rancière presents this crisis as an attack on democracy.[32] By this he does not mean an attack on the state or its functions, but on politics as the bringing of conflicts and antagonisms into the public sphere, and on democracy as the sovereignty of anyone and everyone — or rather a sovereignty that cannot be legitimised *a priori*. This attack entails the privatisation of key aspects of life and, in what remains, the increasing scope of both the police function and the role of the specialist with particular competencies. The crisis of the political takes a similar form to that of the labour process: politics is reduced to the scientific administration of affairs by the state, within limits set by the market. All public collective challenges to domination become excessive, and political struggle becomes an oxymoron.

Liberalism tends towards the side of scientific reason, tolerance of difference, multiculturalism, and rational administration, wanting the state to make politics a matter of management and civility. It involves a secular de-politicisation of social contradiction and antagonism, making of these a province of the state and of experts. Reactionary populism favours explicitly anti-political lines of power such as kinship, religion, and the market, using the state to turn these into matters of personal responsibility, to individualise them. This marks a flight from the public field, the field of politics proper, to that of the private — in both senses of this word — whether as the technocratic domain of rational administrators and specialists or the management of the property of

32 Jacques Rancière, *Hatred of Democracy* (Verso 2006)

individuals or non-governmental institutions. This is also the extension of the police function, of the rule of merit, kinship, wealth. What is sought is obedience to an authority which is objective and therefore beyond reproach or contestation, whether the technical dictates of science, the market or God. For Rancière, since democratic politics is just contestation taking place openly and collectively, as public matters, democratic struggle is the struggle to widen the public sphere, to politicise what is private, and to do so without preconditions for participation.

Though Rancière hypostatises the separation of public and private, democracy and oligarchy, turning these into eternal categories of the human condition, he goes right to the heart of the problem. But he does so only to turn away at the last moment. The savage condition of life at present — unable to stand the thought of politics, and thus suppressing or striking out madly at it — is one where the growing contradiction between the immense capacity to produce material wealth with a minimum of direct human labour on the one hand, and the social form of wealth as capital, as self-expanding value, on the other, is sustained only by denying the possibility of the re-purposing of this capacity for common human ends. The struggle to politicise current conditions — to fight for the problems of crime, violence, poverty, hunger and so on to be expressed as political problems and not as matters of personal responsibility or technical expertise — quickly runs up against the recognition that such a politicisation immediately calls into question the rationality of capital. No doubt this is why any attempt to apply the brakes on runaway inequality or provide free public services is automatically attacked by reactionary populists as socialism or communism, while massive expenditures on the military, police and the repressive apparatus in general — and any associated restrictions on freedom of expression, communication, and assembly — are viewed as protecting democracy.

Consider the recent fight over healthcare in the United States in light of our above analysis. Nowhere is the issue a lack of material ability to provide adequate care. Neither the liberal nor the reactionary side have argued that we lack doctors, technology, the ability to train more people, or the ability to produce adequate medical supplies. The issue is solely the apparent scarcity of money. One side argues that state regulation, if not nationalisation, would regulate care more efficiently so as to reduce costs. The other believes that any human control over market forces is tantamount to questioning the hand of God, and that it will automatically result in greater cost and less efficiency. For neither side is the issue of care itself primary.

LIMITATIONS AND POTENTIAL SUBVERSION

What then are we to do with this? If the city has been largely hollowed out along the lines of the post-WWII suburb; if hollowed city and suburb together give the environmental shape of the current state of capitalist development, in which a workerist class politics has been eviscerated; if this is an era in which identity politics seems to have run its course and largely lost its progressive, not to mention radical, force; nonetheless this need not mean that the city as a site of struggle is dead. The city remains the geographical site of capital's contradictions, because capital, for all its tendency to produce homogeneity, cannot sustain itself except through the constant production of heterogeneity. If Shenzhen is a labour camp, it is one with 10 million people in close quarters capable of disrupting a significant part of global production. If the fastest growing cities in the United States are all sprawl cities, with all that implies, they are nonetheless not suburbs, but complex, relatively dense spaces built upon a potentially explosive combination: dependent on US dominance and the dollar as world money, and on the immense debt-to-income ratio of their inhabitants.

There is no certainty that these places will not succumb to the kind of reactionary populism that has grown exponentially since the 1970s. Despite this, even in the moribund ex-industrial and the suburb cities we find a large portion of the population that is opposed to racist, xenophobic, and misogynist policies. It is probably not accidental that Occupy and the Arab Spring, for all their failings, were overwhelmingly urban phenomena while reactionary populisms like the Tea Party, the Jobbik Party and the National Front in France are overwhelmingly present in suburban and rural areas.

The dispossessed populations of cities — which capital seems to have made permanently superfluous from the point of view of valorisation — often find themselves drawn to the populist and self-help messages of reactionary communitarian populisms and religious groupings, from ethnicised militias to Islamist, Hindu or Christian "fundamentalist" political groupings. It is often the dislocation suffered by being made superfluous and having to survive through "black market" activities — many of which are predatory upon the waged and unwaged alike — which leaves the religious and communitarian groups as the only cohesive social institutions.

If the overcoming of capital is no longer the seizure of the existing means of production by a working class that exists as an estate in a struggle against material poverty and a lack of political and social inclusion, this does not mean the end of the need to overthrow capital. The present situation is clearly unsustainable. The conditions which allowed for the overcoming of the working class as estate, and of what seemed like an inescapable material impoverishment, are predicated upon social relations which cannot maintain inclusion and relative freedom from want. From the side of capital accumulation this cannot be sustained.

In terms of the labour process and therefore the valorisation process, capitalism has survived on an already immense and growing debt on the sides of both capital and labour. We are in the midst of an ongoing crisis of valorisation, because the amount of titles and claims to value, paper money and financial instruments, circulating daily on a global basis, are in the trillions — far beyond the current capacity of capital to valorise. The future is leveraged a long, long way forward. The level of valorisation necessary to solve this problem is unlikely to materialise, since it would require that capital no longer supplant living labour with constant capital — that is, capital would have to find another dynamic altogether. In fact, probably the only imaginable alternative is a catastrophic destruction of existing values — including labour power — on a hitherto unimagined scale.

In terms of material impoverishment, the part of the working class which saw the greatest growth of income and relative prosperity has also seen its debt load rise dramatically. In the United States, average household debt is over 100% of after-tax disposable income, very much connected to rising housing prices, but also to stagnant wages and the reduction of state subsidies for basic social services, such as education and health services. Even more painfully, a larger and larger part of the global population seems to be excluded from formal access to the wage. Over 1 billion people essentially live in a money economy with little hope of access to wage labour in a legal industry, and thus with only tenuous sources of monetary income. Capital is abolishing money, not in the sense of some post-modern "virtuality", but in the very practical, commonplace sense of denying people access to secure wage labour and to the kind of small property that might allow self-employment or sustenance. Material impoverishment is not only returning with a vengeance, but the working class as mass consumer becomes unsustainable the more living labour itself is abolished by capital.

Finally, it is becoming clearer and clearer that capitalism cannot afford the political and legal inclusion of labour. This is not to anticipate a return to the working class as estate, for the material foundation in the circuit of capital upon which that was possible — that is, a certain configuration of the labour process — has gone.

It is important to recognise what has changed. If we have lost the coordinates of the world of the industrial working class, we nonetheless have not seen the overcoming of the contradictions of capital. The very changes to the capitalist labour process which destroyed the old forms of self-activity and the capacity to recognise oneself as part of a coherent working class, seem to be bringing about a crisis in which capital is coming perilously close to abolishing labour in much of the production process — even as it cannot do away with it as foundation of the value form. This contradiction is expressed not only in a tremendous productive capacity that requires relatively little living labour and thus produces crises of valorisation, but also in the forms of spatial organisation. More than ever it seems at least technically evident that we could achieve new forms of spatial organisation that would utilise cleaner power sources, increase population density while decreasing ecological footprints, immediately reduce the hours of human labour, and increase the amount of time available to be lived outside of work. What is perplexing is that while each of these can be imagined apart — and all can be reckoned as rational and feasible — today there seems to be no generalised sense that their combined realisation in a world without capitalism is possible.

AN IDENTICAL ABJECT-SUBJECT?

In *Endnotes 2*, we presented an account of capital's immanent tendency towards crisis that revolved around a theory of surplus population. What follows is an attempt to refine, clarify and develop the central categories of that theory.[1] Our motivation to do so derives from certain misapprehensions we've encountered, which seem to betray a general tendency to directly map the category of "surplus population" onto a singular, coherent social subject or sociological group, with the potential implication that this group is to be viewed as a new kind of revolutionary agent. Far from representing the emergence of a coherent agent, the expansion of the surplus population marks the tendential disappearance of the previous revolutionary horizon.

It was once possible—indeed quite reasonable—to think of the proletariat as an emergent social subject, becoming ever larger and more unified with the global spread and development of the capitalist mode of production, and particularly with the incorporation of a growing portion of the class into industrial employment. Today, in an era of slowing economic growth—which is also an era of general deindustrialisation—the revolutionary orientations of the past no longer make sense. The working class—always internally differentiated—displays a diminishing capacity for unification under a single hegemonic figure, thus realising its always latent tendency to decompose into fragments, facing off one against the other.

At the heart of this fractiousness is the division of the class into two parts: (1) a shrinking one that retains higher wages and social protections, but must constantly fight rearguard actions against capitalist "reforms" and restructurings; and (2) a growing one that faces poor prospects of employment and is offered few social protections.[2] The more secure sector—which is also more organised—often needs the support of the more precarious in order to win its struggles. However,

1 This article is based on a talk given in Berlin in early 2014. Arguments in sections 2 and 3 draw on Aaron Benanav, *A Global History of Unemployment*, forthcoming from Verso.

2 While, in the low-income countries, this second sector is in fact the overwhelming majority, similar divisions and conflicts of interest are also in evidence.

calls for greater "inclusion" of such people may stoke valid fears that this will undermine more secure positions, opening up access to education and training, and thereby increasing labour supply and reducing bargaining power.[3] At the same time, members of the more precarious part may be rightly suspicious of the motives of the more secure: after the sacrifices have been made, won't it be merely the latter's rearguard battles that have been won? After all, those with security rarely take to the streets when it is the less fortunate who are getting screwed. The expansion of the surplus population is important in explaining this division, but it is not the only meaningful one within the class.

There is a potentially infinite variety of such distinctions, so the question of explaining current divisions can in a sense be reversed: What was the unity that is now in advanced stages of decay? How did it come about? This is a question that we have attempted to answer elsewhere in this issue, in 'A History of Separation'. For our purposes here though, it is enough to note simply that there was once a hegemonic identity and orientation among workers that could provide grounds for affirming certain struggles as central, while excluding others as secondary or unimportant. It is equally clear that this affirmation seems less and less plausible today. In place of the identity of the worker, we are now faced with so many competing alternatives, each with its own strategic priorities: those who want more jobs against those who want to stave off environmental catastrophe; those who want to preserve the family wage for unionised male workers against those who want gender equality; those of dominant national or racial identities against those of racialised minorities, and so on.

In this sense, the fractiousness of "identity politics" is symptomatic of an era. In a period of increasingly slow economic growth under the threat of ecological catastrophe, it seems diminishingly plausible to claim

3 Partly for that reason, the more precarious are often rendered as undeserving in one way or another: as upstart youth, illegal immigrants, and so on. See the section on the abject, below.

that fighting the battles of one part of the class will advance the class as a whole. This is why we reject any attempt to find in surplus populations an ersatz social subject that might replace the hegemonic role played by the white male factory worker in the workers' movement. At present there seems to be no class fraction — whether "the most strategically placed" or "the most oppressed" — whose struggles express a general interest. At the same time, attempts to conjure up a new unity from this diversity by simply renaming it as "multitude" or "precariat", for example, merely gloss over this fundamental problem of internal division.

If there is any revolutionary potential at present, it seems that it stands to be actualised not in the struggle of any particular class fraction, but rather, in those moments when diverse fractions are drawn together in struggle *in spite of* their mutual suspicions; *despite* the lack of a stable, consistent hegemonic pole. In such moments, the demands of various sections of the class come into conflict with one another — a conflict that may bring the prospect of destabilising or undermining mutually exclusive demands and identities. The modes by which social life is organised and segmented within capitalist societies can then come to appear as obstacles to further struggle, dividing workers against one another. The question of how to move forward is then at least raised, though with no easy answers. After all, a definitive answer would involve an overcoming of the unity-in-separation that organises social life.

WHAT IS A SURPLUS POPULATION?

The theory of surplus population derives from arguments presented by Marx in the first volume of *Capital*, chapter 25 in particular, on the "general law of capitalist accumulation". Marx defines the surplus population as workers without regular access to work: a worker "belongs to" the surplus population "when he is only partially employed or wholly unemployed".[4] Marx refers to this surplus population as a "relative surplus population", because these workers are not absolutely surplus, as in a Malthusian account (which is to say, it is not a matter of there not being enough food, water, shelter, etc). Instead, these workers are surplus relative to the needs of capital — that is, relative to capital's demand for labour.

4 Marx, *Capital,* vol. 1 (MECW 35) pp. 634-635.

In the history of capitalist societies, large masses of people have been absorbed into the labour market and have come to depend entirely upon earning wages in order to survive. They cannot leave the labour market unless they can get other workers to support them. In other words, workers have to work regardless of what sort and how much work is available. They are at the mercy of capital's demand for labour. When that demand falls and there isn't enough work to go around, workers do not stop working altogether — unless they really have no options, in which case they become paupers. Instead, they enter one or another branch of an extensive and variegated surplus population.

Marx describes "all kinds of forms" of surplus population. Due to transformations of production, workers are constantly being churned out of old and into new industries, depending upon the shifting needs of capital. This gives rise, in Marx's account, to both "latent" and "floating" surplus populations, the latter of which Marx often called the "reserve army of labour". However, as a consequence of this ongoing development, capital also produces a super-exploited "stagnant" surplus population, when it fails to re-absorb displaced workers into new lines.

Marx thought that the problem of the surplus population — ultimately a problem of the growing oversupply of, and under-demand for, labour — would intensify over time and, as a result, people would increasingly find themselves disconnected from labour markets, and hence from regular access to the wage. Indeed, Marx describes this as the "absolute general law of capitalist accumulation". What happens is that capital's ongoing accumulation process leads to rising labour productivity, which in turn expands the "industrial reserve army", causing the "consolidated surplus population" — "whose misery is in inverse ratio to the amount of torture it has to undergo in the form of labour" — to grow, and increasing "official pauperism"; that is, those who cannot make enough in wages to survive, and so must beg for their bread.[5] The overall result is that the accumulation of wealth occurs alongside an accumulation of poverty.

5 Marx, *Capital,* vol. 1 (MECW 35), pp. 638-647.

6 See 'Misery and Debt', *Endnotes* 2, April 2010.

In Marx's account, the main reason capitalist development leads to the growth of the surplus population has to do with what we have called "technological ratcheting".[6] In essence, Marx argues that the demand for labour in each industry eventually falls as labour productivity rises. New industries do come on line, at a faster or slower pace, increasing the demand for labour. However, these new industries never start out from zero: they do not need to reinvent e.g. steam power, the assembly line, the electric motor. Instead, new lines absorb technological innovations that preceded them. As a result, the emergence of new industries is less and less effective in increasing the demand for labour. Hence capital has what Marx terms a "rising organic composition". Marx argues that it is the older lines, which have not yet been technically renewed, which tend to absorb the most labour.

This theory could be fleshed out further by developing links with Marx's notes on overaccumulation in volume 3, but that is another project. Here we simply note that, today, what renders many workers surplus to the requirements of capital is a dual tendency: on the one hand, towards overaccumulation — which reduces profit rates and hence slows the expansion of output — and on the other hand, towards the ongoing growth of labour productivity, which arises out of capitalist competition and results in a loss of jobs in those economic sectors where output does not increase at a rate equal to productivity. The combination of these factors ensures that, in an economy wracked by overaccumulation, the demand for labour will fail to keep up with its supply. That, in turn, will expand the surplus population.

In *Endnotes 2* we argued that these developments would tendentially lead to the reproduction of the proletariat becoming contingent to that of capital. If the post-war settlement had formalised the reciprocal but asymmetrical relation in which the reproduction of the working class is necessary to that of capital, with the end of that settlement and the rise in surplus populations, those who are surplus are effectively reproduced as a sort of "side-effect" of capitalist production.[7] What this means is that capitalist productivity, especially in agriculture, is increasingly capable of supporting sections of the global population far removed from the dynamic industries at the core of capitalist accumulation. But when this happens, the dual interlocking cycles of the mutual reproduction of capital and class seem to make less and less sense. As "Screamin' Alice" has argued, this leads in some senses to "disintegration" of these circuits at the same time as "integration" deepens in other respects — in the financialisation of ever new areas of life, for example.[8]

DEINDUSTRIALISATION, THEN AND NOW

In the 20th century, this idea of the tendency of capital to increasingly produce workers as surplus was largely dismissed as an "immiseration thesis", on the grounds that history had proven it wrong: the working class had clearly failed to become immiserated; on the

7 One should not treat the mutual capital–labour reproduction as if it captured a singular social 'system', valid at the level of each and every nation-state; the basic frame of analysis for such matters is necessarily global. But nor, of course, can we think in terms of an undifferentiated global level: individual national economies must be grasped *differentially* within a global frame. The post-war settlement was thus, of course, not some uniform global arrangement: it applied particularly to the Western industrialised countries, while some analogous arrangements may be perceived in Eastern Bloc countries (and, indeed, the pressure for such a settlement was partly given by the geopolitical polarisation between the two). But insofar as those places in which it applied

contrary, living standards had risen. Industrial employment had grown dramatically, suggesting that the industrial working class would eventually account for the vast majority of the workforce. While Marx appears to have been broadly correct in interpreting mid-19th century tendencies (which limited the growth of the demand for labour in industry), he did not foresee the emergence of new lines of production that would prove capable of absorbing the surpluses of capital and labour that were being produced elsewhere in the economy. These industries — such as the auto and white goods industries — lay at the very core of 20th century capitalist development and industrial employment. The semi-skilled factory worker was the key figure in the old labour movement. But in *Endnotes 2* we posed the question: What if Marx had just been wrong on the timing?

It is now clear that those twentieth century industries have long been in relative decline as employers. Newer industries, although they have emerged, have not absorbed all of the labour being shed from elsewhere. As a result, deindustrialisation has been ongoing since the mid 1970s across the high-income countries. But even newly industrialised countries like South Korea, Taiwan, Brazil, Mexico, South Africa and Egypt have seen the industrial shares of total employment in their economies stagnate or decline since the mid 1980s or mid 1990s. China seems to be an exception to the rule, but even there, construction constitutes a large component of the new "industrial" labour force, and the Chinese manufacturing share of employment actually remained stagnant — at between 14 and 16 percent of the labour force — during the period of rapid growth from 1980 to 2006. New industrial firms were opening up and absorbing labour, such as in the Pearl River Delta region, but this only tended to balance — not reverse — the overall effects of the closures of state-owned enterprises, and the laying off of workers in

represented the bulk of the industrialised world, it is reasonable to think of this 'settlement' as characterising the general nature of capitalist class relations in that epoch. The essential nature of this settlement was that the state would regulate the reproduction of the working class on whom capital depended, since individual capitalists – necessarily relating to that reproduction as an externality – were incapable of looking after it themselves.

8 Screamin' Alice, 'On the Periodisation of the Capitalist Class Relation', *SIC 1*, November 2011.

China's northeast.[9] China's manufacturing employment share only rose beyond previously achieved levels in 2006, reaching 19 percent in 2011 (the last year for which data is available). While the absolute number of people employed in industry in China is certainly staggering, the manufacturing share of employment in the new "workshop of the world" is nowhere near as high today as it was in the West during the heyday of industrialisation. In fact, the Chinese share is closer to the level that prevails in Mexico and Brazil today than to the level of Germany or the UK at mid-20th century (which hovered between 31 and 35 percent).

9 See Ching Kwan Lee, *Against the Law: Labour Struggles in China's Rustbelt and Sunbelt* (University of California 2007).

According to an old developmental narrative, agricultural employment would decline as agriculture became more productive, precipitating lots of potential new workers into towns, who would then be taken up by expanding industrial production. These developments would eventually bring every country into modernity. For orthodox Marxists, this would tendentially form a proletariat unified under the hegemony of its most "advanced" fractions in industry. But as the global peak of industrialisation recedes into history, it looks like something else is now happening. While agricultural employment has not halted its decline, those workers shed are less likely to join the ranks of the industrial working class than to enter a vast and heterogeneous service sector. At the world level, there are now twice as many workers in services as compared to industry: services account for 44 percent of global employment, while industry accounts for just 22 percent. The share employed in factories is even smaller than that 22 percent suggests, not only because it includes the labour-intensive construction sector, but also because a sizable portion of industrial employment in the low-income countries is accounted for by the petty production of informal, self-employed proletarian households.

SERVICES AND SUPERFLUITY

Many commentators will argue that the ongoing stagnation or decline in manufacturing employment, which we described above, is nothing to worry about. It is supposedly a matter of a quasi-natural evolution in consumer demand, driven by market forces. Just as agriculture comes to employ a decreasing share of the workforce, since there are limits to growth in the demand for food, so too with manufacturing: there are supposedly limits to the demand for goods (apparently, there is, however, a limitless demand for services). The result, according to this perspective, is that over time, a rising demand for services will dynamically pull workers into the service sector, just as in an earlier phase workers were pulled into the industrial sector.

In reality, the dynamic draw of manufacturing during industrialisation was unique to that sector. To manufacture something is to take a good — or to transform a service, such as dishwashing, into a good, such as a dishwasher — and to produce that good in a factory, according to ever-more efficient techniques. It is the resulting rise in the efficiency of production within the space of the factory that rapidly lowers costs of production in manufacturing lines. That leads, in turn, to a rapid fall in relative prices. Markets for manufactures expand, making possible a dramatic expansion of output. Concomitantly, huge masses of humanity are pulled into work in manufacturing lines. That is the key to the dynamic growth of manufacturing output and employment: the former is very rapid, and that is why, in spite of high rates of labour productivity growth, the latter expands, raising the manufacturing employment share.

The same does not take place in the service sector. Services are precisely the sorts of activities that cannot be — or have not yet been — substituted by goods. In services, labour productivity tends to increase slowly if at all, and concomitantly, prices follow the same trajectory. In fact, as long as real wages are rising, the relative price of services will itself tend to increase. Since relative prices do not fall dramatically, there is no impetus for markets for services to expand rapidly. Hence, there is no dynamic tendency to dramatically expand output and thus to draw lots of labour into the sector; instead, employment in the service sector expands slowly.

On this basis, it is possible to describe a major distinction between phases of industrialisation and deindustrialisation in the history of capitalist societies. During the former phase, the demand for labour in industry — not during busts, but at least during booms — was very high. That affected the entire labour market, diminishing slack, reducing the size of the surplus population and increasing workers' bargaining power. Once industrialisation went into reverse, the industrial sector became, alongside agriculture, another source of growing slack in the labour market, increasing the surplus population and reducing workers' bargaining power. All the while, the demand for labour in services has been characteristically low. It has expanded, but slowly, due to the fact that more labour is generally needed to increase service-sector output, which is itself growing slowly. The shift from industrialisation to deindustrialisation is necessarily the shift from an economy that grows rapidly, with big booms and busts, to one that grows slowly, tending towards stagnation. In such a context, booms and busts are given merely by financial bubbles being blown up and deflated around the world by surplus capital.[10]

There is a corollary to this theory, which explains why *a large portion of the surplus population ends up in the service sector*, particularly in the low-wage, super-exploited section and in the informal, self-exploiting section. As service work tends to be labour-intensive,

10 The fact that this slowdown is taking place across the world – with, of course, local exceptions – is itself proof against the theory of a simple demand-shift from industry to services.

a large proportion of the final costs are made up of wages. Because real wages do not usually fall across the economy, it is difficult for service sector firms to lower their costs on a regular basis (general tendencies towards falling costs in industry and agriculture are due to increases in the efficient use of more expensive labour). This results in a relatively low level of output growth in services. But precisely for that reason, when workers are expelled from other sectors, it is possible to get much cheaper workers into services—as those discarded as surplus will usually have to accept a lower wage level. This lowers costs and allows for some expansion in demand for, and output of, services. In the service sector, there is greater room to expand the market by lowering wages. By contrast, in most manufacturing activities, wages make up only a small portion of the final cost of the product, so there is less room for manoeuvre.

Of course, this doesn't mean that each and every specific service stands no chance of becoming a basis for dynamic growth. Many jobs which were once performed as services have been at least partially turned into manufactured commodities in the course of capitalist history, either for the individual household or for collective spaces. As mentioned above, the service of washing clothes by hand was replaced by the washing machine, in people's homes or in launderettes. The transformation of services into goods is part of industrialisation, which transforms activities, making them amenable to constant increases of productivity in what Marx called the "real subsumption of the labour process", opening up markets and allowing for long-term growth.

While it is difficult to identify a precise and determinate "logic" as to why some activities become really subsumed and others do not, the fact that certain activities require delicate work or direct human contact, and therefore must remain labour-intensive, is clearly key. There appears always to be a remainder of such activities, an assortment of differentiated tasks, mostly in services.[11] Insofar as services remain services, they tend predominantly to be a source only of "absolute", and not "relative" surplus value. This is simply another way of saying that there are limits to raising productivity. Consequently, economies that are "post-industrial" and concentrated around service work tend to be low-growth.

In such conditions, it is imperative for capitalists to get as much out of their workers as possible, by increasing the duration or intensity of labour. To some extent, the prerequisite for the existence of many jobs becomes pressurised work conditions. If super-exploited sectors take up a growing share of the labour market, this also puts downward pressure on all wages, and increases insecurity, as workers lose bargaining power and bosses are emboldened to demand ever more flexibility. With this, the door is opened for a whole range of abuses to be unleashed upon the worker — sexual, emotional and psychological, as well as the stealing or retention of wages and chronic overworking. Certain positions, such as that of the low-wage service sector worker, thus appear as a kind of special category of surplus worker, akin to the informally self-employed in low-income countries (and in high income countries over the past decade or so). Low-wage service workers must become extreme self-exploiters, as well as being super-exploited, if they are to get work. Many of these jobs (deliveries, house-cleaning, supermarket baggers, and so on) can only exist because the wages of the people performing the service are a fraction of what those consuming the service are paid. Thus, the condition for finding a job in a growing service sector is often accepting a significantly lower than average wage.

11 Not all of these sorts of labour are services. For example, apparel manufacture has always required very delicate sewing work. Since the invention of the sewing machine, it has proven difficult to further mechanise this work, and so apparel manufacture remains a large employer. Whether product or service however, one thing seems to be constant: because wages make up such a large part of the final cost of these commodities, these sectors have been employing overwhelmingly women, whose labour-power can be found on the labour-market at a below average cost. See 'The Logic of Gender' in *Endnotes 3* for the relation between gender and differentiation in the price in labour-power.

SURPLUS POPULATIONS AND UNEMPLOYMENT

As is now hopefully apparent, *the tendency towards increasing superfluity is not a tendency towards a literal extrusion of a part of the working class from the economy*. Surplus workers still need to buy at least some of what they need to survive, and therefore they must earn or acquire money in order to live. Those who are produced as surplus to the needs of capital may still receive wages in super-exploited sectors, or they may be informally self-employed and thus self-exploiting (since they lack access to capital).

Marx clarifies some of these points in his discussion of the "stagnant surplus population". One cannot read his account without thinking of the global informal economy, much of which would have been included, in Marx's time, under the rubric of home-work or "domestic industry". The stagnant surplus population:

> forms a part of the active labour market, but with extremely irregular employment. Hence it offers capital an inexhaustible reservoir of disposable labour. Its conditions of life sink below the average normal level of the working class, and it is precisely this which makes it a broad foundation for special branches of capitalist exploitation. It is characterised by a maximum of working time and a minimum of wages. We have already become familiar with its chief form under the rubric of "domestic industry" ... Its extent grows in proportion as, with the growth in the extent and energy of accumulation, the creation of a surplus population also advances. But it forms at the same time a self-reproducing and self-perpetuating element of the working class, taking a proportionally greater part in the general increase of that class than the other elements.[12]

12 Marx, *Capital*, vol. 1 (MECW 35), p. 637.

It would thus be a mistake to identify surplus populations with "the unemployed". This category is, to some extent, an artifact of 20th century high-income countries' provision of unemployment insurance. In the 19th century, as in most low-income countries today, "being unemployed" in this sense was simply not an option. Unemployment insurance did not exist — and today covers few workers in low-income countries — so workers could not afford to be without work for long: they needed to find employment as soon as possible, regardless of the degree to which their labour was demanded by capital. If there was no demand, they needed to set up shop for themselves, without any employer — by picking through rags, for example.

In the high-income countries, the category of "unemployment" is currently being undermined once again, and appears as increasingly less defined. As a general tendency, the welfare state has been dramatically transformed, such that unemployment benefit, typically paid to a part of the workforce structurally excluded from employment, has tended to give way to means-tested benefits. These are meant to supplement and support incomes only at the very lowest end of the employment scale, rather than support those simply without work, and are contributing to major increases in low-wage, service sector employment. This transformation is of course occurring at different paces in different high-income countries. In many European countries, protections have remained in place much longer, preventing the bottom from entirely falling out of the labour market. For that reason, a major "jobs gap" opened up between the US and UK on the one hand, and continental Europe on the other, wherein the latter have experienced higher unemployment rates, as well as lower rates of labour force participation, particularly for women. This gap can be explained entirely in relation to the relative lack of service-sector employment in continental Europe, and in particular, low-wage employment.

The service sector share of employment is lowest in Germany and Italy, at around 70 percent, as compared to the US, UK, and France, at around 80 percent.[13]

Additionally, in the global economy — in which mobile flows of surplus capital discipline states — high-income states must do everything they can to prevent outright unemployment, and thus unemployment provisions, from growing too dramatically. Welfare expenditures, which are ultimately funded from tax receipts, must be kept to a minimum to avoid worrying bondholders and taxpayers. Current UK government policy, for example, is to try to eradicate, as far as possible, possibilities for unemployment as any kind of stable category, transforming welfare into workfare. As a result, in the high-income countries, many workers fall in and out of relative superfluity during their lifetime, due both to the increasing flexibilisation of the labour market and its destabilisation of categories of employment at a structural level, as well as the falling demand for labour.[14]

Beginning from the identification of specific social subjects typically means reaching for pre-packaged figures who signify to the popular imaginary a simple economic marginality, such as the slum dweller. But "the surplus population" cannot be so easily identified. Though differential positions in relation to the labour process can certainly be empirically identified and taxonomised according to types and degrees of "surplusness", it is necessary to first identify the broader logic at play, before mapping the complexly variegated ways in which this logic plays out; none of this permits a straightforward identification of surplusness with a singular social subject or group.[15] As we have seen, what facilitates the increasing production of workers as surplus is capital's dual tendency towards both overaccumulation and an increase in the productivity of labour, which in turn decrease the number of workers needed to perform many tasks. But from their initial condition as surplus, these

13 The service sector share of employment is also lower in Japan, at 70 percent.

14 This is less true of the low-income countries, in which there are basically no social protections, and where over half of the labour force is often informal, with only a portion of this population ever experiencing the fluidity to move either into, or out of, the formal sector.

15 We have discussed this issue previously in relation to the English riots of 2011. See 'A Rising Tide Lifts All Boats', *Endnotes* 3, September 2013, pp. 118–19.

workers may turn out to compose just a "floating" surplus population — being reabsorbed into production at some later point — or go on to subsist in one or another relatively stagnant part of the economy (the latter is, of course, much more common in low-income countries). In neither case are surplus workers necessarily either unemployed or unproductive of surplus-value. And at a general level "surplus population" refers to a large, massively varied part of the population, characterised by all sorts of internal divisions and stratifications, all sorts of relations to the labour process.

AN IDENTICAL ABJECT-SUBJECT?

On the one hand, this relatively simple theory of the tendential production of surplus population can help greatly in explaining various key aspects of the present global situation. It gives us a basis for explaining deindustrialisation, the relative growth of services, the spread of forms of insecure and flexible labour, and the numerous abuses for which this opens the way. In turn, these tendencies intensify and exacerbate the difficulty of unifying the working class under the hegemony of the industrial worker, in the way traditional Marxism anticipated; it thus gives us a basis for explaining the crisis of the left and present strategic predicaments. It also seems to offer an explanation for declining growth rates over recent decades, as relative surplus value-producing labour has become a diminishing share of global labour. There are other things we could add to this list too, for instance: the difficulty of states balancing between welfare demands and those of markets; the formation of mega-slums; post-industrial forms of urbanism. Or, on the other side: "financialisation", "neoliberalism", and so on. Insofar as these combined tendencies sketch out the major dynamics and outlines of the present global situation, we take the theory of surplus populations to be an important reference point in framing the present.

On the other hand, when a theory has clear explanatory power, it can be tempting to slide into a sort of conceptual overreach, where the theory is presumed to explain things which it really can't explain, or to say things which it doesn't. It may be the case that Marxists have particularly bad habits on this level: for example, "capital" or "subsumption" are concepts that are often reached for too hastily, called upon to do more explanatory work than they are actually able to. For a theory to have real explanatory power, one has to be able to identify its limits clearly and honestly — to say what it cannot, as well as what it can, explain.

What seems to be a standard misinterpretation or over-extension of the theory of surplus population is characterised by a hypostatisation of "the surplus population" as a singular social subject, with the apparent implication that this may be viewed as the new revolutionary agent, or at least that it is the agent behind various forms of contemporary struggle. This involves a conceptual slippage between general tendency and particular sociological or empirical cases. While it would of course ultimately be false to separate the two, it is also important not to identify them too immediately or simplistically. Thus, the theory of surplus population does not involve some kind of neo-Bakuninite romanticisation of a surplus subject "more radical" or "more dangerous" than the organised working class; nor does it involve a reading of present struggles as those of some "surplus" subject.

ABJECTION

Such thinking was in the air in discussions around the 2011 English riots, which we analysed at some length in *Endnotes 3*. Briefly revisiting problematics that were at play at that time will help us to flesh out and specify these points about surplus population.

It seemed back then that for some the riots should be read as a rebellion of "the surplus population". However, such readings appeared in some ways a simple — and disconcerting — inversion of standard and reactionary interpretations of such events, stoked by mainstream media, which held the riots to be the work of a disorderly and dangerous "underclass". The latter is little more than a pseudo-concept, an ideological generalisation from the ungeneralisable. For this reason, it cannot simply be inverted into something positive that one might valorise.

And, in any case, it was clear that the British urban poor who came out on the streets could not be straightforwardly identified with the concept of surplus population. First of all, as we have already seen, the concept of surplus-population is relatively non-specific in sociological terms. It can apply to a large variety of workers, some of whom are fully employed but super-exploited, others of whom are underemployed or informally self-employed. It is reasonable to surmise that a substantial portion of the British working class is relatively "surplus" in one sense or another.[16] Nor can the identity of the British urban poor be easily captured under specific categories of surplusness, such as "the unemployed". While unemployment of course tends to be higher in poor urban areas, the unemployment rate in Britain has been relatively low in recent years, compared to other European countries, and a majority of the urban poor — and of those who rioted — were either employed or in full time education. Nor could they be simply identified with "informality", in terms of the "grey economy", or with illegality, in terms of the "black economy". Early reactionary claims that most of the rioters were involved in criminal gangs predictably proved unfounded.[17] And as we have already seen, it doesn't make sense to see the urban poor as "surplus" in the stronger sense of being excluded from the economy per se.

16 Marx himself even extends this category to orphans and the elderly!

17 Informality is usually distinguished from illegality. The global informal sector includes all those doing *legal* work, but without protections, or in firms consisting of five or fewer people. Thus, it does not include those doing illegal sex-work, or engaged in the drug-trade, etc.

Another often ideological concept that gets thrown around when people discuss the urban poor is that of the ghetto. This has related connotations to the ideas of superfluity that we have already discussed: the ghetto is conceived as a sort of social dustbin where the sub-proletariat is thrown, where state agents often fear to go and where the market is absent. The concept of the ghetto signifies superfluity, exteriority to the (formal) economy, and also tends to link the latter up with the concept of race. Ghettos are, of course, a reality in some parts of the world. But the British urban poor do not live in ghettos in anything other than a metaphorical sense: poor British housing estates are small, often ethnically mixed, incorporated into the broader cities in which they are placed, and managed as well as patrolled by the state. They are not surplus or external in any simple sense to either the state or the market.

If we can say unproblematically that what we've been calling the "urban poor" were a key active agent in 2011, this only works because this is a weak, vague, merely descriptive category. As soon as we try to apply the more technically specific category of surplus population here, we run into problems. Of course, it was not completely irrational to want to do so: there was a sort of intuitive "fit" at least at the level of representational thinking. The palpable, disruptive presence of strata of people on the street who are habitually cast out, excluded in various ways, was one of the most striking aspects of 2011.

This confronted us with three questions. Firstly, how to theorise the social subjects who came out in revolt in 2010–11, and to identify the ways in which these people really do appear as "excluded" or marginal, without collapsing this into the general political-economic logic of the production of a surplus population? Secondly, how to relink this exclusion or marginality with the concept of surplus population once it has been distinguished from it? Thirdly, how might these matters be related to deeper problems of revolutionary subjectivity and organisation?

It is clear when looking at the history of urban riots in Britain that they are distinctly periodisable, and that the period of the real emergence of their modern form is — as are so many things — contemporary with the capitalist restructuring that has occurred since the 1970s. If the tendential production of a surplus population at a global level gives us some basis for explaining this period of restructuring, then this tendency could presumably be linked with the emergence of the modern urban riot in this period, without necessarily needing to establish an immediate identity between urban rioters and "surplus population" as a simple and coherent social subject.

Since the 1970s, we have of course seen growing and generalising insecurity, as stable industrial employment has given way to employment by the state and the service sector. But these developments were uneven, hitting some sections of the working class before others. Prior to Britain's full-scale deindustrialisation, the British working class was of course stratified, with a more insecure, informal, racialised stratum at the bottom, prone to being ejected from employment in times of economic stress, such as occurred throughout the 1970s: a classic industrial reserve army. These workers, at the racialised margins of the organised working class, were some of the first to feel the crisis of the 1970s. They were hit disproportionately by unemployment and they were not to be re-employed in newly emergent lines of production, since these lines did not in fact employ many people.

If surplus population is useful anywhere in this history in identifying an immediate sociological reality, it is here, where it can be used to distinguish a particular stratum in relation to the rest of the working class. However, in interpreting the deindustrialisation that really kicked in from this point on, it is necessary to move beyond the strictly political-economic level on which this theory is forged. This is because the timing and character of Britain's deindustrialisation are inextricable from the particular dynamics of class struggle in Britain, and from the political mediations of this struggle. Though Britain's industrial base had long been in decline, its trashing by the Thatcher government was pushed through actively, at least in part for strategic reasons. If the insecure margins of the workforce grew in England from the 1970s onwards, this is not completely reducible to the general global tendency towards the production of a surplus population. We need reference to the specific political mediations, even if this general tendency can help inform our understanding of what is being mediated by such mediations.

It is amongst these pressurised sections of the working class — the more insecure, informal, racialised stratum, which struggled to be reabsorbed by the labour market — that the riot became particularly prominent as a mode of struggle, from the mid to late 1970s, and it seems reasonable to hypothesise that this newfound prominence is directly related to the absence of possibilities for "normal", regulatory, demands-making of the corporatist type. In developments dialectically entwined with the struggles of this section of the working class, the police in this period increasingly developed new tactics of repression specifically targeted at poor urban neighbourhoods. One might even say that the riot and its repression became a sort of proxy way in which class relations were regulated, in the absence of the "normal" mode of regulation exercised by wage bargaining, etc. This is not a perverse point: historically riots have pushed demands towards which the state has made concessions. This proved true of 2011 just as it did of 1981; more recently it has proved true in the US, after the 2014 Ferguson riots.[18]

In *Endnotes 3* we termed the social logic of stigmatisation associated with such developments "abjection" — a concept borrowed from Imogen Tyler's recent book *Revolting Subjects*.[19] With its in some ways dubious provenance, we were not especially fond of this term, but it seemed nonetheless quite appropriate as a name for certain problematics with which we were grappling.[20] What was useful was that this term named a particular kind of abstract structure in which something is cast off, marked as contingent or lowly, without actually being exteriorised. The relevance of such a structure here should be obvious: the initially racialised communities subject to the forms of oppression that develop through this period are socially marked as a problem — or even as a sort of rejection from the healthy core of the body politic — without being literally exteriorised in any sense from either economy or state. Police repression looms large in the immediate experience of abjection in this sense, but the term is also intended to capture broader social processes, such as the moral crusades of reactionary press, or the constant obsessing of politicians over the various failed subjects of the nation. These are not simply unconnected moments; concrete connections between all of them could be articulated such that we see a particular socio-political *pattern* of oppression.

It seems that abjection may be relatable, in a mediated way, to the production and management of a surplus population in that specific historical moment of the 1970s, as the restructuring began. But the mediations require careful articulation. After all — though there was at least a significant overlap — the stigmatised urban communities who were the "primary abjects" of this new style of policing were of course not composed exclusively of workers at the margins of industrial

18 See 'Brown v. Ferguson', in this issue, for an analysis.

19 Tyler, *Revolting Subjects: Social Abjection and Resistance in Neoliberal Britain* (Zed Books 2013). Tyler has developed this as a general-purpose category of psycho-social theory, through a critical engagement with Georges Bataille and Julia Kristeva, distancing herself especially from the latter's reactionary politics.

20 We also deployed the term 'abject' as a name for some partially analogous – but by no means identical – structures, in 'The Logic of Gender', in the same issue.

employment. Moreover, as Britain deindustrialised, and as broader global tendencies towards the production of surplus population were felt particularly in a generalised decomposition of the working class, the association of these typically racialised communities with a specifically reserve army function declined. Unemployment became highly generalised in the British economy, to then be slowly superseded by a highly flexibilised and insecure labour market. While this association of racialised margins of the working class with a reserve army function diminished, police repression of the poor mounted.

If the development of new styles of policing might be partially linked to the management of a surplus population at the outset then, this tie becomes increasingly tenuous as we get into the 1980s and 90s. One might speak of a developing "autonomisation" of the apparatus of repression and its related stigmatising and racialising logics. By this we mean that an apparatus which initially seems to apply in particular to clear, economically marginal, parts of the class, becomes dissociated from that strict function. While those who are subject to these processes of abjection come to symbolise the limits of affirmable class, these limits are in actuality unstable, shifting and ill-defined. They become more a socio-political, or perhaps socio-cultural, than a political-economic construct. If this is the case, it is doubtful whether we are likely to have any luck constructing the object of this apparatus in purely political-economic terms. Who is "abjected" then? We might provisionally reply, somewhat tautologically: those who are defined as such by the fact that they are the object of these processes of repression. There is no particular pre-existing trait or social categorisation which must, in itself, necessarily or inevitably mark one out as an object of these processes, which is not to say that certain social categories do not end up being reproduced in such positions. Abjection is closely related—though not identical—to racialisation.

If the mechanisms of abjection could once be related to a certain function in the state's management of the insecure margins of the industrial working class, as the object of that management dissipates socially, the function itself would seem to be thrown into question. If something is being "managed" through abjection, it is no longer self-evident exactly what, by who, or to what end. We have blind social patterns of stigmatisation and oppression which are quite general, and can thus not be viewed as the work of some conspiracy. And we also have the continuing operation of formalised structures of power and oppression within these patterns, with police, politicians and media playing important active roles — though generally in part responding to the very real sentiments of the citizenry. In the process a new kind of "function" may be perceived, as the generalised insecurity of the post-industrial workforce is exacerbated by the waning of solidarities here, and people all too readily turn on each other. But this is "functional" only in a perverse sense: it is the product of no design or intent; a purely "irrational" outcome, albeit one which can in some ways prove useful to capital and state after the fact, insofar as it further disempowers their potential antagonists.[21]

21 Indeed, from another perspective – that of a speculative proletarian unity – one may view such developments as a matter of pure dysfunction.

If we are now speaking of the subjects of "abjection" rather than "surplus population" here, how about the abject as a social subject? These developments signify, however, not the creation of a new form of social (or potentially, revolutionary) subject, but rather *the problem of any class subject at all.* In itself, that which is abjected would seem to be by definition unaffirmable, ununifiable, for it is not a positive existence of its own, but merely the negative of something else. Those who are abjected are not something other than the proletariat. More often than not they are workers, students etc. Only, they are workers, students etc who are vilified, cast beyond the pale of social respectability. These developments represent problems for the constitution of a unified class subject; indeed, they are direct expressions of the decomposition of the class. The abject is projected as a sort of limit-concept of affirmable social class, in an operation where that class is itself negatively defined against what has been abjected. "We are not like them" replaces "the workers united will never be defeated". And as such, abjection can have a somewhat fractal quality: not applying uniformly to one social group, but across and between social groups, depending to some extent on where one stands in the social landscape. There is always someone more abject than you.

This is not something that should be valorised or romanticised, or projected as the positive basis for some future social subject. If it is a curse to be reduced to the proletarian, it is doubly so to be abjected. Neither surplus population nor the abject provide any ultimate answer to the problem of revolutionary agency, but both describe aspects of the problem, and it is with the problem that we must start. What seems clear is that whatever shape a future unity of the class could take, it is not one that is likely to be hegemonised by an advanced industrial worker; though it seems equally clear that no "abject" or "surplus" subject offers itself up as an obvious alternative. Nonetheless, the problem will continue to be confronted, as people in struggle strain to compose and extend some unity in order to push forwards. And the combinatory processes of struggle can be endlessly generative.